D1468613

THE
NIPPON
CHALLENGE

日本　日本　日本　日本
日本　日本　日本　日本
日本　日本　日本　日本
日本　日本　日本　日本
日本　日本　日本　日本
日本　日本　日本　日本

PATRICK SMITH

日本　日本　日本　日本

DOUBLEDAY

NEW YORK　　　　LONDON　　　　TORONTO
SYDNEY　　　AUCKLAND

日本　日本　日本　日本

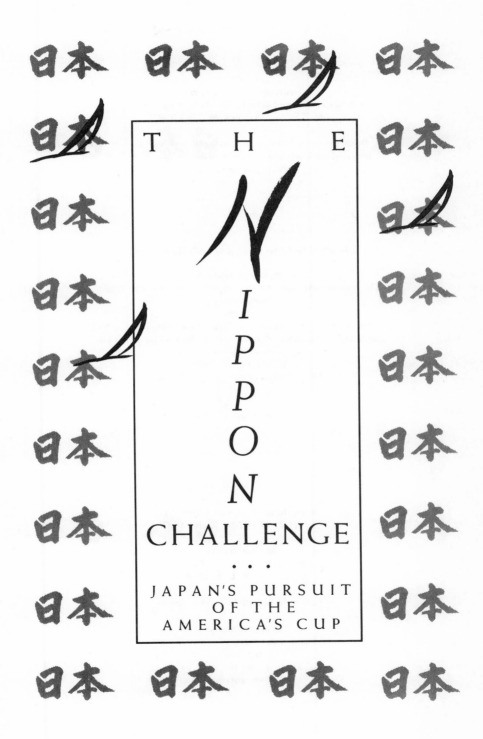

THE

NIPPON

CHALLENGE
...

JAPAN'S PURSUIT
OF THE
AMERICA'S CUP

PUBLISHED BY DOUBLEDAY
a division of Bantam Doubleday Dell Publishing Group, Inc.
666 Fifth Ave., New York, New York 10103

DOUBLEDAY and the portrayal of an anchor with a dolphin are
trademarks of Doubleday, a division of Bantam Doubleday Dell
Publishing Group, Inc.

Library of Congress Cataloging-in-Publication Data

Smith, Patrick (Patrick L.)
The Nippon challenge : Japan's pursuit of the America's Cup /
Patrick Smith.
p.   cm.
1. Yachts and yachting—Japan.   2. Yacht racing—Japan.   3. Nippon
(Sailboat)   4. America's Cup races.   5. Japan—Social life and
customs—1945–   I. Title.
GV817.J3S64   1992
797.1'4'0952—dc20   91-38519
CIP

ISBN 0-385-42171-0

Book Design & Ornamentation by
CAROL MALCOLM-RUSSO

Illustrations by
AHER/DONNELL STUDIOS

Copyright © 1992 by Patrick Smith

ALL RIGHTS RESERVED
PRINTED IN THE UNITED STATES OF AMERICA
MAY 1992
1   3   5   7   9   10   8   6   4   2
FIRST EDITION

FOR
JUDITH EVANS

AND TO THE MEMORY OF
PETER NORTON FINK

Contents

PART III: REACHING

PART IV: RUNNING

OFF POINT LOMA

May is a mild month in San Diego waters. On some days the winds are so slight that the sea starts to resemble a desolate desert shining white under a cloudless sky. Sailors—local sailors, at least— do not dwell unduly upon breezes of four, five, or six knots, conditions in which it is difficult even to move a boat large enough to carry a keel. At other times the winds may pick up somewhat, but then they can be more than matched by oversized swells rolling in from the cold southern oceans. The sea off San Diego, in short, is a tough sea to call, and the sailors who do best in it are the ones who take the principle of flexibility in changing circumstances to its logical extreme. "It's not difficult to predict the winds off Point Loma," a New Zealand yachtsman of considerable reputation once remarked. "It's impossible."

No one who raced the day the experienced Kiwi registered that complaint, not even the skipper and crew who eventually won the event, had put in much practice for the way things unfolded. It was May 4, 1991. If that day's contest wasn't the final word among the nine competitors who headed out at midmorning for the twelve-thirty start, if it proved precisely nothing, its outcome would still suggest a lot of things to a lot of people. It was the beginning of the World Championships in the International America's Cup Class, a week-long regatta in boats never before raced; in effect, it was also the start of the twenty-eighth America's Cup races. A year later, when the final leg of the final event was sailed, one nation would be seen to have produced the world's best yachtsmen and the world's best yacht.

The race, which covered slightly more than twenty-one miles, began conventionally enough. The winds had picked up—from eight knots or so in the morning to twelve or a bit more at the start. Most of the fleet went looking for fresh breezes off to the right as soon as the starting gun went off; only an American boat, *Stars & Stripes*, went on starboard tack. But the Americans, skippered by a local, were first by thirty-nine seconds to round the upwind mark. Behind them came boats from Italy, Spain, and Japan; five others followed farther back.

The Japanese boat, white and trimmed with red, was called *Nippon*. Most of those crewing on it were newcomers to competitive sailing, with almost no experience of the sport, and at the top mark *Nippon* was a flat minute behind the leader. But there are things in every yacht race that spectators never see. *Nippon*'s crew and afterguard were braced for a fight after that first beat. They had chosen the wrong side of the course along with all the other out-of-towners. But in boat speed and pointing—the craft's ability to sail as directly as possible into the wind—*Nippon* had done superbly. Some of those on board thought they had outsailed several of the boats in front of them; they saw a second place easily within reach, and a win did not seem unattainable.

The next two legs, reaches across the wind, suggested they were right. By the second mark *Nippon* had cut its lag to thirty-four seconds. By the third, the Italian boat had overtaken *Stars & Stripes*; the Japanese had advanced to third and were closing fast on the Americans. Tension on board, high from the start, was building. "We were flying," a sailor remembered afterward, "and we were beginning to smell the kill."

At that third mark *Nippon*'s skipper, one of several New Zealanders on board, would make the most important decision he would face all day. The winds, by that time, had picked up to twenty knots, sometimes more, and the waters off Point Loma were becoming uncharacteristically dangerous. Had these conditions prevailed earlier the race committee would have called the day's event. It was beginning to look like a war of attrition. Other boats were blowing sails; the Spaniards had already lost their steering mechanism and dropped out. What sail should they raise for the next leg, a reach to the leeward mark?

On board *Nippon*, the discussion had begun in the afterguard as they approached the mark. "What's the sail call?" the skipper shouted above the din of winches, waves, rigging, and sails. "Let's go with the five," one of the other Kiwis called back. Another said the same thing. After some discussion, so did the mainsail trimmer, a Japanese who had designed every sail the boat was carrying. Five was code for the smallest gennaker on board. These men figured the winds were too strong for anything else. They would catch the Americans no matter what they put up. They would be near the Italians around the next mark, and the race was less than half over. The next leg was upwind; *Nippon* had already proven itself upwind.

The skipper, who had remained silent during the debate he had prompted, broke in suddenly at the last minute. "We're going with the three!" he shouted. Three was K3B, the largest gennaker they carried.

"You're mad," one of the other Kiwis cried.

"We're going with the three!" the skipper screamed again with a finality familiar to all on board.

There are moments in every sailor's racing past when heads has turned irrevocably to tails, when a good race has turned into a disaster and there's no retrieving it. Experienced yachtsmen learn to recognize such occasions, even if they can never fully explain them. "We were moving like a rocket, we blew a sail halfway through,

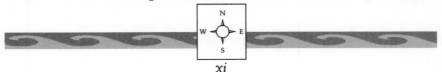

and from then on the whole thing turned into garbage." In one language or another, you can hear stories with roughly the same plot in the bar of any yacht club in the world.

Nippon, once K3B was up, flew again down the fourth leg. It immediately overtook the Americans in second place, and it was advancing fast toward the Italian boat. But *Nippon*'s moment had arrived. It was sailing at thirteen knots, and it was almost recklessly overpowered. All over the boat the crew could see and feel and hear that there was too much strain. It would be close to a dead heat, one crewman was thinking, as to which would go first—the mast, the sail itself, or the spinnaker pole supporting it. His money was on the mast, and he ran toward it from the stern, looking up and shouting, "It's going to go! It's going to go!" The trimmer handling the gennaker sheet overeased at that point to reduce the pressure as much as he could; it was hardly the kind of move one would expect to make midway in a race.

What would go, if anything did, would be more than simply an expensive spar. It had been four years since they began to prepare themselves, far earlier than anyone else and from a far more elementary starting point. This was more than a race to the Japanese. To them, the waters off Point Loma were a proving ground. They were there, which was novel enough to all but a handful of them, and it was an arrival of a sort. But to themselves, at least, they also had to prove it was right for them to be there.

Something no one had planned on happened at that moment. The gennaker halyard, the line by which the sail was raised, snapped two thirds of the way down the leg. *Nippon* was suddenly a shambles. K3B, billowing toward the water, was saved only by the quick reflexes of one of the Kiwis who had called "Five" a few minutes earlier. He ran forward instantly to gather it in. But the boat, heavily heeled, righted itself immediately and sent the mastman overboard. By the time they picked him up, after two awkward roundings, the Japanese sloop was last, four minutes and eighteen seconds behind the leader.

They never gave up. In winds blowing steadily above twenty knots by then, everyone else headed up the next beat with jibs, the smallest

headsails they had. *Nippon* flew a number four genoa, a much larger sail, and proved the fastest boat on the leg. It quickly passed the French entry and took time out of everyone else in front, including the Italians at the lead. Another American boat dropped out when the wind ripped a jib track off the deck. There were seven of them left. We can take *Stars & Stripes*, they were thinking on board *Nippon*, and probably the New Zealand boat, and one other. We could still make fourth.

At the fifth mark, the intent Kiwi skipper swung *Nippon* around the buoy as sharply as an F-1 driver would clear a hairpin curve. It was the kind of risky move a helmsman would make in a flat-out match race if the lead boat was only a length or two ahead and a position in the finals was at stake. Instead of bearing away in a wide arc, gradually easing the enormous loads built up on the boat, the tactic is to turn quickly enough to move inside the boat in front and try to overtake during the next leg.

No one was ready for it. In the stern, one mainsail trimmer had to slip the mainsheet, the line by which the sail was trimmed, quickly enough to allow the main to swing over to match the violent helming. The other trimmer had to release the boom vang, a diagonal piece attached to the mast to stabilize the boom, with equal speed. There was roughly three and a half tons of pressure on the mast at that moment. Neither man was able to ease it on time.

For most of *Nippon*'s crew, the sound and sight of it were not quite simultaneous. The pitman remembered hearing something very like a tree cracking in a forest before he instinctively looked up. A Kiwi in the afterguard, standing amidships at the time, recalled "a crunching, splintering sound, like slowly crushed glass." That came from the starboard winch, and he focused on it briefly before he realized what was happening above. In spectacularly slow motion, it was going over: a hundred and one feet of mast and almost two thousand square feet of sail were headed over the port side.

•   •   •

A little more than two hundred yards to windward of the fifth mark, a comfortable cabin cruiser named *Tariam II* had been bobbing in the swells, waiting for the Japanese boat to make its approach, turn, set its spinnaker, and run down the sixth leg. It had been a trying afternoon, a day of deep disappointments, and there wasn't much being said. In the moments before *Nippon* finished its beat, most of those on board *Tariam II* were watching the Italians, far in the distance, through field glasses; mostly they were trying to distract themselves after the halyard fiasco and the man overboard. At the wheel was an American pilot, and next to him stood a representative of the race committee, a retired dentist who had sailed off San Diego for decades. In the stern were four Japanese, all of whom had given years of their lives to put *Nippon* on the water.

From where they eat, *Nippon*'s final disaster came in total silence and without warning. The sloop was roughly twenty yards past the mark and into the sixth leg when the mainsail started slowly crumbling through its middle. The spreaders, five sets of them at intervals down the mast, were suddenly at odd angles. Then the rigging began to bulge and tangle. Then the main was folding downward like ribbon, and the mast was tilted like a telephone pole on a country road.

"Oh, Jesus!" the race committee's rep exclaimed. "They've lost their stick."

Those were the only words spoken for the next ten minutes. They watched as one of the Kiwis on *Nippon* straddled the mast and then slid down it as far as he could toward the water. All over the boat they were scrambling to detach messes of halyards and stays. The Kiwi on the mast finally went in and began struggling to free the sail before the spar went under.

The skipper stayed amidships, directing and assisting. It had been a tense, aggressive race, and he had made loud, rigid calls throughout. That was his style—quick, intolerant, at times impulsive. Now he was calm, professional, helpful in any way he could be. He was twenty-eight. He had intense blue eyes and curly blond hair that years of wind and sun had already forced back from his forehead. Like many other skippers, he had asked for opinions and then gone ahead and done what he wanted.

From *Tariam II*, the skipper looked as if he were standing on an embalmed corpse. The deck, a bleached white, seemed almost obscenely exposed with no spars or rigging above it. The hull was rolling violently, the huge lead bulb at the bottom of the keel no longer balanced by the weight of the mast. It would be a rough tow back to the base camp.

All the way in, a dense silence prevailed on board *Tariam II*. Only once did one of the Japanese break it.

"Could've been the boom vang wasn't released in time as they made the turn," he said as they made their way past the long spit of land called Point Loma. He was the most experienced yachtsman on board and had been a cold, relentless analyst all day. "Or the mainsheet. Or the backstays."

"We should know soon enough," someone else said.

"There won't be a definite answer. It's probably a simple case of equipment failure. But there's a lesson in it."

There was, but no one asked him about it just then. In the stern, one of the others sat brooding with his chin resting on his folded arms across the transom. He had barely moved since the mast went over. He was the *kaicho*, the chairman of the syndicate behind *Nippon*, and he would have much to explain over the next few days—partly to himself, but mostly to the yacht's many sponsors.

He was fifty-six, with graying hair, glasses, and an acute stare. He had seen dismastings before—they looked far more dramatic than they actually were—but how would he get that across? There *was* a lesson in it—although he hadn't entered into the conversation nearby, he had heard every word of it—but the lesson went beyond backstays and boom vangs. Something seemed very wrong with their approach. First crew problems, then technology problems. It shouldn't have come to this. How could they understand it? How could they fix it? Maybe they didn't belong there after all. Maybe it was too soon for them to compete, despite all the money and technology and effort they had put into *Nippon*. It was as if the entire campaign to race off Point Loma had been aimed incorrectly and had collided at thirteen knots with a wall of wind.

THE
NIPPON
CHALLENGE

PART I

B

E A T I N G

Waking Up

Kaoru Ogimi, like all Tokyoites his age, had his own private memory of how it was when the firebombs started to fall.

Ogimi's father, a Spanish-speaking diplomat who served for many years in Europe and Latin America, had been seconded by the beginning of 1945 to NHK, the government radio station, where he was a division director by day and occasionally worked the evening shift as a watchman. Ogimi was sixteen then. With his parents and his sister, he lived in Yotsuya, a district of central Tokyo then given over to merchants and middle-class houses.

The earliest American air raid on the capital, commanded by Lieutenant Colonel James H. Doolittle, had come three years earlier, on the afternoon of April 18, 1942. Ogimi remembers it well—one of Jimmy's bombs exploded a short distance from where he was standing in the schoolyard after lunch. More than three hundred were wounded that day and thirty-nine were killed, including a thirteen-year-old boy whom the national newspapers elevated into a martyr for the imperial cause. It was Ogimi's first taste of warfare.

The bombs began in earnest in November 1944, and for three months they fell mostly on military targets on the outskirts of the city. Then the incendiary raids started. The worst came just after midnight on March 10, 1945, a date etched in the memory of everyone then alive in the capital. Kaoru Ogimi recalled how low the B-29s flew, and "an almost rainlike showering of fire" that the huge packs of incendiary devices released when they detonated some distance above the ground. Not quite half the city was destroyed that night; between seventy thousand and eighty thousand perished before dawn.

Long afterward, in an office a few miles from the site of his childhood home, Ogimi spent a winter afternoon recounting what he saw. "I went out walking a day or so later, trying to go to school. I saw this vast area of charred moonscape." Ogimi laughed at his choice of words. "That was all we had left. You could actually see the shape of the land, which you couldn't before because of all the buildings."

With his mother and sister, Ogimi started spending more time in Ninomiya, a small fishing and farming village south of Tokyo on Sagami Bay. That was where he was on Friday, April 13, when the family home in Yotsuya, a wooden house like those around it, disintegrated during another air attack. The house was empty at the time—Kaoru's father, Yosoe, having drawn another night shift.

The Ogimis stayed on in Ninomiya, where Yosoe had relatives. Today Ogimi and his own family live in a large, modernized farmhouse not far from Ninomiya's shoreline. What had been a small village of rice terraces, fishing trawlers, and matchstick houses is now a prosperous community of thirty thousand, an hour and fifteen minutes from Tokyo by commuter rail.

One day a year or so after the surrender, Kaoru's father came home and announced that he had bought a sailboat. Yosoe, who had originally studied engineering, had long entertained a mild fascination for the sea. But he knew almost nothing about the enterprise at hand. His previous experience on the water was limited to one occasion during his university years when he had tied a bedsheet to an oar and got lost for several hours on Tokyo Bay.

It was a dilapidated twelve-foot dinghy he had found at the end of a pier in Yokohama, but the price was right—it had cost him almost nothing. By then the whole family was sharing a rented room in Ninomiya. They had lost everything; Ogimi senior was having the same trouble keeping his family clothed and fed as everyone else in the immediate postwar years. But Yosoe still had it in him to change the course of his son's life.

They sailed as often as possible—at least every weekend during the season, sometimes more. And they started buying up yachting books and periodicals as the bookshops in Tokyo began to carry more imports. Among other things, the two of them found and devoured almost the entire set of books published as the *Mariners Library*, a collection of twenty-odd volumes dedicated to long-distance passages and epic sea voyages.

Unguided but for books, manuals, magazines, and each other, father and son taught themselves how to rig, trim, and sail the old dinghy out in Sagami Bay. For Kaoru, the effort struck a chord. He had aspired, as a high school student during the war years, to become an aeronautical engineer and a pilot. He had followed the latest developments in Japanese military planes as avidly as adolescent boys in America dreamed of downing them. With a few similarly inclined friends, he had set up testing equipment that included a primitive wind tunnel, and together they matched hand-thrown gliders against one another to determine the validity of their theories.

"For me, what my father and I did was as much an intellectual involvement as anything else. That was true from the very beginning. All the things that applied to an airplane basically applied to a yacht—the efficiency of sails, the keel, the rudder; drift, lift, drag, wave making."

Ogimi laughed again, a deep-in-the-chest laugh. "We had to try to figure all this out on our own," he continued. "There was no one there to coach us; it was all trial and error."

Almost half a century on the water had made Ogimi, by the early

months of 1991, look slightly older than his sixty-two years. He had long, unruly eyebrows, a square jaw, and a somewhat stern demeanor. But he was as trim as most men twenty years his junior, and he managed, most of the time, to combine his ship captain's solemnity with a look of almost boyish fascination and surprise.

Kaoru Ogimi was a complicated man. Among the many things he didn't explain that February day, at least not directly, was that those first adolescent voyages out on Sagami Bay had also allowed him to redirect a deeper and more abiding ambition.

Kaoru Ogimi's mother, née Mabel Jones and a few months older than the century, came from a middle-class London family that had taken an early interest in the East. Her father had traveled widely in the Pacific as a purser on merchant ships, and Mabel grew up with a variety of visiting Japanese students around the house as "homestayers." The curiosity passed from one generation to the next. Mabel Jones arrived from England in 1921 after her brother was posted to Japan as a correspondent for Reuters, the British news agency. She met her future husband while he was still a student in Tokyo.

By his own account, Kaoru Ogimi was conceived in Mexico, born in Spain, and raised until he was ten in Colombia and Venezuela. It was a background that would serve him well in later years. But, being of a mixed family that could choose East over West, it was a burden as well. This was especially so for an adolescent during the grim days of the wartime dictatorship. Not unpredictably, Ogimi developed what he called "a huge nationalist commitment."

"If the war had continued another couple of years and I had become eligible, I may well have elected to become a *kamikaze* pilot," Ogimi reflected. "For the normal Japanese, 'Japaneseness' was something you were born into; for me, it was something I had to prove."

By the time Kaoru Ogimi recounted all of this, he had long been recognized as one of the best and most influential yachtsmen in Japan. In a suit and tie on land, he worked for a subsidiary of the Seibu Saison group, one of the nation's most prominent retailers, which owned and managed a marina called the Seabornia Yacht

Club. But he lived for the sea and was on it as often as he could be. He was vice-commodore of the Nippon Ocean Racing Club, and he had organized, sailed in, or juried many of the races in which Japan had been represented during his lifetime.

When he finished high school, Ogimi went on to Reed College in Portland, Oregon. He switched from engineering to philosophy at Reed, and after graduating he began a succession of jobs with foreign companies that had opened offices in Japan after the war: eight years with a small American publisher, four as the regional publicity agent for 20th Century Fox, thirteen with the Japanese subsidiary of Reader's Digest, and then on to the Saison group.

While he was studying Descartes at Reed his father bought the family's second boat, an eighteen-foot skiff with a centerboard made of heavy steel plate. Ogimi started sailing it as soon as he got home, and he crewed for an American aircraft executive who had put a thirty-four-foot sloop in the water during the later years of the occupation. Kaoru still sails the Ogimis' third boat, a twenty-four-foot racer called *Serena* that he and his father built in the early 1960s.

Ogimi's life seemed to have unfolded as a series of obvious choices. He, too, chose East over West, as his parents had. Then he looked to the sea because it gave him a way to connect the two different worlds in which his feet were planted and the two that existed side by side within him. And it had enabled him to remain faithful to the lesson in living his father taught him during those desperate days just after the bombs stopped.

"The two of us turned our backs on the dismal conditions around us." Ogimi smiled. "All we had was this open rowboat with one sail, that and our thoughts and spirits soaring. We always dreamed that one day we'd be on the horizon, our sails full. Sailing provided us with a world of our own. It allowed us to shut our eyes to all the misery we saw on land."

•　　•　　•

Kaoru Ogimi has made it to the horizon under full sail many times since then. The story of how he got there, and of how he grew to

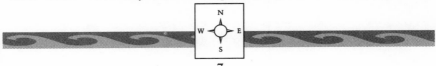

prominence in a world he did much to create, is more or less the story of yacht racing in modern Japan. In a certain way, it is also a kind of back-door account of Japan itself during the postwar years— of what it has thought about and what it has ignored, of what it has sought for itself and what it has shied away from.

The first yachts built and sailed for pleasure appeared in Japan in the 1860s. In those days the foreign settlement at Yokohama, then a few years opened, was swelling with newly arrived traders, bankers, and diplomats. Sailing as a sport was a few decades old in the West. On a clear day with a good wind, a scattering of schooners and yawls could be seen threading their way among the square-rigged merchantmen that crowded the harbor.

But those skippering and crewing in and out of the moorings were as sequestered as the rest of the foreign colony; it would take the Japanese another half century to join in. Even if they had understood the curious way Westerners took pleasure in moving across the water, and even if they had been welcomed, the Japanese were otherwise occupied at the time. Japan was not really a nation in the 1860s; it was a collection of fiefdoms deeply divided against one another. After almost three centuries of isolation, it had just opened its borders. It had to modernize—it had to catch up with the rest of the world.

Yachting began for the Japanese after World War I. The Taisho era, which stretched from 1912 to 1926, was a period of relative liberalism, even exuberance. The politics of the period, now termed "Taisho Democracy," were marked by unusual openness. Japan was feeling a first flush of confidence in its status among the advanced industrial nations, and Western influence was at a height it would not reach again until the occupation era. Cultural currents seemed to run in all directions at once. The scent of European Modernism was making its way across the ocean. Along with it came a new nobility modeled after the German peerage. Families with sons and friends and investments abroad maintained European and Japanese dining rooms and entertained in both with equal ease. Private universities founded in the final decades of the previous century offered degrees considered as good as many available abroad. There was a self-consciousness about 1920s Japan, certainly. To be Westernized was, in part, to put on a mask. Among Tokyo's exclusive new clubs were some run more or less strictly for the purpose of persuading visiting foreigners that their hosts were a worldly and sophisticated lot who knew their glasses and forks.

Sailing, a sport of the refined, was seen as part of the package. It was quickly centered in the small harbors that dotted the shores of Sagami Bay—Zushi, Hayama, Sajima, Yokosuka. Japan's first yacht club was started in 1922. Curiously, it wasn't on the ocean at all but on the shores of Biwako, the largest lake in Japan, in the mountains near Kyoto. A decade later Japan had two university sailing clubs, one in Kyushu and one at Keio University, one of the nineteenth-century institutions in Tokyo dedicated to the liberal values of the age. From then on, collegiate clubs would exercise a heavy influence on the sport as it was practiced in Japan. They taught harmony, team hierarchy, and duty to the crew, much as Japanese executives learned to put obligations to the group before their own achievements.

At the summer Olympics in 1936, hosted with fanfare in Hitler's Berlin, Japan entered the Olympic yachting event for the first time. It was a disaster, the team finishing near to last. (Among Japanese sailors it is still a sore point that their sport is the single Olympic event in which Japan has never won a medal, not even a bronze.) But by 1936 the complex currents underlying Japan's nationalist pride were being radically reinterpreted. What the Japanese call the Fifteen-Year War had begun with the imperial army's invasion of Manchuria in 1931; a coup in Tokyo a few months before the Berlin games marked the beginning of the military dictatorship at home. Once more, the nation turned its attention elsewhere; it would be many years before a yachting regatta would matter much again.

When sailing reappeared after the war, it was again brought in by foreigners. Not long after Yosoe Ogimi refinished his decrepit dinghy and put it in the harbor at Ninomiya in the autumn of 1946, a group of occupation officers, mostly from the U. S. Air Force, started the Cruising Club of Japan in Yokosuka, a base still operated by the United States. The C.C.J. was an informal collection of like-

minded men from Britain and America, but a handful of Japanese
enthusiasts also joined, among them former officers of the imperial
navy. They sailed Sagami Bay in J.O.G.-class boats, so named after
the British classification for them, Junior Offshore Group. In America these modest craft were called Midget Offshore Racing boats;
they were less than twenty-six feet in length, and they couldn't go
very far from home.

The first offshore regatta of any consequence was held in 1950. It
took boats on a seventy-mile course around a volcanic island called
Oshima that sits like a lump of sugar to the south of Tokyo Bay.
Today, exhausted Tokyoites can fly to Oshima in forty minutes for a
weekend on cheap *tatami* mats and walks among the fishermen and
farmers. The Oshima race lasted only fifteen hours, an uneventful
out-and-back exercise with few surprises. To be considered an ocean
race, a contest had to involve at least one night on the water, and
the Oshima competition barely qualified.

But it was a start. Four years later, with the occupation ended,
the C.C.J. turned into the Nippon Ocean Racing Club. It was a small
affair: there were forty-eight boats registered with the N.O.R.C. and
two hundred members. But it soon evolved from a club of sailors
into an organization responsible for setting handicaps, measuring
courses, and organizing and judging races; in short, with the
N.O.R.C. Japan had established what any serious sailing nation has
to have as a piece of basic equipment—a regulatory authority
governing all ocean-racing competition off its shores.

Succeeding races gradually extended the range outward from the
confines of Tokyo Bay and the sailing haunts to its south. But
Japanese sailors were still hugging their shores—most of them,
anyway. In 1962 a man named Kenichi Horie rigged an oceangoing
yacht for single-handed sailing and became the first Japanese sailor
to cross the Pacific alone. It took Horie ninety-four days to reach
San Francisco from Osaka. When he got there he was welcomed as a
hero and received honorary citizenship from the mayor.

Something different happened at home. Trips abroad still had to
be justified to the authorities at the time, and the first reaction to
Horie's feat in Japan was that he was a criminal for leaving the

country without official approval. It was only after news came back of the tremendous reception Horie had received from the Americans that the Japanese government let him off the hook. "They were embarrassed," Kaoru Ogimi said. "Father was still alive then, and he tried to help him out through his ministry contacts. But the authorities still put Horie through the wringer."

Ogimi described Horie's crossing as "the first shocker." Horie had no affiliation with the N.O.R.C. and he had taken the club's close-knit membership by surprise. Horie had also brought the tiny universe of boats and sailors before the Japanese public for the first time. And he had done something, as Ogimi said, that put him "in orbit." In the years after Horie's crossing, Japan developed an elaborate subculture of such people—mountain climbers, polar explorers, latter-day African adventurers—whose accomplishments always made the evening news and who hold the general public somewhat spellbound. Horie, who spent the rest of his career in similar exploits on the water, gave sailing a place in this category. "It's gravity," Ogimi declared flatly. "People like Horie are beyond the gravity of Japanese society."

Two years after Horie's crossing, Japan took its turn as host of the summer Olympics. It was a momentous occasion of a different kind. Nineteen sixty-four was also the year Japan joined the Organization for Economic Cooperation and Development, and these two events were the first to be advanced as signs that the postwar era had finally ended. In fact, the year did not mark the discernible beginning or end of anything. In the quarter century since then, the same importance has been attached to many other milestones, without notable success. But the 1964 Olympics did bring Japanese sailors a certain honor: it was the first time they hosted an important international yachting event.

The pace of change quickened after that. Three years later the N.O.R.C. started the Hachijo race, a three-hundred-mile run around the Izu Islands, specks of lava in a long volcanic archipelago due south of Tokyo Bay. Hachijo took Japanese ocean racers into the open sea for the first time. It was the first competition to cross the Kuroshio or Japan Current, a kind of Gulf Stream in the Pacific;

that added some wide-open water and severe weather to the proceedings.

That was what Ogimi wanted. In 1969 he skippered the first Japanese boat to enter the Sydney-to-Hobart race and placed twenty-first in a field of sixty-nine. More important than the respectable finish was the world into which Ogimi had sailed. Sydney-to-Hobart then ranked among the world's top three offshore events, along with the Fastnet race (part of the Admiral's Cup) in Britain and a contest that runs from Newport to Bermuda. They were all roughly six hundred and fifty miles long, and they involved some difficult conditions. These races meant seamanship, boat technology, maintenance, and pure sport of a kind Japanese sailors at the N.O.R.C. could scarcely imagine. Sydney-to-Hobart was no closed world of unknown enthusiasts; it was front-page news all over Australia and New Zealand.

"That was my first international yacht race, and it was a real eye-opener—a spectacle," Ogimi recalled. "The biggest thing that stuck in my mind was that we needed a serious race—six hundred miles-plus—in our own waters. Offshore racing for Japan meant going around these little islands. We had nothing like what I saw down in Australia."

Ogimi, then the N.O.R.C.'s executive director, soon organized an eight-hundred-and-forty mile race that began in Okinawa and ended four to seven days later at the entrance to Tokyo Bay. But there was one more step before Japan would be truly on the offshore racing map: it had to host a world championship event. The question was whether Japan was ready to do so or not.

Most people in international sailing circuit hadn't even bothered to ask. Ogimi had. Encouraged by a yachting friend from New Zealand, Ogimi started lobbying when he heard that Singapore, an unpromising place of silted waters and mild winds, was scheduled to host the Quarter-Ton Worlds in 1978. The Offshore Racing Council, headquartered in London, was initially skeptical about Ogimi's plan to move the event. "Japan hosting an O.R.C. event?" British members of the council may as well have asked. But Ogimi eventually prevailed.

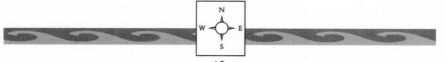

The Quarter-Ton event involved boats of about twenty-five feet—at the time the smallest class raced under the International Offshore Rule, or I.O.R.—but it was a notable success for Japan. Of the thirty-two craft entered, half were Japanese, and the winner was one called *Magician V*, a sleek but not overly sophisticated craft built of Fiberglas. It was designed by the marine division of the Yamaha Motor Company and skippered—on paper, at least—by a young Japanese sailor named Yasuyuki Hakomori.

Yamaha sponsored two boats in that race. The other, *Magician VI*, was skippered by a rising star named Kazunori Komatsu. Shortly before the event, Komatsu had ordered his rudder cut down to reduce resistance and increase speed. He thought he could improve on *Magician VI*'s performance in the qualifying rounds. Instead, the sloop lost its balance and Komatsu had trouble controlling it. He placed ninth.

Komatsu did not like losing. But that wasn't why he viewed the Quarter-Ton results with what he called "deep regret." It had to do with the fraught questions of identity and national pride. Yamaha had entered the Quarter-Ton Worlds to win them—in the months before the series started it became a kind of corporate goal among the marine division's executives—and Yamaha had done whatever it thought necessary to fulfill that ambition. It spent heavily on the design side and the sail program. And it filled out the crew with foreigners. That was a display of no confidence, so far as Komatsu was concerned, and his bitterness endured. "There were two Americans in *V*'s crew," Komatsu explained many years later. "One was a trimmer and one the helmsman. I've never considered the winner a Japanese boat. It was an American boat. The Americans really skippered it, and the Americans won the race."

Even Kazunori Komatsu allowed that the '78 event was a turning point in the local sailing scene. It had focused energy beforehand, and the series itself was a classroom. Many later advances in Japanese yacht design, sail design, hardware, and rigging can be traced to those who contributed to the large Japanese showing at Sajima.

Japan had come a long way since the postwar days. Kaoru Ogimi,

race committee chairman and chairman of the jury, took special satisfaction in knowing two O.R.C. observers had come from London. To him, it was as if a wrapper had dropped from an object years in the making. "We weren't yet world class," he said, "but it showed that we could make it."

•   •   •

Kaoru Ogimi's membership number at the N.O.R.C., the number stitched onto his sails, was 179. Depending on how you looked at it, the nation's interest in sailing had either grown enormously since the early postwar days or it had remained stunted, like so much else in Japan that wasn't directly related to productive capacity. By the autumn of 1990, the N.O.R.C. claimed more than four thousand members. But there was no other club of its kind in the country. There were a thousand keeled sailboats in Japan. The world's wealthiest industrial nation by many measures still had only three hundred and eighty thousand registered pleasure craft, including powerboats and dinghies, compared with sixteen million in the United States.

In certain parts of the Japanese archipelago you can travel the coastal roads for many hours and look directly out to sea. It is a jagged shoreline, with spectacular cliffs that drop straight to the water. Once out of the big industrial ports, what you see are splendid bays, inlets, and lagoons—splendid and empty. It is as if you are driving the perimeter of an underdeveloped island republic. All that is missing are the palm trees and the houses on stilts. First you admire it; then you begin to wonder about a nation so disinclined to partake of its own gifts.

Island dwellers, the Japanese could claim a long history as a seafaring people. The beginning of their tradition in shipbuilding, as elsewhere, was dugout logs. From there, rounded hulls gradually gave way to planked sides and then to flat, planked bottoms. By the sixteenth century, civil wars were raging in Japan, and local powers fought many of their battles in *seki-bune* and *atake-bune*. These were ships fifteen to thirty meters long powered by fifty to a hundred

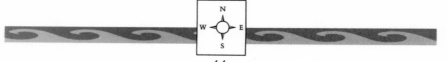

and sixty oars. The *atake-bune,* the larger of the two types, flew a single square sail hoisted athwartships on a yard.

These were ships comparable in size, if not in sophistication, to any of the age. Japan had trade routes that stretched as far as Indonesia and India, and it was well on the way to developing a seaborne empire in the manner of Spain, Portugal, and Holland. But the Tokugawa shogunate changed all that. A few decades after coming to power in 1603, the Tokugawa rulers completed the policy called *sakoku,* or isolation. Foreigners were barred, with the exception of Dutch merchants allowed to occupy an islet in Nagasaki Harbor. Travel abroad, should the sojourner return, was punishable by death. No ship could be built to carry more than a thousand *koku,* five thousand one hundred bushels; in effect, the construction of oceangoing ships was banned.

For the next two centuries the Japanese lived with their backs to the sea. Coastal routes and inland waterways were extensive, but Tokugawa citizens came to think of the open sea as a threat. This was not without justification. The tidal currents washing the Japanese islands, notably the Kuroshio and another called the Oyashio, are strong, and they bring severe and unpredictable weather. The sea is unfriendly—that is partly how Japan now explains the Tokugawa era to itself. A Japanese sailor in Hayama once put it this way: "We didn't look out over the horizon. A few did, but it's the nature of Japanese to look inward. We had no Vasco da Gama, no Columbus. We were satisfied living here by ourselves."

Modernization in the late nineteenth century turned Japan seaward again. By 1905 its navy was powerful enough to defeat the Russians—and to start a sea war for Pacific supremacy thirty-six years later. Shipbuilding was designated a strategic industry during the 1930s, and it became one again after the surrender in 1945. Guided by the Ministry of International Trade and Industry, Japanese builders of cargo vessels increased their share of world orders from less than a quarter in 1960 to two thirds by the middle of the decade. For a time, until the Koreans got into the game, no one could challenge them.

Japan has lived with a sense of urgency since it first began its

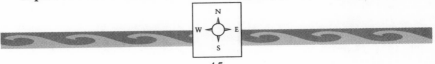

catch-up exercise. Once the shogunate gave way to the Meiji era, in 1868, speed of development and economic efficiency became unchallenged priorities. These were reestablished as national goals twice more in this century—once when war production was dramatically escalated, and again in the fifties, when economic power replaced political and military primacy in the Pacific as the end to which the nation dedicated itself.

None of this did much for sailors.

Kaoru Ogimi, who tended to have two views on every question, once described the postwar sailing scene as "small boats in a small world." There was a specific reason for that. In many ways Japan after the war behaved much like a third world nation. And one of those ways, known to every sailor in the islands, was to tax what were officially classified as luxuries. Any sailboat larger than seven and a half meters (twenty-four feet seven inches) was in that category, and its owner paid a tax of forty percent on its value. It was another form of *sakoku* so far as yachtsmen were concerned. The regulation was altered over the years, but it was rescinded in a series of controversial tax reforms implemented only on April 1, 1989.

"What we were doing did not exactly rate a MITI subsidy," Ogimi said. "On the contrary, sailboats were like diamonds and golf clubs. They were things no sane Japanese could or should even be contemplating. The attitude was, 'Never mind that. Get back to work.' There was no sailing scene the way you're thinking of it. It took a few crazy people who scrounged around and somehow saved enough to build modest little boats. We were like pioneers."

•   •   •

Among the pioneers was a young professor named Kensaku Nomoto, who took his first academic post in the department of naval architecture at Osaka University, in 1950. Nomoto grew up on a remote island called Nogutsuna in the Sea of Japan, and he learned to sail at fourteen by borrowing a boat of coarsely hewn wood from a local fisherman. It measured twenty feet and had a single sail and a local version of a sculling oar. When I first met Nomoto, a few years after he retired from the department of naval architecture at Osaka, he launched eagerly into a scientific analysis of the Japanese-style oar, which had a bent shaft and a wide blade, and explained why it was superior to the straight-shafted object better known in the West.

Kensaku Nomoto never lost his admiration for those boats. He tried to incorporate elements of traditional Japanese ship design in every project he took on. After he retired in 1985, he came to devote more and more of his time to scouring shipyards and libraries for old designs. "All over the world these designs are disappearing, giving way to boats of plastic, steel, and aluminum that are the same everywhere. It's a cultural legacy that I'd like to record. If you're lucky, you can sometimes find old drawings—not even blueprints, just crude drawings—in the corners of old boatyards."

He was a compact man, with a broad face and a warm smile. He managed to combine the reserve and modesty typical of the Japanese with a certain determination. One of Nomoto's sailing friends once said to me about him, "He doesn't like foreigners." He shook his head and laughed. It was late at night, and we had both been drinking for many hours.

"That's not true," I replied. "I'm sure of it."

"*I'm* sure of it," my host said, with a vehemence that brought a brief silence to our rambling chatter about boats and races and the people who sailed in them.

Nomoto was sixty-six when I met him. In our conversations, he often prefaced remarks by saying, "I'm no superpatriot" or "I'm not an extreme nationalist." A "but" usually followed. There is a kind of nationalism in Japan that finds expression in a certain pride in the superiority of Japanese culture and Japanese methods. Nomoto exhibited that often, but he seemed, just the same, to be more interested in what he called "the interface of East and West" than in straight-ahead nationalism of the kind that lingers among some of his generation.

He was a recognized authority in his field. He never worked in a Japanese corporation, but he did as much as anyone else to power the postwar shipbuilding industry. He was a *sensei*, a master. Nomoto's students became the brains behind the industry's postwar boom. They were in the executive offices, the design divisions, and the testing laboratories of every shipbuilder in the country. Once you met some of them, it became clear that Nomoto had troubled to instill in them a deep appreciation of the history of their craft—or, as he put it, their science.

In the 1850s, he once recounted, an earthquake sank two Russian warships off the coast of the Shimoda Peninsula, south of Tokyo. The Russian admiral traveled to Edo, as the capital was then called, to ask the shogunate if two schooners could be built so he and his crew could complete their mission for the tsar's navy. The Edo bureaucrats agreed to supply the Russians with a complement of Japanese carpenters. The ships were produced, they sailed successfully, and schooner construction, unknown until then, began to spread throughout Japan.

"It was the very beginning of Western shipbuilding in this country," Nomoto said. But he balanced his conclusion carefully. "Japanese carpenters absorbed Western techniques quickly. It's one of the great points of a people—to be able to acquire foreign technology that fast. At the same time, without traditional Japanese techniques, I don't think it would have been possible."

Nomoto sailed a thirty-four-foot sloop that he equipped for single-handed sailing when he built it in 1976. He named it *Haru-ichiban II* after a mild southwesterly wind known among Japanese fishermen to herald the arrival of spring each year. It was a cutter, having two headsails instead of one, and it was a remarkable, if slightly peculiar, example of his approach to design. While *Haru-ichiban II* was at home in any marina in the West—and it had seen quite a few of them—it was constructed of wide planks in the Japanese tradition and had the upturned bow characteristic of junks and other locally influenced ships throughout Asia. Its lines were unmistakably of two cultures. At the stern Nomoto had mounted a Japanese sculling oar.

Kensaku Nomoto's N.O.R.C. number was 58. He didn't count himself a founding member, as Kaoru Ogimi did, but it was Nomoto who first organized the club's branch in Osaka and Kobe. Like Ogimi, Nomoto had learned to sail without instruction, and the experience had marked his habits on the water for life. Ogimi preferred long ocean races that started or finished in another

country thousands of miles away—he was a *Mariners Library* sailor; Nomoto liked nothing better than to sail single-handed, alone or with his wife, Nobuko.

He rarely raced. Despite his seniority at the N.O.R.C., Nomoto was never as influential as Kaoru Ogimi in the club's affairs. Ogimi had pulled Japan along like a dinghy on a stern line into the world of international events. Nomoto was a loner. But he was also an organization man in a way Ogimi could never be. As a student and later a professor, he had spent years in the university sailing clubs. If Ogimi's background and temperament made him something of an outsider in his own country, Nomoto was an insider who understood the Japanese system well and preferred it, at last, to any other.

• • •

Kensaku Nomoto and Kaoru Ogimi did not know one another in the very early days. But they had been acquaintances since the 1960s, and it was about the time they met that both were introduced to a relatively new member of the N.O.R.C. His name was Tatsumitsu Yamasaki, and he was a young business executive with a brilliant smile, a magnetic personality, a pronounced taste for living, and a fervor for yacht races that made up for whatever he lacked in experience.

Tatsu Yamasaki did not get his first boat from the end of a pier or from a next-door neighbor who caught fish for a living, but by pointing at it and asking his father to buy it for him. He did his first sailing in the club at Waseda University, another Meiji-era institution. Together with Keio, Waseda maintained a kind of Oxford-Cambridge rivalry called Sokei. Yamasaki enjoyed Sokei sailing events immensely. But after he graduated in 1957, he spent three arduous years doing little other than learning the family business, which was the processing and marketing of curry powder, pepper, and other spices not native to the Japanese diet. The S & B Shokuhin Company had grown into a large and prosperous enterprise since his father started it in 1926; there was no time for sailing while Tatsu Yamasaki, the second of four brothers but the most dynamic of them, prepared to take his place at the top of the company.

One day in his fourth summer as a young executive—"all of a sudden," he recalled much later—Yamasaki decided he had to have a sailboat. He had heard that an American serving at the Yokosuka naval base was trying to sell a Lightning-class craft, and it sounded perfect. It was a small sloop, nineteen feet, but it came with a spinnaker. The price was high for a Japanese: it then cost nearly four hundred yen to buy a United States dollar, and the American at Yokosuka wanted a thousand dollars.

After pleading with his father, Yamasaki took a train to Yokosuka and pounded the American down to nine hundred. That same day he sailed his sloop into Tokyo Bay for the first time. He landed at the edge of an old gun battery, a deserted no man's land set years earlier in the waters beyond the harbor, and cut his feet badly on the rocks. Afterward he carefully avoided the submarine nets that had been beneath the surface during his Waseda days, until an old seaman told him they were no longer there. "That was a great summer for me," Yamasaki, S & B's chairman and chief executive, recalled one day in his office. "I had a boat, and I felt very free."

Yamasaki began life in a big house along the Sumida River in Tokyo. During his student days, most Japanese watched television in the street, through a shopwindow. It was the fashion then to take driving lessons, but since most people couldn't afford a car, they were called "paper drivers." This was life in another world from the one in which Yamasaki lived. He remembers neighbors coming over to watch programs on the Yamasakis' black and white set. They had a car and servants; Tatsu's father had built another big house in another fashionable district after the one near the river was destroyed in a bombing raid.

By the early 1960s, when Yamasaki bought his first sailboat, others were buying their first television sets. Nissan and Toyota cars were finding small niches in foreign markets; Yamaha Motor, an offshoot of a musical instrument manufacturer, had started making motorcycles and along with a relatively new company called Honda was selling them briskly at home and overseas. All of this came amid a decade of feverish economic growth that had begun in 1955. Life

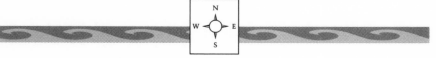

in Japan was returning to—or perhaps first becoming—something like normal.

"The Olympic Games were coming to Tokyo in a couple of years, and we were beginning to get ready," Tatsu Yamasaki recalled. "We were back on our feet again. People started thinking, We Japanese can go on living."

For Yamasaki, going on living meant buying another boat. One weekend he tried to sail from Yokohama to Kamakura, a pretty seaside town a few miles to the south, and the weather forced him to give up in the middle. He began to look for something bigger— preferably something with a cabin—and he found it moored off a Sagami Bay village called Aburatsubo. What struck him most were the provisions stored below deck. "Dry blankets—that was impor- tant to me then. I had been sailing in dinghies since Waseda, and the blankets were always wet and messy." The memory made Yama- saki grimace.

He named the boat, which measured twenty-one feet, *Ako*, the first syllable meaning "Asia" and the second one "light." Ako was also the nickname of Tatsu's new wife, Ayako. Not long afterward, Yamasaki took *Ako* into his first race, the Toba. He finished second. It was the start of a process that would take a few more years and a lot more money.

In 1967, Yamasaki bought a boat he could sail in an international race. The closest such event was the China Sea race, a time-honored contest among colonials that ran from the Royal Hong Kong Yacht Club across the South China Sea to Manila. The first Japanese to enter the China Sea race—or any other internationally recognized yachting contest—was named Shintaro Ishihara. At the time he sailed to Manila in 1966, Ishihara was a best-selling novelist and a young, unaccomplished member of the Liberal Democratic Party. He did badly in the China Sea race, having gotten his navigational strategy wrong.

Yamasaki sailed for Hong Kong with a crew of six in late March 1968. His boat, *Miss Sunbird*, was so laden with provisions from all his friends that he had to stop in Shimoda, south of Sagami Bay, to unload most of it. The journey took almost two weeks, but it was

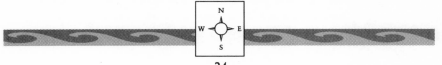

worth every nautical mile of it: Tatsu finished a very respectable ninth. And, as he remembered twenty-two years later, "I've been crazy about racing from then until now."

• • •

Kensaku Nomoto once explained, "My profession was to teach naval architecture and to make scientific studies in theories of motion and maneuvering. Sailing was my hobby."

He never saw the sport as a matter of winning or losing, and most of the N.O.R.C.'s members in the early 1980s felt the same way. They were weekend sailors. They would drive down to Sagami Bay, sail for the day, and then come in early enough to beat the traffic back. They would take clients or office colleagues with them. Keeping a boat in the water was like having an expensive membership at a Japanese golf club. It was as much a business tool as anything else.

For a core group, however, sailing was something more than a diversion to be picked up and put down according to the dictates of daily obligations. On land, they were politicians or executives or bureaucrats or entrepreneurs; but they were not just weekenders on the water. Men like Kaoru Ogimi and Tatsu Yamasaki had also become known, to one degree or another, on the international ocean-racing scene.

They were at the far end of the line through which yachting gossip circulated around the world, but they were accustomed to hearing most of it sooner or later. On September 26, 1983, they were as stunned as anyone when *Australia II*, the boat sailing for Alan Bond in the America's Cup off Newport, Rhode Island, came from a three-to-one disadvantage to defeat the New York Yacht Club's defender, *Liberty*. The Japanese had never been part of the America's Cup scene, of course. But this was a momentous occasion for racing yachtsmen all over the world: the N.Y.Y.C. had lost its most prized possession after defending it successfully twenty-four times over a period of a hundred and thirty-two years. A monopoly had been broken, a torch had been passed across another ocean. A closed field had been opened.

Kaoru Ogimi, by then the N.O.R.C.'s vice-commodore, and Shin-

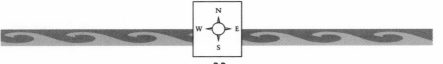

taro Ishihara, who was commodore, were yet more shocked by what began to unfold after the Australian victory. America's Cup rules stipulate that the next challenges must be announced within one month of a Cup competition. Hours before the deadline in October 1983, the Royal Perth Yacht Club, from which *Australia II* had sailed, received a telex announcing the first challenge from a Japanese club in the event's long history.

Once the wire services picked up the news, there was mayhem around the small rooms that served as the N.O.R.C.'s offices in central Tokyo. The reports said the Tokyo Ocean Racing Club had thrown down the gauntlet and that the Australians were only too delighted to accept the challenge. Calls flooded in from around the world.

There was only one problem: the N.O.R.C., the only club in Japan that could seriously consider a challenge for the Cup, had never even entertained the idea. The Tokyo Ocean Racing Club? There wasn't one. A Japanese challenge for the America's Cup? There wasn't one of those either.

The tale turned out to be humorous in a picaresque sort of way. The culprits were two Japanese yachting journalists who, having studied the America's Cup rules, thought they saw an opportunity. Why not submit a challenge that would galvanize the Japanese sailing community into action? Send the telex late, thus getting the best chance of an unexamined, last-minute acceptance. Once past that hurdle, they could form a syndicate and invite sponsors to buy into it. It was cart-before-horse as a piece of logic. But it had, in an unexpected way, something approximating its intended effect.

Long afterward, Kaoru Ogimi would recall these events as "a sudden and rude awakening"—another shocker. Without much humor in his voice, he called the whole ruse "a disgrace—taking advantage of the most sacred and revered tradition in the world of yachting." But he also called it, later in the same conversation, "a catalyst." Speculation had been growing for several years that Japan would eventually mount a challenge. The technology seemed to be there, and so did the money; given the record Japanese sailors had slowly accumulated in other races, it was widely considered simply a matter of time.

"We were incensed with these people," Ogimi said. "But as things unfolded it was obvious that Japan had to launch a proper challenge sooner or later, and preferably sooner. By this time, the '83 window was closed, and thank goodness it was. But we were jerked out of a dream."

NEMAWASHI

ecember 29, 1985, was a crisp and sunny day at the entrance to Tokyo Bay. It was less than perfect for a race—no chop, but almost no wind, either. Afterward, many sailors would say they had trouble getting out of Yokosuka Harbor.

Taro Kimura remembers the date well, because something unusual happened that afternoon. Kaoru Ogimi spoke to him.

Both men, in light sweaters and windbreakers, were on the deck of *Cynara*, a British-built teak and mahogany ketch that the N.O.R.C. chartered for the start of the first Tokyo-to-Guam race, which the club was launching as an annual event. There was a small craft with a few U. S. Navy officers on board—Ogimi had been chatting with them before the race began—but few other boats were out to watch the start.

Nor was it crowded aboard *Cynara*. In a modest, informal sort of way, the club's spectator boat is something of a social scene on such occasions. That day it carried perhaps two dozen N.O.R.C. members.

Despite the dearth of company, Taro Kimura was nonetheless surprised when the older man approached him. They had been nodding acquaintances for some time, but they were never, and never would be, much more.

Kimura was an accomplished man by 1985. He had started his career at NHK, the state-supervised broadcasting company, as soon as he finished at Keio University, twenty-one years earlier. His easy manner, good looks, and newsman's instinct had taken him far and fast since then. He had served as a television correspondent in Beirut, Geneva, and Washington before being called back to anchor the evening news in 1982. He had a gracious wife, two boys in high school, and he commuted daily to NHK's Tokyo studios from a comfortable, chalet-like home not far from Sagami Bay in Zushi.

One of Kimura's American friends—he had many—once called him "the Ted Koppel of Japan," and it was as good a comparison as any. He was not a Walter Cronkite; he lacked what the English would call Cronkite's *gravitas*. But he was well traveled. Born and partly raised in Berkeley, California, Kimura spoke English flawlessly. He was tall, television-handsome, and usually tanned. He could anchor the evening news, as was then becoming the fashion, from Washington or Paris or Cairo, depending on the focus of world events. His experience gave him something not too many Japanese had: an innate understanding of how stories should be told, and the power and benefits that came of telling them well.

Kimura was relatively green on the sailing scene, but he was certain enough of himself to admit it. He had sailed in the club at Keio; when he had time, he had also done some sailing on Lake Geneva and elsewhere during his years abroad. But he was no all-or-nothing competitor; he was only then beginning to understand the kind of passionate commitment Kaoru Ogimi had. Even if Kimura had wanted the kind of double life Ogimi and others like him lived, his profession wouldn't have allowed him to pursue it until he came home in '82.

"I'm a newcomer, a late bloomer among these guys," Kimura

once said in his Zushi living room. He pointed to a picture on the wall behind him. It was a technical drawing that a friend at the Hayama Marina Yacht Club had painted in for him. It showed a twenty-one-foot sloop, white with a pale blue cabin. Kimura called it *Maalesh*, "too bad," or "it can't be helped," in Arabic. It was his favorite expression from his Middle East days; he liked the implied insouciance of it.

"Look at my sail number: 3517," Kimura continued. "I'm a new boy."

By the early nineties, when that conversation took place, the twenty-one-footer was gone, replaced by a larger craft also named *Maalesh*. Kimura was racing regularly himself. He was accumulating experience, but it didn't count with Kaoru Ogimi. Ogimi had a way with disdain. After a while, he made you think it was a talent to be cultivated. The impression began with his height—he was tall for a Japanese, and he simply spent a lot of time looking down on people. But he was also impatient with the cautious, indirect way his countrymen had of expressing themselves. Ogimi was thought too blunt by many of those around him. You don't come to the point right away in Japan; you arrive at it last, after a journey of considerable duration up a spiraled mountain road.

Chatting with Ogimi once about a few of the N.O.R.C.'s members, I happened to mention Kimura's diminutive comparison. "Late bloomer?" Ogimi replied. "He never bloomed at all. Except in the media."

On board the *Cynara*, Kimura and Ogimi conversed briefly and then turned toward opposite ends of the deck. As they did—again to Kimura's surprise—Ogimi suggested lunch. They fixed a date, and a month or so later they met at the Foreign Correspondents' Club, a slightly worn watering hole in central Tokyo. It was a curious choice. The F.C.C.J., situated on the top two floors of a twenty-story building overlooking the imperial palace, was, to Tokyo's foreign hacks, an unexceptional restaurant and a clipping library. Mostly it was a bar, frequented also by diplomats, bankers, and executives. But for the Japanese it had a certain "power lunch" cachet. It suggested that the local diner moved easily in the world of *gaijin*, of "outside people."

An onlooker may have concluded that Ogimi and Kimura were absorbed mostly in making sure they were keeping one another satisfactorily impressed. But as they settled into chairs in the dining room, the older man got right to the point.

"Are you interested in the America's Cup?" he asked Kimura. Ogimi barely smiled. "In my view, I think it's time we entered a challenge, and I'm talking about the next one."

Kimura had little taste for Ogimi's ungentle way of doing things. His reaction, as he took in the notion for the first time, was a nervous laugh. "I agree," he said, "but can we?"

It wasn't the response Ogimi was looking for. It suggested the kind of moist-palmed uncertainty the Japanese often displayed in the outside world, a trait Ogimi despised.

"Isn't it worth at least studying the question among the limited number of people in the N.O.R.C. who would concern themselves?" Ogimi asked impatiently. "Consider it. Would you concern yourself? Are you available?"

Kimura was. And having scrambled onto a patch of common ground, the two men slowly began to converse in a more relaxed manner than they ever had before. Ogimi had particular concerns. One was the Koreans, who were much in the air by the mid-eighties. The Korean economy was booming. Most Japanese were acutely aware that their neighbor was in the midst of a "miracle" at least as impressive as their own, and they knew what theirs had done to the economies of their competitors. "Japan has the wealth it takes now," Ogimi told Kimura. "I can't see this chance go by Japanese sailors. I don't want some other Asians to do it first."

Mostly, they talked about the Cup itself—the history, which both men knew, the Australian victory, and what any syndicate had to put into a credible challenge. Much as two Americans might pass the time assembling their favorite baseball team, Taro Kimura and Kaoru Ogimi spent part of their lunch constructing a crew and an afterguard—who would be up in the bow, who would trim, who would navigate, who would helm.

Lunch ended, and the two made no further plans. Kimura puzzled over that afterward. Lunch, conversation—then nothing. He would not hear from Ogimi again for four months. When he did, it was as if the ten-minute gun had just gone off.

•   •   •

Much of what gets done in Japan, in business, in government, or anywhere else where an agreement among many is required, relies on a process called *nemawashi*. Translated literally, the term means "root turning" and refers to the replanting of trees or shrubs. With extreme care so as not to damage fragile tendrils, the gardener engaged in *nemawashi* will slowly encircle his object by digging each segment of a root system free. It is a delicate process. When it's completed, the transplant itself takes place in a sudden moment. Outsiders are frequently perplexed by the prevalence of *nemawashi* in Japanese society, mostly because they cannot see it. Decisions are made, contracts signed, policies set with no apparent forethought. Board meetings, often embattled affairs in the West, end in easy agreement within minutes.

Kaoru Ogimi may have thought *nemawashi* an inconvenient way of doing things, but he was hard at it by the time he lunched with Kimura in early 1986. During the Quarter-Ton Worlds in '78, he had gotten to know a young sailor whose family name matched that of Ogimi's village. Kinta Ninomiya was a former Snipe-class champion and he had done decently in the Sajima races. The two stayed in touch afterward, and in the autumn of 1985 Ninomiya called Ogimi and asked if he could spare some time.

Ninomiya had something on his mind that was rather less abstract than a Korean challenge for the America's Cup. Since the Australian victory in '83, a flamboyant property developer named Masakazu Kobayashi had appeared on the sailing scene and was looking very much as if he planned to pull together a syndicate himself. Kobayashi seemed to have money—or access to it, no one then knew which—and he was investing heavily in a seaside resort called the Bengal Bay Club. But he was no sailor. Nobody at the N.O.R.C. had ever heard of him.

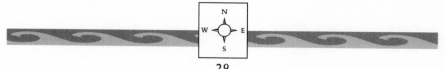

"We can't let Kobayashi stand for Japan," Ninomiya said when he went to see Ogimi in Tokyo. "He doesn't. We have to put together a challenge that truly represents the sailing community. It has to receive the right corporate backing and be a real national effort. It can't be some entrepreneur interested only in the prestige of the Cup."

Kaoru Ogimi's office, where his conversations with Ninomiya took place, was on the fourth floor of a narrow building located in a neighborhood called Kanda, a few minutes' walk from the imperial palace. All around the two men as they spoke were sailing books (in Japanese and English), scale models of yachts Ogimi had raced, and files filled with plans for future projects. A large window behind Ogimi's desk looked out upon an amusement park with a roller coaster of frightening complexity. Any conversation in Ogimi's office was usually punctuated by the shrieks of children thrilled, for a moment, not to know what would happen to them next.

Ogimi naturally agreed with Ninomiya. Ever since the Australian victory, Ogimi had been thinking steadily, and, he had assumed, more or less alone, about what the N.O.R.C.—what Japan—should do. Two years after Alan Bond's success, it had grown into a preoccupation. If someone else from this side of the Pacific was going to leap into the lights, it had to be Japan. And if it had to be Japan, it also had to be the people in Japan who came closest to knowing what they were doing.

But Ninomiya, who looked up to Ogimi as an experienced sailor of international reputation, had come to the wrong man. Ogimi had long ago concluded, as he said later, that the America's Cup "wasn't what it used to be." It had become a huge commitment. It required a syndicate sustained by a financial and managerial structure far beyond his powers to organize.

"There's only one guy we can go to with something like this," Ogimi told Ninomiya. "That's Tatsu Yamasaki. I've had a long association with him at the N.O.R.C. I'm sure I can talk him into it."

•   •   •

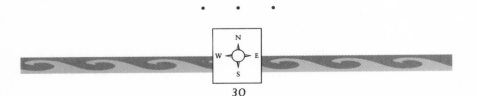

Much later, Tatsu Yamasaki would speak often of an America's Cup challenge as the fulfillment of a dream—not, as Ogimi had called it, an awakening from one. He, too, had thought things through. He also saw what the future held when Alan Bond carried the Cup across the Pacific. But Yamasaki came away from these considerations a skeptic. When he finished watching the Newport race in 1983, he doubted that a hundred Japanese had even seen an America's Cup. No one in Japan had owned a Twelve-Meter boat, the class in which the Cup was contested. It would take Japan ten more years to mount a challenge, Yamasaki reckoned then, and twenty to win one.

Yamasaki's offices, the headquarters of S & B Shokuhin, sat on a narrow side street in Kabuto-cho, a district of small businesses in the Nihonbashi section of Tokyo. Yamasaki's father, who had started the business in a tiny wooden house built the place after the war. Being no more than a mile or so from the center of the capital, the land under the S & B offices was worth hundreds of millions of dollars by the late eighties. But the building itself, a low-rise of brown stucco, was so modest that visitors often had trouble finding it. When you walked through S & B's front door, it was difficult to decide, for a second, whether you had entered the offices of a food supplier or a sporting goods wholesaler. Against one wall there were product samples arranged alongside pictures of curry mixes and instant dinners. More prominent around the room were posters of skiing events, regattas, and marathons.

Tatsu Yamasaki was a slightly built man who managed, nonetheless, to project a certain power when he walked into a room. He moved quickly and decisively among others. He laughed easily, a deep, whiskey laugh, and he spoke in a low voice. It was the voice of a much larger man and one roughened by years of heavy smoking and the obligatory evenings out with clients, suppliers, and colleagues.

Yamasaki was understanding enough as Ogimi and Ninomiya unfolded their case for a Japanese challenge. Understanding but silent. He was a listener, and he nodded assent often. Sometimes he would hold his chin in his hands and it would look as if he had left

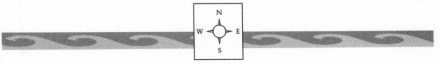

the conversation behind. Although he was usually gregarious, these were moments when he fell back into a recess that was private even when measured against the usual Japanese reserve. Yamasaki listened, but he gave his two visitors nothing. At the end of that first session, Ogimi hadn't talked Yamasaki into anything more than another meeting.

One gathering followed another, usually at S & B, usually a few weeks apart. New people came and went. A photographer named Kaoru Soehata joined. He had covered the America's Cup since 1980 and would depart for Fremantle in October to start shooting the challengers' series. At Newport in '83, Soehata had been on the large cruiser chartered by *Yachting* magazine. It had stayed near the bottom mark, and he remembered shooting *Australia II* as it crossed the finish line in the final race. When he lowered his camera and turned around, he found the Americans on the boat in tears. Back on shore, the Australians were in a frenzy. He wanted to tell the people at S & B about what he called "the reality of it," though he had trouble getting it across. "If you take this seriously, it will change your lives," Soehata said at one meeting. "It raises people very high, and it also bankrupts people. It involves you more completely than anything else you've ever done."

There was the reality of it, and the S & B people wanted to figure it out. They studied things like organization and management. What is a syndicate—a corporation, a club? And the Deed of Gift, the Cup's basic rules: what was that all about? Ninomiya was named secretary of the group, disappeared, then came back with details of a previous British challenge—how they lived, how the boat was designed, how the crew was organized. Yamasaki, for all the sailing he had done, knew nothing of these matters. Ogimi worried about someone else getting in first, and about commercialization at the hands of Japanese sponsors. At one meeting Yamasaki asked, "How much do we think this will cost?" He was the first to mention it. Everyone knew it would be formidable, but no one had much of an idea how formidable. A billion yen, someone answered—six million two hundred and fifty thousand dollars at the time, a million and a quarter more than it had cost Alan Bond to win in '83. A billion yen or two billion or five billion, Yamasaki thought. They were stumbling.

The third-floor conference room at S & B had a hermetic feeling to it. Several windows gave onto the narrow street below, but they were usually closed and curtained. In the center, leather sofas with antimacassar doilies draped over them faced one another in the Asian manner, and matching chairs at either end completed the rectangular sitting area. There wasn't much else. Around the edges of the room were a few brush paintings, a small yachting trophy, and a model of one of the *Sunbirds*.

Just outside the door, Yamasaki kept large bronze busts of his mother and father. They were mounted on wooden pedestals and they looked straight ahead, expressionless, in spectacles and conservative Western dress. Others brushed by these objects, imposing as they were, without noticing them. But to Yamasaki they were constant reminders. In early April, he had finished the books for S & B's previous fiscal year. The results were good, but the yen was climbing in value and the year ahead wouldn't be an easy one. I am trying to run a company with twelve hundred employees and revenues of fifty-four billion yen, he thought midway through one session. These get-togethers are fine, but they are leading nowhere.

Tatsu Yamasaki wasn't used to that. Apart from the war years, S & B had advanced in a more or less steady march since his father set out on his own in the late twenties. Yamasaki could recall the story, and did with pleasure when asked, as easily as he could recall the previous day. In Saitama, a rural district swallowed up by greater Tokyo in the postwar years, the family had produced soy sauce. Yamasaki senior, born in 1895, made his way to the city when the business went under. He worked for a pepper manufacturer until, on a day off once, he bought a bowl of rice flavored with curry.

The stuff was imported at the time. But Yamasaki's father had what later became known as "the founder's spirit," a phrase applied to a generation of merchants and businessmen who, with a foot in the Meiji era, had borrowed ideas to start ventures that would leave lasting marks on Japan. S & B stood for "sun and bird," and it would eventually make *curririce* something approaching a national dish. It also made Tatsu Yamasaki's father a local eccentric. He became so engrossed in smells that his nose turned bright red and his habits peculiar. Toshiuki Kajiyama, a popular prewar writer, eventually published a novel about him.

One of Yamasaki's clearest memories of his father came from a speech Tatsu heard him deliver during the early fifties. Called upon to recount the early days, the older Yamasaki explained that when he built his first factory, at the age of forty, he dreamed for the first time. It was a dream of his own future. When he was fifty, he said, the war was over and he dreamed again, that time of Japan. As his sixtieth year approached, he hoped he would dream once more, this time of the world.

Tatsu Yamasaki inherited much from his father. By the 1980s, S & B had expanded from spices and seasonings into beverages, pharmaceuticals, cosmetics, livestock feeds, liquor, seeds, flowers, medical supplies, restaurant management, stationery, sporting goods, fast food, and, as a company promotion man once put it, "other daily necessaries."

Yamasaki had his father's instinct for the business. Sooner or later, usually straight from the blue, he would ask new friends, "What do you eat when you cook at home?" Of *gaijin* he would ask, "What do you think of Japanese food?" And of Americans, "Do you think American food is good for you?" He thought it egregiously unhealthy—he grimaced whenever the subject came up. The people with the best diet he had ever come across, he considered one day, were the Koreans. He ate Korean whenever he visited his factory south of Seoul. "Very balanced," he said.

Tatsu Yamasaki was living the better part of his father's dreams. He said once that the founder's spirit also meant "the challenging spirit." The question was whether Yamasaki had it. He was a veteran of the yacht-racing scene, but his record was less than impressive. He had never demonstrated the kind of deep commitment that Kaoru Ogimi had. Yamasaki understood that he would make history, of a kind, simply by bringing Japan into the Cup. But he saw no way, as the meetings in the third-floor conference room wore on, that the dream of victory could be made a reality.

"We had no real sailors to speak of back then," Yamasaki said when he talked about the beginning. "We had no real technology to build a Twelve, no real capacity to study sails, no real experience in match racing.

"These were all reasons for me to be negative, and I was. Back then, I was a bit of a coward."

•   •   •

As the summer of 1986 drew to a close, Tatsu Yamasaki was also a bit of a loser.

He had sailed in the 1977 Admiral's Cup, in the Southern Ocean Racing Conference a year later, from Sydney to Hobart in 1981, and in the Pan Am Clipper Cup the year after that. He had done reasonably well in some of these regattas. *Miss Sunbird* had long ago been consigned to history; it gave way to *Sunbird II* in 1971, and by 1986 Yamasaki had replaced *Sunbird V,* which was decidedly behind the design curve at the time, with *Super Sunbird,* a forty-one foot prototype sloop built by Yamaha; Yamasaki saw it on the water one day, liked it, and paid twenty million yen for it.

That summer he set out for the Kenwood Cup in Honolulu—the Clipper Cup until Pan Am dropped its Pacific routes and Kenwood Corporation, the Japanese electronics firm, picked up the sponsorship. Before he left, in a gesture typical of Yamasaki, he took his crew out for an evening at a geisha house in an old quarter of Tokyo. Kagurazaka, prominent among the city's pleasure districts in the last century, had long ago given way to Ginza and Roppongi; supermarkets, restaurants, and stereo shops had whittled the geisha scene down to a few hard-to-find cobblestone alleyways; but it was a few minutes' drive from Yamasaki's home, and it still had a certain old-fashioned charm.

During the evening, a long and lively occasion, Yamasaki promised his crew a return celebration if they came home from Hawaii victorious. Just before departing, the crew had T-shirts printed with the slogan, *"Katara mata,"* or "If we win, Kagurazaka again,"

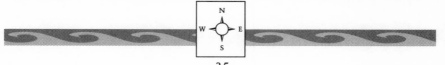

stenciled across them. They wore them throughout the Kenwood event.

It was that kind of trip. They were half serious and half clowning, but that was enough for Yamasaki. He enjoyed himself; he met Dennis Conner, then preparing a rematch with the Royal Perth Yacht Club, for the first time. He loaded *Super Sunbird* with new hardware, including an expensive set of spreaders dispatched from San Francisco. Then he watched his sloop place twenty-sixth. It was an improvement over his last appearance in Hawaii, when he came in forty-second. But you couldn't say much more for *Sunbird*'s crew. They didn't do too badly in the two Olympic course races, but they looked awful in the third event, an overnight ocean race of a hundred miles. The navigation was terrible; most of the crew fell asleep.

"Good experience but no power," Yamasaki said in a not very rigorous postmortem of the performance. "My crew was a nice bunch of guys. They were just too old."

He tossed off the Kenwood disaster with his usual aplomb, but Yamasaki wanted another boat when he got back from Honolulu. He wanted to take it back to the next Kenwood, or to the Admiral's Cup in Cowes again. He had no more enthusiasm for the America's Cup than when he had left. But he took his place once more in the leather armchair at the end of the S & B conference room. And it wasn't far into the autumn before he allowed that, yes, he could put into a challenge at least what he would have spent building his next *Sunbird*.

•   •   •

Taro Kimura was there when Yamasaki made that decision. Over the summer, Ogimi had finally decided the time was right to telephone and bring him in. He was a lightweight, Ogimi figured, but a Japanese syndicate would need a man like Kimura, someone who understood the media and was well placed within it, someone who might know how a syndicate from a country that cared little about sailing could win national attention and support.

The situation was changing—it looked that way, at least, from within. The core group, at that point, came down to Yamasaki, Ogimi, and Kimura. They invited a consultant in from Dentsu, the powerful advertising and promotional giant, and they got a *bucho*, a section head, to listen. This was a modest coup. Dentsu doesn't simply place ads and advance people and products; it has a powerful influence on the news and programming that gets on Japanese television and into the nation's newspapers. It is, in a sense, the national PR agency. The *bucho's* name was Nakasu. He came over to S & B, heard the proposition, and he said he'd get back to them.

Bucho Nakasu didn't return for the follow-up session. He sent an assistant instead, and the message was simple: raising the kind of money they would need for an event most people had never heard of would be, as they say in another country, tough sledding. At S & B they took it badly at first, then the other way. He didn't call us crazy, but he might as well have," Taro Kimura said. "I felt challenged. I thought, We don't need Dentsu to do this."

The whole thing seemed to drift in and out of their grasp in those months. They did have some numbers by then. They heard that some American syndicates had defended with four to five million dollars in the past. The sailors were all volunteers, their wives did the cooking. That seemed manageable. A billion yen or so: by then they were ready to accept that.

But then the challenger series began in Fremantle—it was October—and they started getting rather different reports. The Americans, it was said, were spending ten million dollars and they would probably go higher than that before the end. (They did, to fifteen million.) One of the American boats was rumored to be carrying a forward rudder, a technological development no one at S & B even understood. (It was Tom Blackaller's *USA*.) There was talk of intensive tank testing and computerized performance analysis. None of this surprised Kaoru Ogimi, but the others at S & B were still wondering whether Japan had anyone who could build even a rudimentary Twelve.

Videos were arriving from Australia, too. They showed challengers sailing in rough seas and winds of twenty-five knots or more— both standard conditions in Fremantle. The on-board cameras

showed bowmen handling jibs and spinnakers as if they were dinghy sails, and winch grinders who looked like neckless bar-bouncers. Who in Japan can do this? Kimura wondered to himself. At one meeting he asked the question aloud. Everyone else nodded; they were wondering the same thing themselves.

•   •   •

At Taro Kimura's urging, NHK was broadcasting feeds from Fremantle in the autumn of 1986. There had been no interest among Japanese networks when the Australian television people came to market the rights. But Kimura thought it was important to put the event before the public, and he had enough influence at the station to push through a deal. "Are you crazy? Buy it, buy it!" Kimura had shouted to the network's programming executives as the price went down. The Australians had arrived expecting a million dollars or more. In the end, NHK paid one hundred thousand dollars and combined the Cup coverage with American baseball games.

Kimura's judgment was proven right over and over again. One day he heard through friends that Yamaha was looking into the Fremantle competition. That made sense: the marine division was growing. But there was no way, Kimura thought, that Yamaha could organize a serious syndicate; it was unlikely that they were even contemplating it. They could build boats, but what did they know, really, beyond that? Kimura telephoned anyway, and a Yamaha man named Takao Takagi agreed to sit in on the next meeting at S & B.

The meeting turned out to be an important one. Takagi, a ranking executive in his fifties, could confirm that, yes, Yamaha was indeed interested in the America's Cup, but no, it had not thought of a challenge. It was watching. Only a few days earlier, Yamaha's president, Hideto Eguchi, had called a board meeting to ask just what the Cup competition on television was all about. Takagi, in fact, had been detailed after that meeting to fly to Fremantle for the final series and report on what he saw.

Hideto Eguchi, a silver-haired man who had spent all of his adult life at Yamaha, occupied a large office atop the company's headquarters in Hamamatsu, a couple of hours by train south of Tokyo.

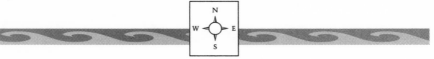

From his windows Eguchi could look out over a sprawl that was divided into what looked like city blocks. These were Yamaha Motor's main production facilities—low, gray buildings of enormous size. There were blocks where motorcycle engines were produced, blocks for chassis, and others for packing and shipping. The complex stretched as far as the horizon; scattered along its sides were baseball diamonds, soccer fields, and company dormitories.

After ordering Takagi to Fremantle, Eguchi had also sent for Kohtaro Horiuchi. Horiuchi was a stocky, contented man approaching sixty, and he was credited inside the corporation with putting the marine division together almost single-handedly in the seventies. Horiuchi rarely wore the blue-suit-and-white-shirt uniform of the Japanese *sarariman*, as management-level employees are known. He dressed halfway between a lab technician and an auto mechanic. But he lunched with others of his rank, and one day in the executives' cafeteria in Hamamatsu, he, too, was told to get himself to Fremantle to inspect the situation.

The approach was much in the Yamaha mold. There could hardly be a purer example of a Japanese company that had lived on learning from abroad. When it started in 1887 as the Yamaha Music Company, clarinets, pianos, and violins were coming into the country in volume. They were part of the Meiji era's enthusiasm for imported Western culture. Yamaha would make instruments at home, and it would make the market, too. It started the first of what company executives now call "soft businesses"—a network of music schools that taught people how to play the things Yamaha was making and selling.

The strategy had scarcely changed. When Yamaha began building motorcycles in 1955, it again opened schools and went quickly on to sponsoring racing events—small ones at home, then world-class contests abroad. In 1970 Yamaha built its first sailboat, a fifteen-foot dinghy, under license from a West Coast company called Columbia Boat. A year later Columbia Boat was out of the picture: Yamaha was producing its own version and calling it the Y-15. Yamaha later became the exclusive manufacturer in Japan of 470 dinghies, an I.O.R. class. By the time Takao Takagi walked into the

S & B conference room, marine products—powerboats, sailboats, jet skies, and many others—accounted for almost a quarter of Yamaha's corporate revenues. There was a Yamaha Yachting Association, a nationwide network of Yamaha sailing schools, and a growing number of international sponsorships.

Marketing was the ultimate objective, of course. But along the way Yamaha gained an upscale, edge-of-technology image and access to every new development in the field. What it learned at a regatta or a motorcycle rally eventually found its way into the plants at Hamamatsu or elsewhere, and from there into Yamaha subsidiaries around the world. "We get a lot of technical experience from racing," Kohtaro Horiuchi once said. "Racing has also been made part of the company spirit. It integrates dealers and distributors, and it makes the technicians and other employees enthusiastic. It's why we can talk about 'the Yamaha family.' "

The Yamaha input, though brief, made things click in the conference room at S & B. Maybe a roomful of sailors couldn't bring off something as complex as an America's Cup syndicate, they thought. But a few amateurs in combination with a corporation such as Yamaha might. No one at S & B had any illusions about the company's capabilities: Yamaha was well developed in the twenty-five- to forty-foot range, but it had built few hulls larger than that—and none larger than fifty feet or so. A Twelve was seventy-five feet long. But if the technological gap was going to be crossed, Yamaha was the one to do it; apart from a few small independents, it was the only possibility.

At S & B, they no longer seemed to stumble after Takao Takagi's visit. They had hit on something solid.

•　　•　　•

Each December the N.O.R.C. holds an annual party for its members, and in 1986 it took place on the twenty-eighth in a banquet room owned by a wealthy Tokyo retailer, a former commodore of the N.O.R.C. named Tokubai Furuya. He was a close friend of Tatsu Yamasaki. Furuya was aging and retired by that time, but he kept a boat in the water and his club membership alive.

As it did every year, the whiskey flowed that evening, and Tatsu Yamasaki had little difficulty speaking for his share. There were three hundred people in attendance. As his circle of sailing cronies was draining its second bottle and starting on a third, Yamasaki, in high spirits, spotted a Yamaha man named Isao Komiya on the other side of the room. At that moment, a thought of ineffable clarity passed through Yamasaki's mind. I'm the guy, he said to himself, who should challenge the America's Cup! He grabbed two fresh glasses, filled them, and started on a slightly unsteady starboard tack in Komiya's direction.

Komiya, a thin, stone-faced figure, was friendly enough, but he rarely, if ever, displayed enthusiasm for the business at hand. He and Yamasaki knew one another distantly from the *Super Sunbird* transaction, and from a dinghy-class competition in which both had been involved some years earlier. Komiya knew next to nothing about sailing—he was an executive with a product to build and sell—but he was quite senior in the marine division at Yamaha, and he was bound for a corporate post as a director working closely with Hideto Eguchi, the company president.

"Will you help me?" Yamasaki asked a little too boyishly when he reached his destination.

It was the first time the two men had spoken of the idea directly, but Yamasaki was fairly certain at that point that discussions about a joint venture of some kind had begun at Yamaha after Takagi's recent visit.

"If I tell my people that we'll be cooperating to get into this," Komiya replied carefully, "our situation now is such that no one would oppose me."

They started chatting about Masakazu Kobayashi, whose name was all over the room that evening. Kobayashi had by then anchored a hundred-and-fifty-foot motor yacht off Fremantle, and the stories coming back to Japan were not heartening: lavish shipboard parties, a rumored deal with Alan Bond to buy two Australian Twelves after the finals. "It's not really right," Yamasaki concluded.

Komiya turned to face Yamasaki. "Why don't we make a team?"

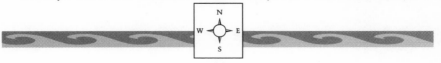

he asked at that point. "Our people can take charge of the technical side."

Syndicate Chairman Tatsumitsu Yamasaki.

As he resumed navigating that evening, Yamasaki went public with his brand-new intentions for the first time. The support was loud and unanimous—"We'll help!" everyone said, and "We're behind you!" It was Tatsu Yamasaki's moment, and it continued into the following day in call after call to S & B. One was from Kimura, who had been broadcasting the previous evening and missed the party. *"Daijobu!"* Kimura exclaimed, a much-enlarged rendering of "Okay!" Another came from Nobuo Fukuyoshi, an advertising executive Yamasaki had known for years.

"If you start now, maybe you'll have a chance three challenges from now," Fukuyoshi chided him.

"I've already been through that calculation. Take it back."

"You know, once a man says something there's no taking it back," Fukuyoshi said. "There's no way out but forward."

He was sixty, an old sailing friend. "Let's leave it at this," Yamasaki said by way of ending the conversation. "I'll take the America's Cup while you're alive."

• • •

Tatsu Yamasaki had indeed done his calculating. Once, sitting in the S & B conference room, he thought silently for a long time and then explained what it was that finally changed his mind. "To be frank— and this may sound funny—I think it was my age," he began. He thought again, and then continued:

"After I finished school, I was trained, I studied hard in the business world. I had achieved, somehow, in my work, and in my private life I enjoyed the life of a sailor.

"I was fifty-two. It was too early to start talking about 'the rest of my life.' But once again I thought, I'll make another challenge, take a chance, make my stomach ache once again. I wanted the experience of it. I thought, I'll do it three times. I'd be sixty-five the third time. I could manage it at sixty-five. We'd have a chance to get the Cup to Tokyo and have a race for it in Japan.

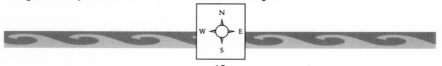

"Again, it may sound funny to talk about the next ten years, but I thought, The America's Cup is something I could put all my energy into for the rest of my life. It's something worthy of that. I knew, though, that I couldn't tell my wife until some time after I made my decision."

Yamasaki laughed. "I knew I'd be spending a lot of money, and maybe she was thinking of a more stable and secure life. For years she said often, 'Again?' to my yachting projects. It was like when I was racing *Miss Sunbird* back in 1967. I was using a wooden mast, and I bought an aluminum one. It cost two million yen—big money back then. We nearly had a fight, because she said, 'We could have bought a nice diamond for that.'

"And I answered, 'A diamond is very small, and a mast is this big, so there's really no comparison.' "

• • •

In the end, there wasn't that much to say. Yamaha sat on one side of a long, polished conference table and the S & B crowd on the other. It was January 10, 1987, sunny and cold. Two years of *nemawashi* were coming to an end.

Yamasaki, Kimura, and Ogimi made their way that morning to the Pacific Hotel in Shinagawa, a busy neighborhood south of Tokyo Tower, and took the elevator to the Opal Room on the twenty-ninth floor. Like many other corporate deals in Japan, this one would be made in neutral territory. Isao Komiya was there from Yamaha, in a dark blue suit. Hideto Eguchi, along with Kohtaro Horiuchi and a few other Yamaha people, had come with him. Each side understood that the task was simply to edge the other side forward. No one would be out on a limb; no one would be responsible for the decision or the commitment. No one would do anything alone.

They talked about finances at length. But the money question, by this time, was so large and perplexing that they simply put it aside as unfathomable. The rest was easy. The S & B people would enter the challenge on behalf of the N.O.R.C. and take responsibility for raising funds. They were the sailors. Yamaha would build them Japan's first Twelve.

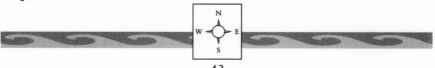

Everything will be new, Hideto Eguchi was thinking. But we did it in motorcycles, and we did it again with dinghies and then keel boats. We already know it's the most efficient way to develop a new technology.

Afterward, Eguchi would remember it as "an instant agreement." So would Horiuchi. But it was Kimura who sensed that the moment had arrived and finally broke the ice. "Why don't the two of you, Yamaha and S & B, raise your hands?" he asked abruptly. "The rest of us will do the running around. We'll make it all work for you."

He turned to Yamasaki and started his stage business. Everyone was ready to play his part. "Yamasaki-*san*, you can afford the entrance fee. It's twenty-five thousand dollars. What do you have to lose?"

"Yes, I can manage that. But can we do it?"

Kaoru Ogimi felt slightly impatient with all this. Were they talking about winning a yacht race or launching a product line?

"We should try," Ogimi said. "At least that."

"Why don't we announce the challenge and see what we can do?" Kimura asked.

Komiya turned to Yamasaki. "Shall we?" he asked.

"Let's give it a try."

•   •   •

By his own admission, Tatsu Yamasaki had developed a strong psychological dependence on Taro Kimura during the long months of groping conversation. He would always say afterward, "It was Taro who pushed my arm up." And as the new year got under way, Yamasaki was still a man who needed to be prodded. He was still carried by events; he had not learned to shape them.

Not long after the Pacific Hotel meeting, Kimura hosted an American friend on a four-day visit to Tokyo. Gary Jobson was a noted sailor by then. He was Ted Turner's tactician when the flamboyant Southerner sailed *Courageous* to victory in 1977, and he had sailed in every Cup after that until Fremantle. He had watched the international match-racing scene evolve and the world

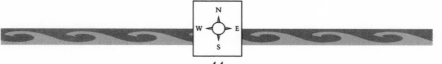

of amateur sailors begin changing into a professional one. Jobson was something of a star. He continued to sail, but he had gone on to larger roles; he was organizing regattas and commenting on them for ESPN, the all-sports network. And he was advising others about how to launch and run contests of their own.

The previous summer, Jobson had invited Japan to send a team to the Liberty Cup in New York. Kimura, as sensitive as any other Japanese to the slights or kindnesses of *gaijin*, had appreciated the gesture—no one else in the match-racing scene had ever thought to extend such an invitation. After the races, when Kimura started wondering whether Japan could host a similar event, he felt entirely comfortable turning to Jobson. Jobson was in Fremantle covering the challenger series by then, but he was generous with his advice and time, and there was no condescension in the way he offered either.

Match racing was more or less unknown to Japanese sailors. Like Kaoru Ogimi, most of them preferred the drama of ocean racing to the finesse and tactics required to beat toward an upwind mark, jibe around it, reach across to another, and run downwind to a finish line. But Kimura could see that a new international match-racing circuit was growing in prominence—the Liberty Cup was included among a so-called "Big Eight"—and he wanted Japan to get into it before it was too late.

Jobson arrived in early February, and he felt, as he said later, "as if a needle had been put into my brain and sucked it dry." There were meetings with N.O.R.C. people, broadcast and press people, yacht club managers, and boat designers. He was invited to sail a Yamaha 30, and there were pleasant dinners to attend in the evenings. He ran a clinic on match racing one day, and another on organizing a race committee the next. Elaborate notes were taken; each morning his hosts would produce transcripts of everything said the previous day, including an English version for Jobson to review. "It was impressive," Jobson said, "and exhausting."

Just before Jobson left, Kimura took him to lunch with Yamasaki at Prunier, an expensive French restaurant on the mezzanine floor of the Imperial Hotel. It was a well-paced occasion—it lasted almost three hours—and Jobson was up for it. Having flown straight from

Fremantle after covering Dennis Conner's 4–0 victory over the Australians, talking about the America's Cup over a fussily correct French meal was simply a matter of slipping back into his on-camera mode.

All the questions posed in the S & B conference room, where there had been no one qualified to answer them, came tumbling out again. How does it work? Why do you do it? What's in it for the winner? How much money do you need and how do you raise it? It was day one again for the Japanese, as if the previous year's labors had never taken place.

"My first piece of advice is, don't do it," Jobson began when it was time for him to speak. "It will infuriate you, it will be harder than you can ever imagine—it'll be an emotional roller coaster ride."

He paused, warming to the task. "It's an event, however, that brings phenomenal rewards if you win. And please understand that you don't have to win the America's Cup to win the America's Cup game. History is everything in this, and it's how you are perceived at the end of it that counts. You will gain tremendous respect in the world. If you did win, you could expect a billion-dollar industry to come to Japan. You would serve as a fantastic example for anyone even remotely interested in sailing. You'd bring a lot of new people to the sport."

Yamasaki listened intently. You don't have to win to win. That was interesting, Yamasaki thought, though he wasn't sure just how Jobson meant it. Yamasaki remained as quiet as he had the day Ogimi and Ninomiya had first approached him.

Jobson could see that Yamasaki's mind was racing forward, soaking in every word. As the courses came and went, both men found it convenient that Yamasaki spoke only in Japanese and insisted that Kimura, who sat in the middle, provide a careful translation of what Jobson was saying. It gave each of them time to think.

Jobson had two specific pieces of advice for Tatsu Yamasaki, and toward the end he put them carefully on the table. One was about money. "It's a designers' race, it's partly a sailors' race, it's a

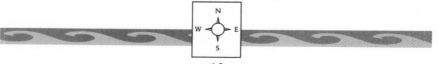

logistical contest," he said. "But it's a race for funding. You need the most powerful people you can find to raise money. My counsel is to ask for a lot early, because once you get a million-dollar sponsor, they'll all come in for a million; if you ask for a hundred thousand, they'll all come forward with that."

Jobson's other point had to do with management. Keep the command flow clean and simple, he urged. And put as small a number as possible at the top. One would be best, three the maximum. Races took place on the water, but they were won or lost, to an important extent, on land. He had just seen it all in Fremantle: the syndicates that did poorly were usually those with too many people making decisions; the N.Y.Y.C., Jobson considered, was the outstanding example.

Jobson sensed a new confidence in his hosts as their lunch drew to a close. He was right. The big question had finally been answered. They were going forward. Others remained, of course, but they would be resolved, Yamasaki and Kimura had come to feel, not standing at the edge of the arena but in the middle of it all—when answers were needed.

"Money and things. Those are Japan's two big advantages," Jobson had said. "Prepare properly and you may surprise yourselves and the rest of the world with the result."

The bill came and Yamasaki paid it. As they left Prunier, Jobson went upstairs to his room. The two others satisfied themselves with the prospect of surprise. As they walked through the lobby together, Yamasaki turned briefly to Kimura.

"Maybe," he said, "I'd better start learning to speak English."

WAKON YOSAI

Tatsu Yamasaki and Taro Kimura were silently turning over three words as they stepped through the Imperial's revolving doors into the cold February air. *Hito, mono,* and *kane*—people, things, and money. True, Gary Jobson had been encouraging about the latter two. But he did have reservations about Japan's ability to produce the right people. He didn't think Japan had sailors ready to race for the America's Cup. And there was the management issue, as well.

At that moment, they had no crew, no boat, and no money in any event. But they had a syndicate, and they understood a little more, at least, about the expensive and oddly obsessive world of the America's Cup. The doubts and questions were already flooding back. But the doubts were less to be shared now than the certainties, Kimura said to himself as he made his way across the city to prepare for the evening broadcast.

As these men saw it, the America's Cup was to be a wholly new challenge for Japan. It would be a learning exercise from start to finish. Everything, as Hideto Eguchi would say, was going to be new. Among the S & B crowd, the sheer scale of it evoked comparisons with quests such as Everest. There was something outsized about the idea of competing for such a prize. They had felt their way only a few feet along the trail. But they sensed already the mixture of fear and exhilaration—the ache in the stomach—of which new endeavors are made.

Neither man gave much thought to the past that day. But any eavesdropper could have understood that Yamasaki and Kimura were embarking upon a path worn smooth by countless others over the previous one hundred and twenty years.

•   •   •

Japan in the mid-1980s was a nation that flitted from one fad, one *bumu*, to another. There was a *bumu* in old American cars, huge Chevrolets and Fords with fins, which turned into a *bumu* in old Japanese cars. There was a *bumu* in James Dean posters, another in tin Coca-Cola signs, and another in films that featured furry animals. In Otemachi, the Tokyo district of glass and concrete towers, there was a venture-capital *bumu*. The idea of an executive turning himself into an entrepreneur, competing out on his own, was one that captivated Japanese business circles.

There were two other phenomena that fitted into roughly the same category. One was the appearance of what the Japanese called *shinjinrui*. The term translates neatly as "new breed," although native speakers usually insist it more accurately means "new species of human being." The *shinjinrui* was a generation—from mid-teens to mid-twenties—whose values were a puzzle to most of the nation. They consumed rather than saved. They cared little for lifetime employment with the large blue-chip corporations. And they traveled a lot. The *shinjinrui* suggested the notion that something had snapped in Japanese society. They did things for different reasons. They displayed no interest in dedicating their lives to furthering the

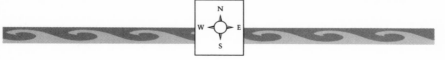

nation's economic strength; Japan's superiority in the marketplace was something the *shinjinrui* seemed to take for granted.

There was also a *bumu* of sorts in Tokugawa history. Everyone knew that in the years of Edo Japan, from 1603 to 1868, the Japanese lived under an inflexible hierarchy. It was a period of oppressive rule by a family dynasty, punctuated regularly with famines and peasant riots. But the essence of the *bumu* was the portrayal of a past as uncomplicated as a woodblock print. In movies, books, and television specials, the Tokugawa centuries were advanced as a long period of pastoral tranquillity. It is easy to see the appeal. Nostalgia has long been a powerful emotion among the Japanese. Shuttling by overcrowded subway from cramped home to cramped office and walking the unyielding streets of modern Japanese cities, the average city dweller likes to think there is still a little mud on his shoes. It isn't too much different from the myths maintained about the simplicity of life in small-town America.

Something like the Tokugawa *bumu* had been going on among scholars for many years by the time it hit the television screens. It was almost axiomatic by then that the great seedbed of modern Japan was a far more dynamic period than historians had thought just after it ended. After 1868, when Edo gave way to the Meiji era, there was a natural desire to seal the backward past in a box, the better to display the sprung-from-nowhere accomplishments of the early modernists. Then the pendulum swung the other way. Scholars began writing about the great changes that took place beneath the stagnant surface of Edo society. It was a brand of nationalism, a reclamation project. To stress the shock Japan felt when it suddenly opened to the West was a Eurocentric approach that unfairly discounted advances made during the premodern period.

Certain things were clear. Education and literacy spread widely during the Edo period. Roads and communications systems were extensive and efficient. Almost ninety percent of Japan's people were peasant farmers, but industries such as textiles, ceramics, mining, and paper took root in rural districts. In the towns and cities, merchants exhibited a lively entrepreneurship—groundwork for the full-tilt industrialization that was to follow. A prescient *samurai*

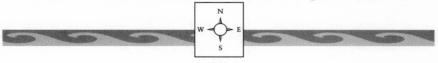

named Sokubei Mitsui began brewing soy sauce and *sake* in the second decade of Tokugawa rule, started financing his customers, and then went into the textile trade; a century later the Mitsuis organized themselves into the world's first diversified corporation and drafted many of the management principles upon which modern Japanese giants have built their success.

In the end, however, any notion of a society that progressed at anything like the pace evident elsewhere has to be pushed aside. What didn't happen in Edo Japan? The descendants of Ieyasu Tokugawa had preserved the hard-won order that the warrior who began the age established after a century of civil war and near complete anarchy. They did so by putting the archipelago into a bell jar and turning the thirty million Japanese under it into figurines.

The European Renaissance was two centuries old when Ieyasu established himself in Edo. On the other side of the globe, the authority of feudal institutions was becoming a thing of the past, replaced by a belief in man's ability to exert himself upon the world around him. Locke was soon to initiate the Age of Enlightenment. Reason, the power by which man understands the universe and improves his place in it, would be celebrated. The divine right of monarchs gave way to a new social contract. "Freedom of men under government," as Locke defined it in 1690, "is to have a standing rule to live by, a liberty to follow my own will in all things where that rule prescribes not, not to be subject to the inconstant, uncertain, unknown arbitrary will of another man."

The American and French revolutions coincided with the reigns of the tenth and eleventh Tokugawa *shogun*, Ieharu and Ienari. The period was known as the Tanuma era after an Edo elder who devised an innovative and entirely ad hoc method of extorting the merchant class. Whatever else the Tokugawas gave modern Japan, they carried the static institutions and psychology of the feudal age to the very edge of the modern transformation.

The contrast could hardly have been more stark. Confucian rationalism taught not the rational exertion of power over the world but a rational accommodation to it. The Japanese had no encourage-

ment to think as individuals, only as members of one or another class or group. There was no question of anyone acting, out of an inner conviction, upon the world into which he or she was born; experience was not seen to shape character. One was either a *samurai*, a peasant, an artisan, or a merchant—and ranked in that order. What in the West were becoming matters of individual choice were dictated by social status. Descartes was turned upside down. It wasn't, "I think, therefore I am," but "I am, therefore I think."

Among the most enduring developments of the Edo period was the emergence of an institution known as the *ie* ("EE-ay"). As a loose form of social organization, the *ie* had been around for centuries. But in late Tokugawa it became the most important point of identity in people's daily lives. An *ie* is more than a family; it is best translated as "household" in that those not related by blood could be adopted or apprenticed into it and could advance through its ranks. The *ie* was ubiquitous by the mid-nineteenth century. Villages were organized as groups of *ie;* those with a common occupation were in the same *ie,* and commercial concerns such as Mitsui were structured as *ie.* Loyalty to the *ie* was like loyalty nowhere else in the world. Loyalty had always been a Confucian virtue; but when the Chinese teachings crossed the Sea of Japan, loyalty in accordance with one's conscience became loyalty at the sacrifice of it.

The *ie,* which contributed much to the period's advances by strengthening the social fabric, has survived—or been manipulated to survive—more or less intact to the present day. Modern corporations are conceived of as extended *ie;* so are community groups, sports clubs, political organizations, and the regulars at local bars. The notion is still used to impart a profound sense of belonging and security to members of groups conceived of as *ie.* With this, of course, comes an estrangement from those who do not share the same notion of oneness. Possibly, latter-day nostalgia for Tokugawa tranquillity was a sign that the *ie* psychology is beginning to fade; in the face of more individual choices, it is natural, perhaps, to idealize an age when there were none to be made. But whether one is *soto* or *uchi* "outside" or "inside," remains among the defining dualities of the Japanese way of doing things. Others—*omote* and *ura,* "re-

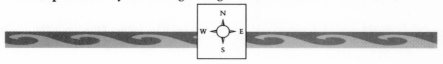

vealed" and "concealed," and *tatemae* and *honne*, "spoken truth" and "reality"—are not unrelated.

We have few photographic records of life in late Edo Japan. At mid-century the camera was eleven years old, but the Japanese knew nothing of it. There are the prints of Hokusai and Hiroshige. A novel called *Shank's Mare*, a Chauceresque account of two adventurers on the road from Edo to Kyoto, had been published between 1802 and 1809. Its satiric wit showed the Tokugawa hierarchy in a state of deep decay; but it was still inconceivable that *samurai* or peasants or merchants would think of themselves as part of the same form of life. A few Japanese were beginning to ask how things worked on the other side of the ocean. But as late as 1850 Edo bureaucrats thought it wise to suppress a proposal to publish a Dutch-Japanese dictionary.

Officially recorded events tell more. In March of the same year the *shogun* formally prohibited clandestine trade with China— suggesting, of course, the extent of it. The following month the imperial court ordered seven shrines and seven temples to pray that foreigners be driven away. It was a well-timed idea: in June a Dutch ship docked at Nagasaki with news that United States Navy vessels would soon arrive to ask for open trade. In 1851 the shogunate's concern was starvation. In March it distributed free rice to the poor and ordered merchants to do so that June. In September the powerful Osaka rice brokers who controlled the market were obliged to lower prices.

Who inhabited the world on which the famous *ukiyo-e* artists based their work? Yukichi Fukuzawa, an early Meiji scholar and educator, attempted to answer that in a work called *Outline of Civilization*, a title typical of the period's preoccupations. Fukuzawa, an advocate of liberal values but no slave to "Westernization," appears today on the face of every ten-thousand-yen note, looking stern and slightly wistful wearing a somber kimono and a Western haircut. One senses he is looking forward in that pose, but in the two-volume work published in 1873 he looked back to describe a people atomized but not individual, private but not free:

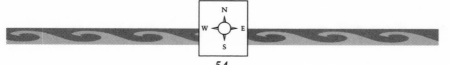

They all depended on the government and did not concern themselves with national affairs. Among a million people there were a million different minds. Each person shut himself up in his own house and ignored the outside world as if it were a foreign country. They failed to consult one another even about the best way to clean their wells, let alone ways to repair the roads. If they chanced to come upon someone stricken by the wayside, they sped away in haste. If they came upon a dog's excrement, they went around it. They were so preoccupied with trying to avoid getting involved in anything that they had no time to discuss things together. This long-ingrained habit became a custom and produced the present sad state of affairs.

Many thousands of miles from the slammed shutters and unattended dung of late Edo Japan, the sounds and smells were of a different order.

America at mid-century was restless with energy. Six hundred textile mills in New England employed sixty-two thousand workers. California was admitted as the Union's thirty-first state, and New Mexico wanted to be next. The first cast-iron building went up in lower Manhattan. Three hundred seventy thousand immigrants arrived in 1850. The big social issues were slavery and women's rights. The New York *Times* was founded the following year, and Melville published *Moby Dick*. Horace Greeley printed an editorial headlined, "Go West, young man, go West." New York City was connected to the Great Lakes by rail, and San Francisco, flooded with prospectors, had a crime problem.

England was approaching its height as the world's factory, banker, and trader. In mid-1851 it invited other nations to compare their accomplishments to its own at a Great Exhibition held in Hyde Park. The latest developments in machinery, chemistry, metallurgy, farming, architecture, and art were all represented. The Great Exhibition, catered by Schweppes and housed in the Crystal Palace, drew six million visitors in the six months it was open. The Americans surprised everyone with the Colt revolver and the McCormick reaper.

In June of that year six New Yorkers—John C. Stevens, his brother Edwin A., George L. Schuyler, J. Beekman Finlay, James

A. Hamilton, and Hamilton Wilkes—took delivery of a ninety-five-foot yacht named *America*. The craft's designer, George W. Steers, was, at thirty, considered a master in the field of small sailing vessels. American-born, Steers was the son of a noted English naval architect and had done well catering to an emerging taste for yachting among well-to-do Easterners.

It was not much of a sport in the United States at the time. In 1835 a handful of merchants formed the Boston Yacht Club, but it died after two years. In 1902 a man named Thomas W. Lawson published the first more or less official history of the cup to be named for the schooner George Steers built. He described the mid-nineteenth century as well as most scholarly historians:

> The national life had not reached a point where time and money could be spared for pleasure sailing. The temple of the nation's industrial greatness was being built. . . . The people were too busy and too much absorbed in the development of their fortunes and those of their country to care for the sport of racing boats.

Seven years before *America* was constructed, on July 30, 1844, John Stevens had taken eight other yachtsmen out on his schooner, *Gimcrack*, for a day's sail off the Battery in lower Manhattan. The son of an army colonel who had helped pioneer steam propulsion, Stevens was a financier and the founder of the first day line between New York and Albany. Those he assembled off the Battery voted the New York Yacht Club into existence before touching land again, and they elected themselves, naturally enough, the original members. It was the only such club in America. The minutes, recorded at five-thirty that afternoon, show that a committee was appointed to draw up club regulations and that Stevens was assigned to lead an exploratory cruise to Newport, Rhode Island, the next day.

There are no further accounts extant of that session in *Gimcrack*'s cabin, but it must have been exuberant. It marked the beginning of competitive yachting in the United States. Stevens, elected the N.Y.Y.C.'s commodore, saw through the development of an impressive program of racing and cruise events in the years that

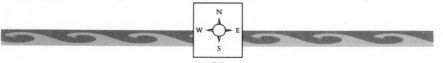

followed. And it was to his specifications that *America* was completed in the spring of 1851.

The bill for the boat came to thirty thousand dollars—high for a yacht at the time. But the builder, William H. Brown, delivered the boat so late—three days before it sailed for Europe—that he had to accept payment of only two thirds that amount. Brown included several curious clauses in his contract with Stevens and his N.Y.Y.C. partners. "If she is not faster than every vessel brought against her it shall not be binding upon you to accept her at all and pay for her," Brown had written in laying out his terms. "You are to have the right instead of accepting her to send her to England, match her against anything of her size built there, and if beaten still reject her altogether."

It was the kind of deal that could be cut only in a young nation of confident risk-takers, among people who were there and who had prospered, almost by definition, because they were good for a gamble and who felt all around them the release of an enormous power. *America*, as its name suggests, was built to represent an insurgent nation. One of the surviving photographs of the craft, now in the Naval Academy Museum in Annapolis, shows it in full sail on a reach, starboard gunwales at the waterline. The sails and halyards, a pattern of geometric curves and diagonals, are precisely the image Charles Sheeler, the American Cubist, would paint seventy years later to capture the dynamism of a nation in perpetual motion.

America had a specific purpose from the start: to bring the N.Y.Y.C. into competition with the reigning yachtsmen of the day. The notion began when John Stevens and George Schuyler were shown a letter from an English merchant inviting American sportsmen to mark the Great Exhibition by sailing in a few English regattas. Two months after *America* was launched it arrived at the Isle of Wight, an affluent speck off the southern coast of England, to race for the Hundred Guineas Cup at Cowes. The decanter-like trophy, its long neck and bulbous middle expressive of the age, would be awarded to the winner on August 22 by the Royal Yacht Squadron, as the local club was known.

Queen Victoria and Prince Albert watched from the deck of the

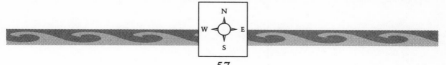

royal yacht, a two-masted, steam-powered paddle-wheeler. The course was "round the Isle of Wight, inside No Man's Buoy and Sandy Head Buoy and outside the Nab," the Nab being a light off the eastern tip of the island. There was none of the pre-gun positioning that can prove so decisive in fleet competition today. The race began, as was the custom in those days, with all entries dead at anchor, sails stowed below.

No one else came even close. After taking the lead and adding to it, *America*'s crew, skippered by Stevens, could look back on a comedy of errors among its English competitors. The *Volante*, a forty-eight-footer, collided with *Freak*; *Arrow* ran aground and *Alarm* stopped to give aid. Late in the race *America* had a mile-long advantage over the nearest yacht still under sail; although the wind died at the end, the schooner from the former colonies crossed the finish line six minutes before *Aurora*, its only serious contender all afternoon.

The English must not have understood what now seems the historic inevitability of the result. Why else would they have shown sufficient confidence toward their upstart guests to declare *America* the winner without dispute? *America*'s skipper had sailed inside the Nab, not outside it, and claimed the course was so described in the instructions he had received. *Aurora* seems to have been the rightful winner that day.

Everyone at Cowes was aware, however, that something new had come across the ocean. The "commoners from the new world," as their hosts called them, won on the basis of superior technology. *America*'s design shocked its English hosts. The schooner's masts were raked toward the stern at an extreme angle. Its hull was narrow and elongated at the bow—a feature emphasized by a seventeen-foot bowsprit; its maximum beam, the vessel's widest point across, was well aft of where naval architects of the day normally placed it. Once the Hundred Guineas Cup began, Commodore Stevens stunned his competitors again. In contrast to the voluminous sails and loose trim typical of the day, *America*'s sails were flat and lashed tightly to the boom; they were made of machine-loomed cotton rather than the flimsy flax canvas then widely in use.

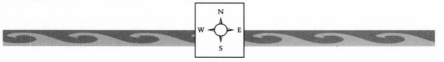

America spent ten years racing and cruising in Europe after it astonished the polite spectators at Cowes. Then it changed professions: the Confederacy bought it early in the Civil War and made it a blockade runner. In 1862 it was sunk in the St. John's River; raised, *America* joined the North until the war's end. Then it returned to civilian life, but its best days were behind it. Although it raced frequently until 1893, it was described during those later years as "a monument to the skill of her designer"—a form of flattery equipped with a second edge. *America* ended the century drydocked in Boston and was then given to the Naval Academy, which sent it on its final voyage—to the shipbreakers—in 1945. What survives today is the rudder, which can be seen in the America's Cup Museum in San Diego.

The Cup that bears its name, of course, suffered no such decline. It was not intended to be a trophy that could be challenged or defended again. But its new owners saw things otherwise. In 1857 they presented it to the N.Y.Y.C., which faced its first "America's Cup" challenge—against the English, of course—in 1870. The field was slightly one-sided: a single schooner, *Cambria*, crossed the ocean to compete against seventeen defenders on a course that ran through the New York Narrows and around Sandy Hook Lighthouse, off Brooklyn. The *Cambria* met the same fate as one of its predecessors: it collided with a defending schooner in a traffic jam at the Narrows, losing a sail and some of its rigging. It finished eighth, a long way from taking the renamed Cup back home.

• • •

Eighteen-seventy was an important year in Kaoru Ogimi's family. His paternal grandfather, a fallen *samurai*, left Japan for what turned out to be a twelve-year stay in the United States; he would return an ordained minister with a degree from Princeton Theological Seminary. The adventure was typical of the time. The Meiji era was two years old. The Edo order was being washed away, and there was no place for the warriors of Tokugawa times. The frenzy to catch up had begun.

We can only imagine how discouraging the situation must have

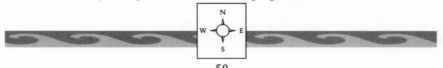

looked to Japan's new leaders. There was almost too much to be done. Men such as Yukichi Fukuzawa stressed the need to create a national consciousness among sixty-three thousand villages where no such notion had ever existed. There was much talk of democracy and independent thought, but this was a complicated business. Individual striving was good because it was good for Japan; it would help Japan in its rush to meet the threat from the West. The new leadership was not to govern so much as "to inspire," one prominent thinker wrote, while the citizenry was "to yield as the grasses before the wind."

Japan became, in the early Meiji years, the first modern example of what are now known as Asia's "learning cultures." Its methods were various. Studying abroad was the rage. The number of Japanese in universities overseas approached six thousand a decade after Meiji began. There was traffic in the other direction. By 1874 more than five hundred *gaijin* occupied senior posts in the Tokyo bureaucracy. The Kobusho, the forerunner of MITI, accounted for almost half that number by itself. They were paid well for their services; when the skill was learned, of course, the *gaijin* were quickly dismissed.

The most curious learning exercises, though, were the missions Japan sent abroad in the first years after it opened. These groups, composed mostly of diplomats, scholars, and specialists, would fill countless notebooks with descriptions and diagrams as they traveled throughout the United States and Europe. In a way, they anticipated the thousands of agents who posed as salesmen, shopkeepers, or students throughout the Pacific during Japan's period of expansion and preparation for war. The early Meiji travelers, however, were innocent recorders. They learned to take the best each nation had to offer and to leave the rest with notable discrimination.

Meiji bureaucrats were fallen *samurai*, given to weaponry rather than poetry and the Chinese classics. Centuries before, Japan had felt inferior to the Middle Kingdom, and then it came to feel inferior to the West. *Sakoku* was the Tokugawa answer. The Meiji ethic was to catch up, but catching up was seen purely in terms of industry and science—in terms of *mono*, things—and was accompanied by a

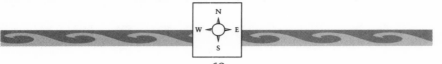

profound rejection of Western concepts having to do with the spirit. The drive was different. While Western capitalism developed as a consequence of the individual desire for autonomy, in Japan it developed to close a material gap and, in the end, to triumph. To triumph did not mean winning in open competition, but dominance after careful preparation while sequestered at home. The method would be apparent again after the Second World War. It made the Japanese strong in a short period of time, but it did not allow them flexibility in response to change.

The Meiji creed was *wakon yosai*, "Japanese spirit, Western things." Japan would learn from the West, but it would manage what it learned according, to tradition. Modern companies would be in the image of the old village, *ie*. management would be centralized, but clarity of purpose was not its strong point. All communication was vertical, not horizontal: everyone reported to the one above; there were no loyalties forged sideways. Employment, like residence in a feudal village, was for a lifetime.

As to the *gaijin*, no lesson was too great or small. England taught its visitors how to run a navy, the French an army. They studied German engineering and borrowed the Prussian constitution of 1871 to fashion one of their own (which Prussian scholars judged an abomination when it was published). In America they studied manufacturing methods. Along the way they were careful to observe the baking of bread, the brewing of beer, and the building of iron bridges.

The most important of the missions abroad began in 1871 and lasted nineteen months. It was called the Iwakura Embassy after Tomomi Iwakura, the foreign minister and ambassador plenipotentiary who led it. The notebooks copiously kept by members of the mission are remarkable less for their factual accounts than for the light they cast on the diarists. They are filled with the peculiarly raw insights of complete strangers. Everyday economic competition was odious, "warfare in peacetime," wrote Kume Kunitake, secretary to Iwakura and author of the mission's official report. "The white race," he wrote elsewhere, "are avid in their desires and zealous in their religion, and they lack the power of self-control."

Kido Takayoshi, second in rank to Iwakura, wrote in a guileless style that might be called blank slate. That was appropriate, since he would visit, among many other places, a freak show, an aquarium, an exhibition of hot-air balloons, and a central bank—all for the first time. The mission's stay in Washington was especially long, and in April 1872 Takayoshi went to a navy yard in the capital, where he saw "a rubber suit for use in the water":

> If air is pumped in between the suit and the body of the person wearing it, when he jumps into the water, he does not sink. A man leaped into the water wearing the suit to demonstrate it for us; and I must say that it is a useful device.

A few months later Takayoshi was taken—for reasons not explained—to view the facilities at an insane asylum, also in Washington. Among other things, he observed an air conditioner:

> We looked at steam laundry equipment. In addition, in a separate place a gas engine has been installed, and next to it a device which blows out air. By the time the air emerges from an underground hole, it is free from heat.

The Iwakura mission was a long adventure for a people who, as if in an experiment with time, were born into the modern world but had seen little of it. Above all, its members brought home a sense of amazement at the way Western individuals lived. They were challenged to determine the sources of Western power and intelligence and how these could be developed in Japan. But it was not all wide-eyed wonder, as Kunitake, the more insightful of the two diarists, observed before he got home:

> Since the Western theory of progress is being transmitted and planted in Japan, things are being carried out carelessly and without forethought. The old is abandoned and there is competition for what is new. These "new things" cannot always be obtained. What should be preserved of the old is destroyed, and in the end there is no trace of

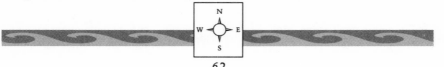

it. Ah! how indeed can this be spoken of as daily advancement? How can it be called progress?

So began more than a century of ambivalence. A desire to learn from the West—to equal it by imitating Western ways and then to surpass the source by making the method Japanese—would alternate with rejection of the outside world and retreat into traditional culture. *Sakoku* would turn to *kaikoku*, "the open country," and then back again. The individual would be glorified, but never to the extent that it be permitted to surpass the sense of group belonging. Again and again, attraction and a feeling of inferiority would finally induce resentment, distaste, and assertions of superiority; it drove Japan inward and eventually helped push it to war.

The currents can still be traced. As early as the 1890s those in reaction against industrialization and liberalism idealized the old life as an alternative. Typical of the impulse was a turn-of-the-century novel called *Furusato*, or *Hometown*, a third-rate attempt to praise the virtues of rusticity. With historical echoes no doubt in mind, Noboru Takeshita, during his beleaguered prime ministership from 1987 to 1989, instituted a program called *Furusato* to revive the prefectures and the economy. Takeshita's plan, of the same quality as the novel, went nowhere. But the canny politician knew the soft spots in the popular imagination, and he showed they hadn't changed much.

By the 1980s, however, the feeling was growing in Japan that the long period of catching up with the West was nearing completion. Economic affluence began to induce a sense that Japan had finally made itself the equal of any Western country. The postwar national guilt that had colored the decades of reconstruction was beginning to fade. Inferiority turned over again to become superiority: "techno-nationalists" advanced the idea that Japan was better equipped than any other industrial nation to cope with the challenges of a postmodern world. A certain arrogance appeared; the intellectuals popular on late night television called it "soft nationalism," positing that the firmer stuff was a thing of the past. Shintaro Ishihara, still a yachtsman but by this time also a well-known if

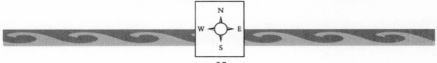

little-followed politician, caught much of the mood when he published *The Japan That Can Say No* in 1989.

In economic terms, at least, the phenomenon can be dated earlier.
By the early eighties Japan had accepted "voluntary" restraints,
trigger price mechanisms, quota agreements, or other export limitations on textiles, steel, color televisions, and autos. The implication was clear to the Japanese, if not to European and American
consumers: *gaijin* notions of open competition were no match for
the Japanese method. Then came *endaka*, or "high yen," the
doubling of the yen's value against the dollar, which began in late
1985. Intended to encourage imports and restrain sales overseas,
endaka did little to balance the chronic Japanese trade surplus and
much to unleash a flood of investment overseas. Partly in consequence, *kokusaika*, or "internationalization," became the most
popular idea of the late eighties—if, possibly, the vaguest: everything had to be international, from the car in the driveway to the
location of your company's newest factory.

Yasuhiro Nakasone, the tall, elegant, English-speaking prime
minister through the eighties until Takeshita took office, actively
encouraged these currents in Japanese thinking. Broadly stated, his
intention was to increase Japan's integration into the global community and prepare it to assume responsibilities that reflected its
status as an economic power. Under him, a retired central banker
named Haruo Maekawa issued a policy statement that advocated a
fundamental overhaul, not just of the economy, but of the nation's
way of life. It encouraged leisure, consumption, and imports while
discouraging overtime, manic export drives, and the overwhelming
emphasis on saving and "economism," as the scholars call it, in the
postwar ethos. The Nakasone years were important for the questions
they raised, if not for the ones they answered. Nakasone effectively
placed himself at the end of one era in Japan's postwar evolution
and the beginning of another. In speeches he called it *sengo seiji no
so kessan*, the postwar stocktaking. We have rebuilt our nation, he
told the voting public; we must now seek new goals for ourselves.

They had achieved, and they had done it their way. But there

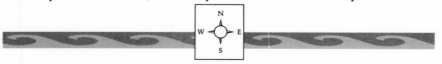

were things they still needed to learn. There were questions they still needed to ask.

They could make cars that threatened General Motors, but they could not build a Porsche. They could play tenor sax or create sculpture on a monumental scale, but with exceptions such as Sadao Watanabe or Isamu Noguchi (who became an American anyway) they could not transcend their materials. They became obsessed with their entries in the Guinness Book of Records, but that only demonstrated what it was intended to refute.

It was all done by committee, by process. It was all borrowed, and it was all science and no art, technique without inspiration. These became popular criticisms, and most Japanese became accustomed to them. It was as if they had run up against a wall. There was nothing in the water and nothing in the genes; it was their chosen method. They wanted victories in the outside world, but they didn't want to compete in it. That was where *wakon yosai* had gotten them. The essential issue was creativity. They had not yet entered the realm where art and inspiration and the individual's inner drive counted for as much as all the rest.

And that was where they next wanted to go.

KYOKI

*I*t started as a sporting event," Taro Kimura once explained in a coffee shop near his office. "All the rest came after."

When it started, in the spring of 1987, Tatsu Yamasaki turned to the most reliable young sailors he knew. These were men who had sailed with him or for him in most of the great races of his career—in Hawaii and off the Isle of Wight, along the Australian coast from Sydney, and south from Florida through the Keys. They knew Yamasaki well, and they knew his boats better. When they got together they could talk among themselves about the *Sunbirds* as if they were textbooks they had shared in college. *Sunbird II* was a classic wooden hull designed by Sparkman & Stephens. *Three* was a beautifully clean quarter-tonner by Bruce Farr, the noted New Zealand designer, and it sailed like a rocket. *Five* was a gleaming white fifty-four-footer also drawn by Sparkman & Stephens, but it was a dog.

One of the sailors Yamasaki had begun putting at the helm of his boats was Kazunori Komatsu, who had skippered *Magician VI* at the Quarter-Ton Worlds. And in early April, Yamasaki telephoned Komatsu at his office in central Tokyo with a new proposal. Komatsu was to find a crew for himself among the old *Sunbird* veterans and skipper them through the Citizen Cup, a Big Eight match-racing series held each spring off the New Zealand coast at Auckland. They would be called the Seven Samurai, and Yamasaki wanted, he said, "the best yachtsmen in Japan." There would be no *Sunbird* this time: the Citizen was a one-design race, meaning a fleet of identical boats would be provided. In this case, they were Stewart 34s, boats whose design dated to the late fifties.

Afterward, Yamasaki told his helmsman, he wanted a written report about everything Komatsu and his crew saw, heard, and experienced. The enterprise had specific objectives, and Yamasaki listed them:

a. To experience match-racing techniques.
b. To communicate with other match racers.
c. To observe a match race in operation.
d. To confirm the relationship between match-race participation and a Twelve-Meter challenge.
e. To grasp the position of match racing in New Zealand and its relation with the mass media.
f. PR for Nippon Challenge.

It was time to start sailing. The N.O.R.C.'s official notice to the San Diego Yacht Club had gone out two months earlier. Neither Ogimi nor Kimura, the resident English speakers, was at the club that day: "We sich to lodge challenge for the forthcoming America's Cup," the club had cabled on February 16, complete with typographical error. Yamasaki had written his check for twenty-five thousand dollars. Now they had to start putting their mouths where their money was—what little of it they had at the time.

Komatsu was a logical choice to head the Auckland foray. He had skippered for Yamasaki in the '86 Kenwood Cup, and he had

accumulated an impressive record for a Japanese sailor. He had raced in world championship events for ten years in a row and he had Olympic experience in the 470 dinghy class. Komatsu had his down moments, certainly—his performance on *Magician VI* was only one of them—but he was as close as any Japanese had ever come to being a world-class sailor.

Komatsu was a rarity among Japanese sailors: he was a professional. You never saw him without the glow of the wind and sun on his angular cheeks. He had been a test pilot for Yamaha's new designs, working and racing full time on the water, for much of his career.

That worked well for Yamasaki, too. With the Yamaha people's backing, he had appointed an old attorney friend, Shingaku Takagi, to structure the legal and fiduciary aspects of the syndicate. They wanted to get contributions going as swiftly as the Tokyo bureaucracy would allow, and they wanted to minimize the tax consideration, preferably by making contributions deductible. But they discovered a regulatory system wholly ungeared for the kind of enterprise they were launching. A nonprofit corporation, the first choice, would have taken more than three years of administrative review. "The race would've been over," as Takagi put it.

They finally settled on a profitmaking corporation called NCAC Inc., Nippon Challenge America's Cup, with paid capital of ten million yen. Yamasaki and Hideto Eguchi were named cochairmen and presided over a nine-member board. Yamasaki knew sailing, and he managed well; his partner represented blue-chip Japan. Yamaha was many times the size of S & B, but Eguchi would rarely object to any of Yamasaki's policies, and he never overturned one. But it was a delicate balance. Yamaha wanted its money's worth, and part of that was full representation in almost every phase of the project.

Sending Komatsu to Auckland was a good start, even if it meant a complex set of relationships on board the Stewart 34.

Kazunori Komatsu had developed a reputation over the years. People tended to tiptoe around him. "He is by nature very sincere to himself," Kensaku Nomoto, the cautious professor from Osaka,

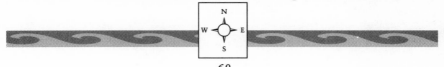

once said of him. "At the same time, he demands everyone to have the same sincerity, and to push themselves as hard as he does." A sailor named Makoto Namba put it this way: "Even when I met Komatsu many years before, I noticed that there was no one around him." Namba made a gesture with his hands, as if drawing a moat around his chest. "He was isolated, he had no sailing friends." Komatsu was driven, ambitious on his own behalf. Somewhat like Kaoru Ogimi but for different reasons, he was too direct for many of those who knew him.

Makoto Namba was among those whom Komatsu chose to take with him to Auckland. So was Robert Fry, a quiet, balding New Zealander who had sailed for Yamasaki since he moved to Japan in 1973. Namba and Fry, family men in their late thirties, had occasionally sailed with one another, and sometimes against one another, for several years by then. Neither could be called a professional sailor, but each had found a trade that provided for plenty of time on the water. Namba, a tall, earnest, and deferential man with a long face and gentle eyes, headed the Osaka branch of Sobstad Sails, a loft headquartered on the Connecticut shore. Fry was managing the Japanese branch of a family trading company that specialized in imported yachting hardware.

By Makoto Namba's reckoning, the '87 Citizen Cup was the first match race anyone in Japan had ever sailed. They were dog-paddling at the deep end of the pool. "It was a smart way to go about it," Namba said much later, "to take on high-powered racing from the very beginning."

It didn't seem so to anyone aboard the Japanese sloop at the time. It seemed, as Namba acknowledged with characteristic reserve, "not a comfortable regatta." Komatsu, typically, called it "a huge mess, a disaster from start to finish"—a description to be counted a closer rendering of reality. They went zero for nine that week, never finishing even remotely close to the winner. They were another team of Japanese also-rans.

The atmosphere in Auckland, "the city of sails," was a shock of itself. Komatsu and his crew had been in ocean races outside Japan, but none of them had mixed much in the international yachting

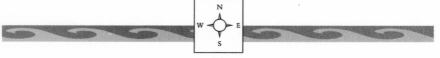

crowd. Sailing, of course, is the national sport in New Zealand. When Sir Michael Fay brought the Kiwis into the America's Cup for the first time—in Fremantle that year—the boat launching was the occasion of a parade to rival St. Patrick's Day in New York. At the Citizen Cup, there were commodores and skippers and yachting hacks everywhere. Komatsu discovered, to his anguish, that he was expected to make a speech at the opening-night party. The Japanese felt out of it. No one spoke their language.

The Auckland autumn was like nothing they had prepared for. Out on the water the winds were never lower than fifteen knots and reached thirty the second day. That was close to Fremantle conditions. Komatsu kept thinking, It's obvious to anyone looking that we don't know the ABC's of this sport. To him the event was a particularly deep embarrassment. In any contest where wind and water figure, luck can always impose itself on the result. But one-design racing is as level a field as sailing offers. Skippering and sailing skill count for as much as they ever can. Nobody has a hidden edge.

Nothing went right. Sail handling, starts, maneuvering, tactics, turns—Komatsu's team did badly all around. They lacked what only time and effort could provide. They lacked experience, and money couldn't buy that.

There was never even a moment to which they could cling as evidence that they belonged in the same league as the others. Once, beating upwind, an avid young Kiwi skipper named Chris Dickson pursued them deep into the jungle of spectator boats lining the course. It was no man's land, far off the layline. When Komatsu tacked over suddenly, Dickson lost sight of his prey and wound up ramming a spectator craft. "It let us off the hook," Fry remembered, "but only briefly."

Not long into the series, Komatsu and Namba started drawing the same conclusion: apart from all the other difficulties, they weren't physically strong enough. Stewart 34s were light but difficult to sail. That made matters worse. The Japanese were also sailing against crews in top condition. Five of the ten skippers there had just raced for the America's Cup in Fremantle. Every boat but their own had three to five crew members with America's Cup experience.

In the end, it was mostly the deep, unfamiliar water of winning or losing—a deliverance too cut and dried for the Japanese. There is too much risk involved out there, they kept saying to themselves, and too much loss of face for the defeated. These were things the Japanese liked very much to avoid. In sumo wrestling, there is not just a winning trophy but a *kanto-sho* for "good achievement," a *doryoku-sho* for "good effort," and a *gino-sho* for "good technique." But this was a world where the delicacies that counted at home counted not at all.

Gambatte, meaning "do your best, persist, try harder," is one of the keys to Japan's success. Long campaigns are the preference, not the sudden death of a match race. In wars of attrition, the Japanese are battle-tested. They are perfectly prepared to sacrifice a short-term showing for the distant goal. They hang in as the stakes drift higher, learning what they can for the next time around and forcing competitors to pull out of the game. *"Gambatte!"* is a familiar salutation in the corridors of corporate Japan. But races aren't raced by industries—not directly. The Citizen Cup wasn't the North American market for transistor radios or steel bars.

Kaoru Ogimi understood that, though few others involved in the new syndicate did. Yacht racing would require the Japanese to compete in a way they never had before. It would often look, to Ogimi, like a lambs-to-slaughter endeavor. But there was something in it he considered essential for the Japanese to learn.

Makoto Namba would return to those first moments of recognition often in his conversations. "The feeling was different in Auckland," he once recalled. "You survived or you didn't. No more middle of the pack. It was very easy to get frustrated, very easy to panic, very easy to blow it. And that's what we did."

• • •

Tatsu Yamasaki and Taro Kimura were having truth sessions of their own, not unlike Makoto Namba's. To ask for money, Kimura discovered, you had to have money. To complicate matters, there were others who seemed already to have it.

Everyone knew that the America's Cup was a brand-new scene

since the Australians had won, even if Dennis Conner had just taken the Cup back to San Diego. San Diego wasn't the N.Y.Y.C. The newcomers were piling in—the Germans, the Spanish, the Swedes, the Danes were all said to be challenging—and they hadn't anticipated that in Tokyo. They felt enormous pressure at S & B, which continued as the informal clubhouse of the Japanese syndicate. Most of their anxiety, in fact, came from their own side of the ocean, where Masakazu Kobayashi was mounting a highly visible campaign.

After the N.O.R.C.'s year-end bash, they had run a sort of security check on him. There was a Kobayashi listed at the club, a wealthy doctor from Osaka whose boat, large and expensive, fitted the description of the one that appeared in Fremantle. But it wasn't he. They kept inquiring around the sailing circuit and still found no one who had ever heard of Masakazu Kobayashi. Through Yamasaki's friends in financial circles, they tried to find out where he banked: no record of a relationship. They tried the tax rolls: nothing there either.

Kobayashi was not atypical of his time. Land prices, always high in Japan, were skyrocketing by mid-1987. And with the yen climbing steeply against the dollar and other major currencies, land was creating a collection of new Japanese dealmakers who were multimillionaires in whatever denomination they cared to keep their money in. Suddenly, shopkeepers who had passed grim lives in rooms measured in tatami mats were buying, selling, or building expensive properties in Hong Kong, Sydney, and Los Angeles. "Japanese money" became the broad-brush explanation for the newest skyscraper in town; the phrase hid some peculiar stories.

There were any number of them about Kobayashi. He and his wife, it was said, had started out in the sixties in a noodle shop opened with savings and borrowed funds, and they had worked hard, cooking, serving, cleaning up. Then they invested wisely. That tale, an East Asian Horatio Alger story commonly applied to come-from-nowhere entrepreneurs from Seoul to Jakarta, had gained currency, in Kobayashi's case, abroad as well as at home.

The facts were harder to come by, but there were a few. His father, it seemed, had managed a munitions factory in central Japan

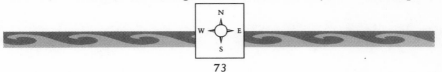

before the war, turned to other things after it, and taught his son
the manufacturing business. Masakazu began producing batteries
on his own during the sixties, but the effluents created a mess
intolerable even by the slack standards of booming Japan; environ-
mentalists forced him to close the operation in 1970. Kobayashi
moved the factory to Taiwan and used his vacant land to get into the
property game. He grew steadily, if unremarkably, after that. Then
came the high-yen eighties. Like many others, he had started living
on easy money and leveraged speculation. Among much else, he
owned eight hotels in Nagoya, twenty-three cars, and the gaudy
cruiser that had appeared, Gatsby-like, off Fremantle.

The Bengal Bay Club was Kobayashi's prize. It was his passport
to another world, the fifth star on his visor. He conceived of it as a
resort, marina, and condominium complex along Ise Bay between
Osaka and Nagoya for the super- (and newly) rich—people like
himself. Bengal Bay was still in development, but to give it the
desired polish Kobayashi had challenged for the America's Cup in
Bengal Bay's name. It was barely legal. The club had run a regatta
to qualify, but one that could hardly be called an annual event,
which is required of any club entering a legitimate bid. Nonetheless,
Kobayashi was already calling himself the Alan Bond of Japan, an
analogy that would be truly appropriate a few years later, when,
like Bond, he would sink in a sea of debt. His other model was the
Aga Khan, who had brought Italy into the America's Cup by
challenging twice, in 1983 and 1987, in the name of the Costa
Smeralda Yacht Club, a refuge for the very well-to-do on the
Sardinian coast.

While Kobayashi was consummating his deal to buy two Twelves
from Alan Bond, the tone at S & B was rather different. They had
scarcely started to tell people who they were. Taro Kimura was
cadging forgotten footage from the NHK video library and assembling a promotional brochure to go with it on a borrowed four-color
photocopier. The Nippon Challenge America's Cup would stretch to
the limit what contacts it had, what small advantages it enjoyed.
Like any other corporation in East Asia, NCAC would do business
on the basis of whom it knew.

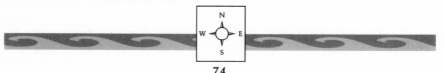

Months before, Kimura had begun to think about a logo. The fees Dentsu would ask were out of the question, of course. A young graphic artist Kimura knew had begun donating some of his time to the project, but after seventy or eighty drawings he was stuck on the notion of sails and was delivering right triangles in every configuration he could think of. His proofs looked like oversized party napkins.

Kimura wanted something Asian, something palpably Japanese, something foreigners would understand, and something that implied motion. The sails were dropped, and a rising sun appeared; then the word "Nippon" in brush strokes. "It's not right," Kimura said when he first saw it. "It tells too much of the story." One day they met to review new ideas in a busy coffee shop at Tokyo Station. Among them was a refined version of the *hinomaru*, the rising sun. The first three letters of "Nippon" were white across the red ball, the last three in red on a white field. It hit Kimura immediately. He taxied to S & B, and Yamasaki concurred. Nippon Challenge had a public identity, and they got it for free.

These were the tools with which Kimura and Yamasaki, like two Fuller Brush men, began canvassing Tokyo to explain their cause: video stock of past sailing events edited into takes of Kimura doing a stand-up narrative with Hayama Harbor in the background; a slightly blurred pamphlet; a do-it-yourself logo.

The best they could hope for, by way of sympathetic hearings from prospective sponsors, were people with an enthusiasm for powerboats or fishing. It wasn't sailing. Yamasaki and Kimura would have to start with the most rudimentary explanations: how match races worked, the hallowed history of the America's Cup. But they had a good strategy: to lay out the commercial and public relations benefits that would accrue to those supporting Japan's first real America's Cup challenge.

The time seemed right for such an approach. By mid-1987 one of Van Gogh's *Sunflowers* was at home on the top floor of the Yasuda Fire & Marine Insurance Company, and large portfolios of foreign assets were accumulating in Tokyo. Investment in the United States was booming: it had nearly doubled the previous year, to ten and a

half billion dollars, and would rise by an additional forty-seven percent before 1987 was out. Honda was racing in the F-1 circuit, and other companies were sponsoring new soccer cups, golf tournaments, and tennis matches everywhere you looked. "It had to do with the times," Kimura said later. "There was an inevitability about it. Everyone felt, Now we can do this. Now we can afford it. That was a common perception among the Japanese."

•   •   •

There were other common perceptions. One was that the Americans' ire over their continuing trade imbalance with Japan was reaching dangerous levels. *Endaka* was almost two years old, the yen had nearly doubled in value against the dollar, yet Japan was still almost fifty billion dollars to the good in its annual merchandise trade with the United States. There was a new kind of friction in the air, and the more astute Japanese business executives sensed it. The takeovers of Columbia Pictures and Rockefeller Center were a few years off, but all Kimura and Yamasaki heard from business friends was, "What if we win this thing? What then?"

One afternoon in Zushi, Kimura allowed himself to free-associate in his living room for a few hours and came up with a list. It ran to nearly two dozen entries. One was, "Beer: summer, freedom, coolness." Others were, "Cosmetics: sun, youth, health," and "Banks: team play, human relations, sincerity, *kokusaika*."

Armed with this collection of loose ideas, Taro Kimura headed for his first mark, a man named Makoto Iida. Iida ran a highly successful concern called the Secom Company, which specialized in home surveillance systems ("Security: secrets, technology, precision"). Iida was a good friend of Yamasaki. He fished avidly, owned an expensive powerboat, and knew something about the America's Cup. He gave Kimura more than an hour in his office. Together they watched the Nippon Challenge video on a portable player with a pop-up screen that Kimura brought with him. Iida approved of the challenge, he told Kimura when the meeting was over. He would get back to him.

Kimura was encouraged. He reported to Yamasaki that Iida-*san*

sounded like he would come on board. But when Kimura heard
from Secom the next day, it was the Dentsu routine all over again.
It wasn't Iida on the phone, but the assistant who had set up the
interview. Iida, a wealthy man whose company was privately owned,
did like the idea. But if he wanted to be involved, Kimura was told,
he would've challenged the Cup himself. The answer was no.

Yamasaki was getting roughly the same response. The Bank of
Tokyo seemed interested when he paid the institution a visit, but a
public relations man called back and reminded Yamasaki that
government regulations prohibited banks from advertising on television. Nippon Challenge was looking for a hundred million yen,
about seven hundred thousand dollars, from each sponsor. What
good would an expensive sponsorship do if the bank couldn't put it
in front of the public?

It was early days yet—these calls could be put down to market
research—but Kimura and Yamasaki sensed they were up against a
barrier. Structuring the syndicate had been a minor nightmare with
the tax authorities. Japan was a maze. How many other narrow-
minded executives and regulatory difficulties would block their way
in the hunt for backing? The country simply wasn't ready.

They needed a stocktaking, their own little *sengo seiji no so
kessan*. In February they had set the syndicate's budget at one
billion seven hundred thousand yen, eleven million three hundred
thousand dollars at the time. To get it, Kimura had structured a
multi-tier group, an *ie* of sorts, consisting of official sponsors,
honorary sponsors, official suppliers, cosuppliers, and individual
supporters. Each would have its contribution. They wanted ten to
twelve sponsors at the time, for a total of a billion yen or more.
Suppliers would come in with in-kind commodities—anything from
plane tickets to noodles to cranes—and individuals would contribute
ten thousand yen each.

Now they needed a new ideology. They were behind the curve.
Let's look at this project from a different perspective, Kimura urged
the group at S & B. Let's say, okay, there are no tangible gains
here, but it's time we Japanese tried something new. It's time we
demonstrated that we're hot-blooded people, just like the *gaijin*.

One evening Kimura decided to write an imaginary editorial. It was his idea of what the New York *Times* would publish the day after Nippon Challenge won the America's Cup. It was the clearest statement of purpose the syndicate would ever come up with, and it answered all the concerns they had so far heard—trade friction, return on investment, public relations value. Kimura and Yamasaki would include it among their marketing devices ever after, and it read:

Japan, long pushed to increase its imports, has just spent $15 million to bring home an old vase. It won't reduce the trade surplus, but it surely is more significant than $15 million worth of purchases overseas. The vase proves that the Japanese are not monsters, economic animals, but human beings like ourselves.

The America's Cup is, in a sense, the world's greatest meaningless event. You invest millions, but all you get back, if you win, is this old silver vase. It requires the latest technology, but it is technology that does not necessarily enrich our daily lives right away. The young people who fought in the race won't even get a medal, as in the Olympic Games. However, we in the West have pursued this race because we think man is distinguished as the only creature that can be enthusiastic about meaningless things.

Japan has given us the best in television sets, Walkman stereos, and cars, but sometimes we have found it difficult to decide whether the Japanese are really human beings. They seem to have sacrificed their individual lives to contribute to their companies. They are rational people, a people who are careful not to waste, but they seem too inhuman.

Now the Japanese have made a huge investment in the world's greatest meaningless event, and they have done so even more enthusiastically than we have. They have happily returned home with the Cup that bears no correspondence to their investment in getting it.

The meaning for us is simple: we have discovered through the America's Cup that the people upon whom much of the world's future depends are also human beings.

There would be other first-time challengers in San Diego. And they would bring as much national pride to the occasion as the

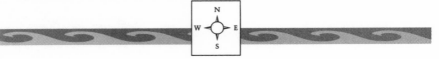

Japanese. But from this point onward none would invest so much beside money. No newcomer would set out to prove as much to a world that did not know them—about who they were and their worth as people, what rung they stood upon in a world they saw as a hierarchy, and, as it would turn out, the superiority or otherwise of their way of doing things.

.   .   .

Kimura had struck a new chord. His editorial fantasy, more attractive still for the hook of hubris with which he concluded it, was readily received as a stirring declaration in Tokyo's corporate quarters. The Nippon Challenge would be more than just a sporting event, and more than a promotional event, too. Some observers would wonder throughout the challenge precisely what happened to these sentiments once corporate money started mixing with sailboats and sailors. The principle was well stated. The Japanese were going to compete as Westerners did. But as Kaoru Ogimi was beginning to wonder about Tatsu Yamasaki and Taro Kimura, was the commitment to the principle there?

The first to come in as a sponsor was the Sanyo Securities Company, whose president and chief executive, Yoichi Tsuchiya, was another friend of Tatsu Yamasaki and much in the Yamasaki mold. The two men golfed and occasionally partied together. Tsuchiya was a youngish executive, prematurely gray, with a plump face fixed in an almost constant grin. He was born into Sanyo. His father and Yamasaki's had been friends for many years before they retired, and Sanyo had underwritten S & B's initial share offering when Yamasaki senior decided to take S & B public in 1961.

As so many others would, Tsuchiya recalled his decision as more or less immediate. He knew nothing about sailing. But he had seen the NHK broadcasts from Fremantle, and he had been talking to Yamasaki about the financial side of the venture ever since things began to get serious. "I knew it was Yamasaki-*san*'s dream," Tsuchiya remembered much later. " 'I can't finance the whole thing,' I told him, 'but I can help get the right people together.' That's how it started."

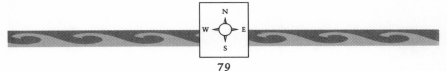

Sanyo, an affiliate of the Nomura Securities Company, wasn't in the top tier of Japanese brokerages, alongside Nomura and others in the "Big Four." But it was a good catch for the Nippon Challenge people. By August, Yamasaki and Kimura had gone past their goal to fifteen sponsors, and a month later they had gone to twenty. Among the quickest to follow Yoichi Tsuchiya in were the Haseko and Kajima corporations, both leading contractors and developers, Japan Air Lines, the Marui retailing chain, and Mitsui & Company. Then came Sapporo Breweries, Fujitsu, Omron (a computer maker) and the Nikka Whisky Distilling Company.

By the autumn, however, even twenty was no longer enough. The syndicate's nascent bureaucracy, located in an office building in Shimbashi, a neighborhood of sweatshops and shabby businesses, reported in September that crossing the finish line in San Diego would cost three billion yen—almost double the initial budget. With the approval of those already behind him, Yamasaki quickly decided to go for thirty sponsors. In the end, between sponsors and suppliers, there would be seventy-five companies behind Nippon Challenge. The names would never be less than top drawer. But it would be more than two years, until the autumn of 1989, before the thirtieth official sponsor, the Central Japan Railway Company, signed on.

• • •

Spring is the season of annual meetings for most Japanese corporations. And as the syndicate's sponsors grew in number, Yamasaki found himself faced with a phenomenon that emerged every year in Tokyo with the regularity of cherry blossoms. He was being followed, he discovered, by *sokaya*.

Sokaya have an unusual way of making a living. They are small groups of people who, having purchased a few shares in a given corporation, assign themselves the task of disrupting board meetings on behalf of the silent majority of stockholders. Investors in Japanese companies have plenty to complain about. Dividends paid on Japanese shares are among the world's lowest; corporate directors are notorious for taking decisions that are not in the interest of

individual shareholders. But the long-established abuse of small
investors is only part of the point. It is far from unheard of for
money to change hands before a company's *sokaya* contingent
desists.

By the spring of 1987, *sokaya* were pestering many of the sponsors
Yamasaki had recruited. And the argument was identical in all
cases: "Why are you diverting funds," the *sokaya* shouted at their
boards, "that should rightfully go into shareholders' dividends by
putting a hundred million yen into a meaningless sports event?"

Yamasaki would spend six months coping with noisy *sokaya*
disruptions. But what he later remembered most about that period
was an opinion piece that appeared one day in *Nihon Keizai Shimbun*, Japan's leading financial daily, in which an executive named
Sadao Tokumasu went public with a position similar to that voiced
in Kimura's "editorial." The America's Cup was more than recrea-
tion, Tokumasu argued. "Let's realize a dream together," he wrote.
"We can show a new Japan to the world."

Hideto Eguchi, the Yamaha president, had put Yamasaki and
Kimura in touch with Tokumasu early in the campaign for support.
A thin, gray-haired man who had fought his way up the corporate
ladder after the war, Tokumasu was an old business friend of
Eguchi, and he was about to advance from president to chairman at
the Sumitomo Marine & Fire Insurance Company. His life at
Sumitomo had given him a fair measure of exposure abroad over the
years. The *kokusaika* wave had come late in Tokumasu's career, but
he was fascinated nonetheless by all it seemed to portend for Japan.
He, too, made a quick, instinctive decision to back Nippon Challenge. He had met neither Kimura nor Yamasaki. He had simply
read the brochure they dropped off at Eguchi's suggestion, said yes,
and pushed it through two board meetings. It took him nine days.

Tokumasu was in his mid-sixties. He wore simple suits and a
Sumitomo button on one lapel. He had the smile, the manner, and
the outlook of a man whose important battles were well behind him.
He worked in a new office tower high above a neighborhood of cheap
postwar housing along the Sumida River near Tokyo Bay. On the
wall behind his desk, shaded from the sunlight streaming through

an expanse of windows, was a small Rouault; two Impressionist oils hung elsewhere in the room.

Tokumasu articulated much of what captivated corporate Japan about the America's Cup. He wanted it to signify a deep metamorphosis in the way Japanese companies behaved. In Tokugawa Japan, merchants were ranked the lowest of the four classes. Peasants existed to serve the nobles; merchants had no such higher calling. It was considered that they had no purpose other than the lowly ones of accumulation and self-interest. By the late 1980s the rest of the world was consigning them to this ignominious status all over again. In 1987 the Toshiba Machine Company prompted an international uproar by selling sensitive submarine technology to the Soviet military. Such incidents were frequent, and they did not serve the corporate cause well. "People in Japan are willing to change," Tokumasu asserted, "but there hasn't been any general recognition of this yet."

Sadao Tokumasu had a vision of what Japanese corporations should become, and he explained it by dividing management's responsibilities into two parts. "One is science—a corporation's effort to generate profits—and the other is art. By 'art' I mean a corporation's culture." It was only by keeping science and art in harmony, in balance, that a corporation won "the respect of society," as Tokumasu put it.

"There's a nice word in Japanese, *kyoki*, which is hard to define," he said. "It describes something that is extremely pure. Like a chivalrous spirit, or a pure friendship between men. In my view, a corporation should be thirty percent *kyoki*. There is another word like it, *bigaku*. It means 'aesthetics,' aesthetics of a very idealized kind.

It was the sort of thing Japanese executives learned in the eighties to spout like water from faucets. And it usually reflected no more than the speaker's assessment of what a visiting *gaijin* should go home thinking. But Tokumasu was a little more direct.

"As a business enterprise, of course, to pursue the 'art' of a corporation is not possible without considering profit, the 'science,' " he continued. "I can't deny that there was a fellow up here

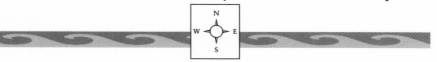

from marketing who found this project quite useful. But who wants to go forward only that way?"

Tokumasu wasn't bound by the past, as many sailors are. He did not have the nostalgia one can usually find haunting a typical sailor's psyche. In fact, he never sailed. But, like many who sailed as children and stayed out on the water well into adulthood, he had something of the same longing to relive old experiences, to sustain or recreate youth. It was a characteristic of many of Tokumasu's generation.

Early in his career Tokumasu spent a year at the Philadelphia offices of the Insurance Company of North America, learning a business then not much developed at home. One holiday, he traveled to Miami and received what he called a pleasant shock when he saw the city's beaches and marinas. "I thought, Japan is a marine country. It could be this way in the future. Thirty years later, I still don't see it. But sponsoring our America's Cup challenge is, in some small way, like realizing the dream I had then."

Dreaming. Sometimes it seemed to be all anybody connected to Nippon Challenge wanted to talk about. But to Tokumasu, dreams were important in the Japan of the late 1980s.

"Some say young people, those born after the war, are hardened realists," Tokumasu said after musing about Nippon Challenge for much of an afternoon. "We've gone through some tough times, and perhaps that accounts for it. We're wealthy now, but we're not psychologically satisfied. I don't think a dedication to materialism is going to make people happy. And that will lead to more dreams. My generation, you know, is sometimes called the 'Taisho Romantics.' We still believe in dreams."

Yamasaki, Kimura, and Eguchi went to Tokumasu's vast office nineteen floors above the mouth of the Sumida on April 23. Neither Yamasaki nor Kimura had met him before. Tokumasu had not yet written his opinion in *Nihon Keizai Shimbun*.

The encounter was brief. When it was over, the syndicate had another hundred million yen in its pocket. It was just about the time Komatsu and his crew were blowing it badly in Auckland.

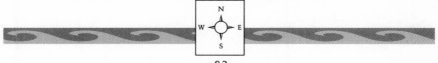

• • •

Kazunori Komatsu's prose style was no match for Kido Takayoshi's a hundred and fifteen years earlier, but he was the Meiji diplomat's equal, if not his better, when it came to his capacity for surprise. "Full-grown men devote themselves to yachting. It is not a sport just for youth," Komatsu began his post-Auckland report to the syndicate. "A Twelve-Meter boat is neither a cruiser nor a dinghy. It has the speed of the dinghy but requires the power of the maxi-boat."

Komatsu had made some elemental discoveries in the course of his first match race. There were passages in his report in which he all but fell on his sword. "The motive force of yacht racing comes from each man on the boat," he observed. "Again and again, I felt a sense of crisis in this regard. We could not manage the machine."

Komatsu was worried about individual motivation. Where, he wondered, were the Japanese going to get it? The point was essential, but his report also reflected Komatsu's pride, which came in two varieties. His impulse to distinguish himself from other Japanese was strong; at the same time, he wanted just as strongly to win respect for Japan. He wanted to communicate the deep feeling of inferiority that had come over him when he faced Western professionals on the sea. As he had considered on the boat, it came down to strength. "Technique must accompany power, but technique without power is like Little League baseball—or like the Japanese playing American football."

The Japanese reserve a peculiar reverence for the defeated. All through their history they have elevated to hero status the lone fighter ungiven to compromise and the crusader who persevered to the end in the face of impossible odds. In a world ruled by conformity and precedent, it is another vicarious celebration of freedom and individuality. Kazunori Komatsu, with an expression that conveyed determination and vulnerability at the same time, might have fallen neatly into that category. He had his own mix of humility and defiance. "I recognized my own racing experience as no more than an extension of child's play," Komatsu concluded the opening

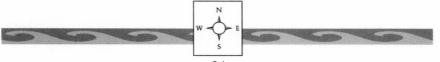

section of his report. "All of what I write is common sense. We can't climb Mount Everest by training on Mount Fuji."

But he was no glorious loser, no *kamikaze* flyer. Defeat was not on Komatsu's final agenda. In his report he went on to propose a course of action that he thought would enable a Japanese racing team to "surpass existing teams within a year." It included a detailed curriculum for improving what he considered the essentials of the endeavor: knowledge, muscle, and skill. He wanted a full schedule of match races, video gear for reviewing daily practice, and a well-equipped tender craft to follow the sailboats in practice. He wanted decent salaries for crew members and assurances that corporate positions would later be opened at sponsoring companies "to reduce the crew's anxiety about the future."

Komatsu also recommended "long-term employment of foreign crew and coach." This presupposed his own position at the helm, of course. And he intended to sail with a few *gaijin*, not a boatload of them. He wanted them, in essence, to participate in building a new kind of sailor in Japan. This led to the most novel proposition of the many Komatsu advanced: no recruit would need experience. He would build his team from the bottom up. "Even if we recruit experienced sailors," Komatsu wrote, "we can't catch up with the others unless we improve the pace of training significantly. And it's difficult to alter the pace."

In the end, most of Komatsu's proposals were accepted. The criteria for recruitment would be the simplest imaginable. A recruit would have to meet two lower-limit numbers: 165 pounds in weight, five feet ten in height. That was all. Komatsu wanted "one hundred percent devotion to racing." He would find it, in part, through want ads in the newspapers.

He filled five pages in longhand. In his final entry Komatsu reached for effect by adopting the device employed at about the same time by Taro Kimura. Like Kimura, Komatsu had something important and new to say, but he had to find the right way to say it. He decided to write an imaginary address to the unchosen and unknown crew members who would challenge for Japan in the America's Cup. It read:

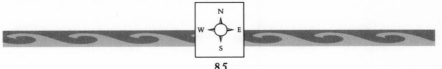

The America's Cup is a battle in which sea-loving men have made desperate efforts for 130 years. It cannot be won without intellect, physique, and technique.

Sailors, some more than six feet and more than two hundred pounds, fight one to one after years of hard training. One to one means not only one boat to one boat, but one person to one person among the entire crew of eleven. Only when each individual makes the greatest imaginable effort can the one-to-one battle be won.

I believe we can form a group to discover the inner essence of our young men—even in today's Japan, where people tend to get lost in easy dreams. Living and training with foreign crew and coaches and racing overseas several months a year, I believe, would be a great opportunity for each of us not only to improve racing techniques but also to acquire the character of an international person and become the individual Japan needs for the twenty-first century.

Above all, it is only through effort that we Japanese, small in stature, can equal the big guys. Why don't you make history with us?

CHAPTER V

NEW BREED

azunori Komatsu wasn't the only one in the new syndicate who wanted to separate the dreamers from the makers of history. Kaoru Ogimi saw the entire campaign as one part of a vast social passage through which the Japanese would leave behind a confining past in favor of a brighter and freer future.

This may have been a prescient vision of the way ahead, but it did not make Ogimi popular within the syndicate. These were matters that didn't concern Tatsu Yamasaki and Taro Kimura, things they simply didn't want to hear about. Through the offices of Taro Kimura, Ogimi had been excluded from executive management by late 1987. "Smartest thing I've ever done for this project," Kimura said over lunch one day at the Hayama Marina Yacht Club. Kaoru Ogimi remained, however, an undeclared house philosopher; as the only one who could cast Nippon Challenge's search for crew against some larger backdrop, he was also the only one who understood what was really at stake.

"The object isn't to create a new type of being, though that's in fact what we're doing," Ogimi said once. "The object is to win a race. But to win it we need people who can transcend the 'group mentality' and share an intense individual commitment to winning."

Ogimi's office, where he usually conducted his Nippon Challenge business, had a new look since Kinta Ninomiya first came to see him in 1985. Intermittent screams still came from the roller coaster across the street. But in the spring of 1987 Ogimi had added two conspicuous silver bowls to a shelf next to his desk, both acquired in the same event. The first Melbourne-to-Osaka race, sponsored by Yamaha, was sailed that season, and Ogimi entered with a powerful sixty-footer called *Nakiri Daio*. It was an awkward tag: the first word meant "wave cutter," and Ogimi got it from the name of a small fishing village near Nagoya he had once visited in *Serena*; the second word meant "great king." Ogimi skippered, and he won a bowl for finishing first overall and another for winning the Class A division, the big-boat category. In the sporting world, it made him something of a national hero.

Scattered across Ogimi's desk one day much later were plans for another project: the purchase of a refitted square-rigger on which young Japanese sailors would train. It would be years in the making, but it was an undertaking to which Ogimi would devote more and more of his time as the months went by. Proper training was where, he thought, the most fundamental challenge to the Japanese lay.

"On the hardware side, you've got a set of problems having to do with getting the fastest boat designed and produced. Look at it that way and Nippon Challenge is more or less a generic exercise in technology transfer. We've been doing it for nearly a hundred and thirty years," Ogimi said. "But there's one big difference. A boat is only a tool placed in the hands of the crew. Sailing is a sport in which yachtsmen use a yacht to try to beat other yachtsmen using other yachts."

Ogimi paused and laughed. "To put it another way, sailboats are driven by wind—an obvious point that's often missed. Speed is

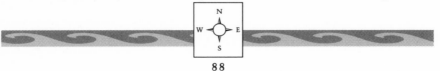

achieved on the human side, by individuals able to understand the laws of science and nature and to sustain top performance to drive the boat forward.''

For many Tokyoites, the *shinjinrui* phenomenon of the late eighties was identified with a small strip of street in a trendy neighborhood called Harajuku. Harajuku was dense with clothing and record shops, restaurants and fashionable coffee bars. Every Sunday, weather permitting, a few hundred of the "new breed" would assemble nearby to play live music, dance, and carry on in a generally un-Japanese fashion, which is to say, with little or no reserve. In the late afternoon, as if a bell had gone off, they'd all go home to get ready for work or school on Monday; some changed into conventional clothes before boarding their trains. It made good magazine copy, but it was something of a laugh to those who had seen it, a not untypical exercise in style without substance.

Not for Ogimi. He saw in the *shinjinrui* the promise of the kind of sailor Nippon Challenge needed, and he was expansive when it came to discussing it. "Japan is only three generations a modern state," he would begin. "Material achievements in industry and technology have been phenomenal. But at what price? All that has to do with individual happiness has been subordinated, first to the nation and since the war to the company.

"If you go beyond the superficialities—Harajuku and all that— this is not a normal generation gap," Ogimi said. "The radical difference with the new species is that they're the first generation that's not security driven. The older generation was motivated by money and things. To the *shinjinrui*, time is the most important asset they have. They do things not because they have to but because they want to.

"I think what's taking place in Japan is a cultural revolution of major proportions. For the first time, we're removing the fetters that have hindered the flowering of individuality. It's only quite recently, after our crisis-driven 'catching up' has been substantially achieved, that Japan has started questioning this hundred-and-thirty-year commitment. For Nippon Challenge, it goes two ways. We're not trying to create a new kind of person in Japan, we're having to. At the same time, the campaign for the America's Cup is a product of change in Japanese society. It's a radical departure for Japanese people."

Ogimi agreed with Komatsu as to how Nippon Challenge should find its crew: given the objectives, it would be the most unorthodox recruitment drive of any America's Cup campaign. They had assembled an inner core—Komatsu, Robert Fry, Makoto Namba—and now they would search for unmolded clay. Komatsu may have wanted inexperienced underlings because, as he saw it, he could shape them in his own image. It was no good going after "veterans" anyway, Komatsu figured, because the best of them had trained on boats appropriate for high school students.

Ogimi understood that, but he viewed it differently. He considered the inexperienced *shinjinrui* the key to the psychology the campaign would need to succeed. To him, thinking individuals were essential. True, sailing is a team sport; the Japanese, accustomed to group effort, should be naturals. But there is a difference between a group and a team. A team isn't made up of homogeneous equals, and if it has a hierarchy, it isn't one based on the strict law of seniority. A team consists of individuals, each with a special talent and a commitment that comes from within.

To Kaoru Ogimi, what had to be avoided was the tradition apparent even in Komatsu, who was as inner-driven a sailor as Japan had produced. Kimura and Yamasaki had nothing but fond memories of the university sailing clubs. To them, Nippon Challenge should derive directly from the university tradition. Ogimi thought differently. Off in Oregon, he had missed the clubs in his days at Reed College, and he never regretted it. So far as he was concerned, they transmitted all that he wanted to keep out of Nippon Challenge. "The clubs don't teach sailors to develop any keen sense of how to get the maximum out of the machine in changing wind conditions," he once complained. "The driving ethic is simply to obey those above. Succeeding means learning to become an efficient cog. The yacht, the machine, isn't owned by the sailors but by the school. It's beyond the individual to tinker, test, and tune it to his satisfaction.

In the clubs, you're not taught to elevate your art. Quite frankly,
you'll never win a yacht race that way."

•   •   •

The syndicate started expanding from the core group outward by
word of mouth. All along Sagami Bay, the yacht clubs that dot the
shore—Seabornia, Hayama, and others—were abuzz with news of
the Japanese challenge in the spring and summer of 1987. The clubs
were pleasant places by then. You no longer got a sense of being
among pioneers. Each club had its bars, restaurants, boutiques full
of yachting gear, its palm-shaded lawns. The berths and moorings
were well built and well protected. Condos were going up nearby.
The Japanese had become powerboat crazy. For many of those able
to afford the investment, being out on the water meant white
trousers, the proper hat, plenty to eat and drink, and a hired crew
to handle the messy business of moving around. But there were lots
of sailors, too. On a day with decent wind, Sagami Bay was a forest
of masts and sails, with flocks of 470s and Finn-class dinghies
moving like schools of minnows among them.

The syndicate found some healthy-looking prospects along the
bay. But it began to spread the net wider over the summer, the
traditional induction season for Japanese corporations. Logically
enough, Nippon Challenge first advertised in sports newspapers and
yachting magazines. Then, as if it were simply one among many, it
enlisted the services of the Recruit Company. Founded in the 1960s,
Recruit was playing a key role in the Japanese economy two decades
later. Its core business was what its name implied: it helped locate
fresh graduates and ease them into their lives as *sararimen*. Outside
of Japan, Recruit is known almost exclusively for the central place
it held in a shares-for-influence scandal that eventually toppled the
government of Noboru Takeshita in 1989. In corporate Japan, that
was a sideshow. Labor at all levels was so short by the mid-eighties
that recruiting was an industry of its own, and Recruit's share of
it—almost seventy-five percent—made the company nearly indispen-
sable to the smooth functioning of the economy. Such was its lately
cultivated pedigree that it was also a Nippon Challenge sponsor.

In August an initial group of candidates, sixty or seventy of them, was gathered at Hamanako, a large, pine-bordered lake not far from Hamamatsu. Yamaha kept a marina and a testing facility there, and for several months it would be home for those finally selected as crew members. The initial tests and interviews, run by Komatsu, Namba, and a couple of shoreside managers, were almost perfunctory. They watched videotapes of the races in Fremantle, the same ones that had brought silence briefly to the conference room at S & B. Then they simply hoisted themselves on a chin-up bar while Komatsu paced past them like a drill sergeant; at last they filed into a room, three at a time, for Komatsu's questions.

"Have you had any previous sailing experience?"

"None at all," a tall, almond-eyed tryout replied.

"What other sports have you participated in?"

"I planned to play professional soccer until I damaged my ankle. Now I teach swimming part time."

"Why do you want to join Nippon Challenge?"

He was twenty-two, with tousled hair and the looks of a youthful movie star. His name was Takeshi Hara, and he went by the nickname Ken. Hara answered the last question this way: "I like winning and losing. You put yourself into it completely. You can see the results of what you've done."

Ken Hara was straight from the textbook as written by Kaoru Ogimi. He was a small-town kid from Fukushima Prefecture in the northern part of Honshu, where his father taught English in junior high school. When he graduated from Tsukuba University, an institution an hour or so west of Tokyo devoted to science and high technology, Ken Hara's world caved in: his parents cut him off financially and an injury ended the only ambition he had. Hara became a *freeter*, a recent Japanese coinage. It is a combination of "free" and "*arbeiter*," the German word for laborer. In Japan, an *arbeiter* is a temporary worker; a *freeter* is a *shinjinrui* type, unwilling to enter the *sarariman* maze, attaching himself to little, rejecting the values of the past even if his own are inchoate.

Hara was temping in Tsukuba: junior school tutor, swimming instructor, athletic club attendant, bartender, weight-training coach. One day at the local A.C. one of the members, a wealthy sailor, told him about Nippon Challenge. "Hara-*san*, you should try this," he said. It was simply a matter of sending a picture and a résumé to Tokyo.

"It was easy to decide. I was sick of what I was doing and I was drinking too much," Hara said. "It was the idea of putting yourself on the line, knowing whether you can do it or not. If you enter a company, you never feel whether you are successful, you never know. Before long your whole life is wrapped up. Most Japanese are trapped that way. A sport like sailing is different. You can't do it unless you really want to."

There were others like Ken Hara. Hitoshi Matsubara, known to all as Jin, was a *freeter* in thought if not in fact. Jin was a free spirit waiting to be born. He had grown up around boats in Yokosuka, and, like Hara, was two years out of university in 1987. He had studied at the Yokohama College of Commerce and afterward worked his way up to planning manager at a Toyko printing company. He had done a little sailing—a friend in the university club had a dinghy, and after finishing school he crewed a few times on an old cruiser out of Yokosuka—but it wasn't sailing or the sea that made him answer an advertisement in *Kaji* (*Rudder*), a monthly magazine. "The company was okay," Jin said, "but the small frustrations were building up. I could see what I was heading for at sixty or sixty-five, but I couldn't imagine all the years in between. I was twenty-three then. I wanted to do something big before I was thirty. I wanted to hit a high point."

Everyone who was tested that hot day at Hamanako remembered one thing about Kazunori Komatsu. It was the way he stopped and locked his blazing eyes on theirs as they hung suspended on exercise bars. "I knew he was trying to see inside of us, to see who we really were," Ken Hara said later. The look in their eyes and the third question—Why?—were all that seemed to matter to the passionate man who would be their skipper. "Thinking back, I realized those very first applicants had the best qualities," Komatsu said later. "It was a question of morale and spirit and enthusiasm. The people who came afterward applied because Nippon Challenge's reputation was spreading. The first ones had a purer interest. If I could do it over again, I'd take half of those sixty or so and select the entire crew from among them."

There was another tryout in the autumn, that time on a cruising yacht docked in Yokohama Harbor, and a third later on that included a number of young Yamaha *sararimen*. Nippon Challenge would make decent sailors out of some of its later recruits. But the complement from Yamaha grew large, and that wasn't, finally, to the good. It was always said, though never admitted, that there were sailors in the syndicate who had arrived at their desks within the Yamaha group one morning to find they were simply reassigned to Nippon Challenge. Grinding a winch, trimming a sail, working the bow or the mast would be merely jobs. Reporting to the sailing camp was like reporting to the subsidiary in Brazil or Norway. There would be a beginning, a middle, and an end.

Then came the strays, the dreamers who managed to climb on board. Takashi Kawahara, twenty-seven at the time, was flipping idly through the pages of *Kaji* in mid-1988 when he saw another version of the Nippon Challenge ad. Kawahara, an intense, wiry, sharp-featured man, was a pig farmer in northern Honshu and was taking a day off from his pens. It was early June, and as he read the ad's peculiar request, he found that the deadline was the end of the month. "I was too small and I didn't weigh enough, so I sent a picture that made me look bigger," Kawahara recounted. "I didn't think I'd make it, but I thought, I'd like to sail for a living. I remember at the time there was a national campaign to recruit astronauts. Sailing seemed like the same thing."

On September 4, 1987, before all the later recruits arrived, Tatsu Yamasaki received the first batch in his office on the second floor at S & B. It was an expansive room, with sea-green carpet, a large desk at one end, and a small conference table in the middle. It was Yamasaki's inner sanctum, and all around were the relics of his racing life: plaques and bowls, photographs, a large model of *Sunbird V,* one of the Sparkman & Stephens boats. The first recruits came to nine, seven of whom would go the distance. Hara was there, and Jin, whose hair was already sixties-style long and unkempt, and

others named Shimizu, Sakaki, Okabe, Yaji, Yoshizawa. In age they
ranged from twenty-two to thirty-three, and they made up a fair
sampling of the nation's youth.

Tatsu Yamasaki wasn't the sociologist Kaoru Ogimi was. He lacked
an understanding of what the syndicate was after on "the human
side," as Ogimi put it, and he looked upon his first recruits as if
they were no more than candidates for positions at S & B. Who *are*
these people? he asked himself while smiling out from behind his
desk. Can we hire people like this? Long hair, dirty clothes, shaky
backgrounds? *This* is what they've come up with?

He warmed to them, though. Their attitudes seemed serious.
"We've had no enthusiasms in our lives before this, "they told the
kaicho. "We want to strive, to burn out."

A few weeks later, on October 1, that's what they started doing.

·   ·   ·

Nobody in Japan had anything on Tatsu Yamasaki when it came to
acquiring boats. He had been through eight of them in his sailing
career—that first nineteen-footer he bought in Yokosuka, then *Ako*,
Miss Sunbird, the four numbered *Sunbirds*, and *Super Sunbird*.
(There was no *Sunbird IV*, one term for the numeral *shi*, also
meaning death.) Now, however, he had to buy two pieces of machinery larger and more complex than any of those.

Yamasaki had already discovered there were plenty of Twelve-
Meter boats on the market. The previous April he had taken a
business trip through the United States, and it included stops on
each coast and in Chicago. In Manhattan he dropped into the
N.Y.Y.C., an elaborate edifice on West Forty-fourth Street built to
recall a ship. There and elsewhere, Yamasaki was nearly attacked
with offers. These were ominous encounters. The Fremantle event
over, he soon learned, every syndicate that had raced was trying to
clear its debts. In Chicago he met Buddy Melges, whose *Heart of
America* had lost to Dennis Conner in the challenger series. Melges
was an especially keen salesman. During a stopover in Los Angeles
on his way home, a crew member from the Chicago syndicate

knocked on Yamasaki's hotel-room door with a two-hour slide presentation to show him. It was 5 A.M.

None of these propositions would do. Time was of the essence, Yamasaki knew. They had to start practicing on Twelves as soon as possible; more important, they had to start building one, and the only way a Japanese designer was going to draw the lines of a Twelve was to have one next to him as a starting point. "Reverse engineering" was nothing new in the East, of course. But Yamasaki didn't want *a* Twelve; he wanted two of them, and they had to be identical.

America's Cup contenders had sailed against trial horses for as long as the Cup had borne its current name. *America's* was named *Maria*, which shellacked it before *America* went on to shellac its English opponents. But the first syndicate to train on two identical craft was New Zealand's debut campaign in 1987, and the strategy helped make up for the Kiwis' lack of experience in the Twelve-Meter class. Having two craft of the same specifications brought undeniable advantages. It was a perfect test bed. Any appendages (rudders and keels), spars (masts, booms, spinnaker poles), sails, rigging, or winches—anything, in short, not part of the basic hull— could be tested against any variant with reasonably scientific results. All one had to do—and it was often no easy task—was sail both craft in close to identical conditions. So long as you had a realistic assessment of how your boats should sail, you could also judge your crew against other sailors in the class.

The only place Yamasaki could find what he wanted was New Zealand, since the Twelves built for the '87 campaign headed by Sir Michael Fay, a flamboyant Kiwi financier, were the only ones in the world that matched. Fay had money, and the Royal New Zealand Yacht Squadron, from which the Kiwi challenge sailed, was the toniest club in the country. But there was a spit-and-baling-wire aspect to the Kiwi operation nonetheless. The only way the Kiwis managed the two-boat approach financially was to eschew aluminum, the standard material for Twelves, and build "the plastic fantastics," Fiberglas hulls from the same mold. Now Fay held out a deal for the Japanese; if he had gone to an American business school, the term "synergy" would have found its way into the pitch.

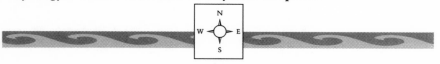

Fay was interested in a sort of mutual-aid arrangement that would have amounted to a joint campaign. The Kiwis would contribute boats, sailing expertise, and access to local companies versed in the construction of hulls, spars, sails, and hardware. The Japanese were short, if not unversed entirely, in all of those categories. In return for what it offered Nippon Challenge, the Fay syndicate would gain access to what it most sorely lacked: laboratories, scientists, technicians, and an industrial infrastructure. The consideration to Fay would be seven hundred thousand American dollars. (The yen and the New Zealand dollar were then too bouncy to negotiate in.) That would have covered the purchase of the Twelves and a collaborative campaign of up to two years, after which the two sides would go separate ways.

Nippon Challenge knew it had to find foreign expertise somewhere and, in the best Meiji tradition, it was looking to the nation that did best what the Japanese wanted to learn. Kaoru Ogimi, knowing the depth of the Kiwis' sailing culture, nurtured the Fay deal in Fremantle during the '87 Cup and in Auckland afterward; by telephone and facsimile, he urged it on Tokyo up to the moment he shoved off from Melbourne in *Nakiri Daio* in the race to Osaka. He thought the arrangement "an ideal combination, a winning strategy." The choice of foreigners from which to learn is an important decision for the Japanese, because it will naturally leave its stamp on all that comes of it. To Ogimi, Nippon Challenge's choice went the wrong way at this point.

The buzzword among the syndicates in Fremantle that were looking to the future had been "technology exchange," and that was where Ogimi thought Japan's best interests lay. But when Yamasaki arrived in Auckland in October 1987 there wasn't much talk of cooperation. All Tatsu recalled seeing was a flock of busy attorneys around Fay's offices, though he didn't quite understand what they were up to. Yamasaki had traveled with his wife, and he met Gary Jobson as soon as they touched down. Jobson had brokered a simpler deal with Fay: eight hundred thousand American dollars for the two Twelves. There would be criticism later that the price was too high, but Jobson brooked none of it; eight hundred thousand

certainly compared favorably with the seven million dollars the
Bengal Bay crowd had paid for Alan Bond's Twelves a few months
earlier.

Fay's interest in any kind of tech exchange had apparently cooled,
replaced by his absorption in his corps of lawyers. But Ogimi,
looking back afterward, blamed the missed opportunity on Taro
Kimura. Kimura had introduced Jobson to the syndicate, and
Jobson's influence, particularly on Kimura and Yamasaki, had been
immediate. After his visit to Tokyo the previous winter, Jobson
remained attached to the syndicate as a consultant. Much later he
would take to referring to Nippon Challenge as "my baby," and to
a certain extent it was. Fay made sure the boats were painted—
complete with the new Nippon Challenge logo—before they left for
Japan, and he sent a couple of Kiwis with them to get them ready to
sail again. But there would be no sailing instructors from the Fay
camp. As it had in almost everything since the war, Japan would
again hitch its wagon to America's. In fact, Kimura and Yamasaki
had already enlisted Jobson's help in finding a suitable team of
coaches from the States.

Yamasaki was awed by what he had bought. "I felt their great-
ness," he remembered later, "but I also wondered, Can we handle
these?" That was understandable. *KZ-3* and *KZ-5*, the "plastic
fantastics," hadn't sailed for the America's Cup; but the boat that
did race in the challenger series, *KZ-7*, had been developed from
the two-boat testing program and was judged by many to have been,
results aside, the fastest craft in Fremantle. Twelves of any design
are a stunning first sight. They are long—sixty-five feet (not twelve
meters)—and heavy, about twenty-six tons. They sit low in the
water, and when first boarded they exude the power for which
they're known among sailors. A Twelve's hardware—winches, rigging—is huge by the standards of most cruising boats. To sail one is
to know why. The loads that build up as the boat approaches an
effective maximum speed of nine knots or so are massive. They
require crews of eleven, with work enough, by today's standards,
for twenty. Twelve-Meter yachts are "wet" boats, to say the least; in

powerful winds, racing one can mean trying to get your job done knee-deep in seawater.

•   •   •

What Yamasaki imagined, as he gazed at the syndicate's purchases, was far from the scene then unfolding off the shores of Lake Hamana. Hamanako was a large body of water slightly inland from the coast, large enough to present sailors with three-foot swells. The recruits—there were fifteen of them by then—were taking the waves in two Yamaha 30s, I.O.R.-rated boats less than half the size of a Twelve. Even those were a mismatch. Komatsu, who was setting the agenda along with the newly arrived *gaijin*, was teaching "infants," as he later called his charges, and expecting perfection of them.

Among the Americans Jobson found were Stu Argo, an easygoing, broadly built blond who could have stepped out of a men's underwear ad, and Hank Stewart, a less striking and less sympathetic hired hand. Both were accomplished sailors; Argo would later go on to one of the American defense syndicates against whom Nippon Challenge was hoping to sail. A week after arriving, Argo and Stewart accompanied a small crew to the Australia Cup match-racing series off Perth. It was the new crew's first match race, and they had sailed exactly four days before leaving. They placed sixth of ten entries—a notable improvement over the Citizen Cup debacle earlier in the year—but it was chiefly an exercise in experience and in learning how far they had to go.

The routine at Hamanako, well established from those first four days onward, was stiff and repetitive, and it ran from Monday through Saturday. It consisted of a combination of blackboard sessions and work on the water. They would drill on, say, starts, and then on shore cover what they had done right, what wrong, and which rules applied. Argo said, "What made it tough was they had no attention span." They had no knee pads or sailing gloves, either. The crew would remember exhaustion and the outer layer of skin peeling off their palms. They learned by rote and imitation. In the beginning, they couldn't even moor the boats properly unless they were in the same place every day.

Nobody had a set position. Instead they rotated, as if they were in a Japanese company, where *sararimen* move from one department to another for their entire careers. Nobody was in one place too long, and, just as no one could build a power base under such circumstances in corporate Japan, no one became proficient at any one job on board the 30s. But proficiency wasn't the aim then. It was staying on the boat and getting it to sail.

The format on the water always included match racing, Komatsu skippering one boat and Makoto Namba the other. But it was a comedy of errors nearly every day. One boat would win the start and hold the lead until the first mark; then it would blow the turn and the other boat would overtake. It was the same at the next mark, and the next, until the race was over. Komatsu was relentlessly aggressive. One afternoon Namba was racing exceptionally well against him. After an even start in the last race of the day, the two entered a tacking duel in winds that were hitting sixteen knots. Namba was heading out to the right and holding a marginal lead. His fifth tack was perfectly on the layline, the line straight to the upwind mark, and Komatsu was pointed directly at Namba's port side. Komatsu would have to tack over himself or dip below Namba. Either move would have cost Komatsu the leg, but there was no chance of crossing Namba's bow.

Jin, who was port trimmer on Komatsu's boat, yelled back to his skipper, "It's getting close. Which way, dip under or tack?"

Komatsu, his eyes straight ahead, said nothing. They were two boat lengths from Namba's side when Jin called back again. "We're still on port tack. What should we do?"

Komatsu was still silent.

What is this guy thinking? Namba began wondering. On his boat it was clear a few seconds later that Komatsu was trying to cross his bow.

"You can't make it!" Namba's crew started screaming over. "You can't do it!"

Then Komatsu rammed them. Namba took considerable hull damage, while Komatsu's bow pulpit was destroyed and his mast snapped, falling over his leeward side. Repairs to the two 30s would

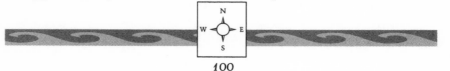

keep them off the water for a week. But Komatsu never said a word about the incident.

He wasn't entirely humorless. One day he fell in the water while stepping from one boat to the other and came to the surface laughing at himself. But Komatsu could also force a sailor over the side to solve a problem with the appendages when the day was over and there was no earthly reason for it. He was, the crew soon found, the nasty piece of work they had judged him to be during the recruitment exercises, but they had respect for him nonetheless. "He'd bark at them more or less constantly, always in Japanese, of course," Argo said later. "But the crew looked up to him. They took their places under him as if they were heads on a totem pole."

What the syndicate got, in fact, was a powerful dose of the routine famous among university clubs. Komatsu had sailed a 470 dinghy, a two-man boat, to All-Japan championships for a decade, but never with the same partner. Even when he raced overseas, it was rarely with the same crew twice. Now the syndicate understood why. Komatsu was a different person on the water. His face would tighten, his eyes blaze more brightly. Beatings were common. He'd spit in a sailor's face if he was angry enough, uncommon even for those who had sailed under the most hierarchical of college skippers.

Komatsu viewed all this as part of the required regime. "When we first started, they couldn't even do simple things like tie lines," he summed up the early months. "When we finished at Hamanako, they had reached the level of fifteen-year-olds. We had poor facilities, and our training methods weren't well developed. But I think Hamanako was the best time the sailors would have."

Hamanako was an interlude; it didn't last much beyond the beginning of 1988. By January of that year the Twelve-Meters were arriving. These were monsters from another world, the largest sailboats the Japanese public had ever seen. They would eventually be put in the water at a small port city called Gamagori, but that year's Tokyo Boat Show was an obligatory stop on the way. Grant Spanhake, a New Zealander Fay sent to help rig the boats, was preparing *KZ-5* for display when he got a taste of what the coaches were in for. Although the boats had been painted, they needed cleaning after shipment from Auckland, and in the course of directing that duty Spanhake found a small patch aft of the keel that needed a light sanding. A typically quiet and congenial Kiwi, Spanhake patiently explained the detail to a Japanese technician, mostly with his hands, and left to attend other tasks.

When he returned, the rough spot that required ten minutes of smoothing over was a neat rectangular hole straight through the deck. It wasn't the syndicate's last mess, or anything like the largest, that would be filed neatly under the heading of "cross-cultural communication problems."

• • •

When Tatsu Yamasaki and those centered around S & B went looking for a suitable place for the campaign's base camp, the first place they tried was along the coast south of Tokyo where the Japanese sailing scene was centered. What quickly caught their eye was an old boatyard on an islet off the uneventful town of Miura. The location, at the tip of the peninsula that formed the northern edge of Sagami Bay, seemed perfect, and Miura's mayor was quick to see the benefits of having an America's Cup challenger on his shoreline.

Japan, however, was still a nation of local fiefdoms. Manufacturer without peer in many industries and creditor to the world, it often thought like a farmer or a five-and-dime merchant. Tokyo's international airport, opened in 1978 and overused almost from the start, is still subject to violent disputes because building it meant trimming the surrounding rice paddies by a few square kilometers. This time, it was the Miura fishermen. Having Nippon Challenge around meant nothing in terms of global image, national pride, or advancement in the community of nations; it meant sailboats coming and going, and that would disturb the fish. Negotiations with local associations dragged on for months, and Yamasaki finally had to scratch the site.

By then the *kaicho* had turned to a gruff, salty fellow named Arthur Wullschleger, another of those Gary Jobson had introduced to the syndicate. Wullschleger had agreed to jury the first Nippon

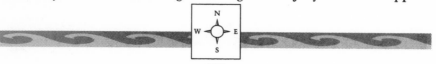

Cup in 1987—Taro Kimura's dream having come true—and afterward he began assisting in the search for a camp. Wullschleger was a *personage* on the international sailing scene. Born into a wealthy family with a private textile business, he was a longtime member of the Larchmont and New York yacht clubs and had raced in countless Trans-Atlantics, Fastnets, Bermudas, Trans-Pacifics, and Hobarts. A gravel-voiced, grandfatherly man in his late sixties by the time he came to Japan, Wullschleger was "umping and judging," as he put it, around the world—San Diego one week, St. Lucia the next. Having taken up fishing in his later days, he was known familiarly as "Captain Tuna" in just about any country where there was a lively yachting scene.

Wullschleger was perfect for the task at hand. During the war he had constructed bases around the Pacific islands for the Army Corps of Engineers. It gave him a lasting frame of reference—"The Japs are funny," he'd say often. By the time he judged the Nippon Cup, in November 1987, he had already begun combining his experience with his passion. Setting up the America^2 camp in Fremantle, Wullschleger developed his "barren rock theory," which was a plan, really, by which he could build a sailing camp from scratch much as a manufacturer builds a "green field" factory.

Blunt and gentle at the same time, Wullschleger took one look at the Miura arrangement and said they were better off elsewhere anyway. "It might be close to Tokyo, but you've got fishing boats twenty-four hours a day and an incredible surge," he pointed out. "Dock a Twelve against one of those concrete piers and you'd have it in for repairs every time the tide came in." Wullschleger started combing other parts of the Honshu coast and stumbled on Gamagori during a visit to a nearby Yamaha factory.

Once again the mayor and his municipal officials would open their arms to Nippon Challenge. But there would be more fights with fishermen, too, and as a result of them the city's shoreline was gerrymandered extensively before any agreement could be reached. "What was left after everyone else was finished was the shittiest part of the port, and we got it," Wullschleger said in characteristic tones.

"But the bay looked like a great place to trial. It was calm, and the surge wasn't bad." Nippon Challenge had found a home.

Gamagori was typical of the many towns and cities that Japan had passed by with great momentum in the 1980s. No one in the syndicate had ever heard of it when Wullschleger first proposed it as a site. The Japanese rust bowl, unlike its counterpart in the American Midwest, was spread gulag-like around the country, and Gamagori was unmistakably part of it. It had a long history as a textile center, and by the early fifties, its heyday, the city claimed fame as the producer of nearly sixty percent of the nation's output of synthetic rope. It was down from the summit after that. Gamagori never made the leap from basic industry to high tech, or, as the Japanese liked to put it, from *ju ko cho dai* (heavy, thick, long, and big), to *kei haku tan sho* (light, thin, short, and small).

To reach the place from Tokyo you took a *shinkansen*, a bullet train, to either Hamamatsu or Toyohashi, lively industrial hubs nearby; then you caught a local that dribbled through a series of minor hamlets. What you saw first were dozens of aging factories with peeling chimneys and streets that were empty most of the time. Eighty-five thousand people still lived there, but you never encountered many of them abroad, and when you did it appeared that there was no one in town under fifty-five or so. The port gave onto a modest-sized bay called Mikawa. Apart from its population of fishing trawlers, it was still used to import wood for the Japanese housing industry and to export cars from a factory operated by the Mitsubishi Motors Company in a nearby town.

The two Twelve-Meters, renamed *J-3* and *J-5*, arrived at Gamagori on April 5 and sailed for the first time in Japanese waters a week later. It was every bit the shock the Americans, who now numbered several, had anticipated. As the pressure builds on a Twelve, the craft reaches a point when it's so close to "maxing out" that wind translates less into increased speed than as an intense load on the sails and rigging. The new recruits simply didn't understand the forces involved, and a Twelve could quickly turn into a dangerous piece of gear in the hands of the uninitiated.

They would learn, and with what some considered impressive

speed, but not before blood was spilled and teeth broken. The essence of the problem, as the *gaijin* began to see it, was a lack of basic feel for the boats among the Japanese. They did everything mechanically. They could duplicate, but the difference between good sailing and bad is the development of finesse and timing— talents that had to be learned but couldn't really be taught. In short, the crew had developed no flexible responses. And that was especially clear among the sail trimmers. Their timing was terrible.

It was deeply frustrating for the American coaches. Once, tacking up and down Mikawa Bay in unusually fresh winds, the trimmers had been late releasing the jib all morning. That was a dangerous mistake in a breeze, because the jib sheets on a Twelve are wire, not rope. Easing the sail too late into a tack meant the sheet could whip across the boat and lash a hapless sailor in the face on the way. After it ripped into a grinder's nose, Argo and Stewart stopped to lecture the crew on the importance of an early release. Then they tried again, Namba at the helm, Stewart behind him coaching in a nonstop monologue. On that next tack the trimmers were egregiously late, their worst effort of the day, and the jib sheet whipped far enough back to wrap around Stewart's neck. Argo, who had seen it coming, was peeling the wire off as Stewart fell to the deck.

"Are you all right?" Argo asked, standing over Stewart and peering down into his face.

Stewart was gazing up at the mainsail and the sky. "How do I look?" he shouted back.

"Well," Argo said, "yeah, you *look* pretty good."

• • •

The morning of April 24, 1988, was clear and fresh along Mikawa Bay. All the sponsors' names were posted on a bright, white board at the base camp's entrance; inside, thirty flagpoles advertised thirty corporate logos. The sail loft was up, along with the physical training center. There were a front office, a mess hall, and space for some offices. It was opening day.

Among the first to arrive were a local marching band and a flock of Gamagori schoolchildren, who lined up along the fresh concrete

of the base camp quai. Opposite, all red and white but for their light blue decks, the Twelves bobbed side by side against a pontoon-supported pier. As the crowd gathered, *meishi*, business cards, began to change hands in volume, and men and women were bowing to one another everywhere you looked. Blue-chip Japan had come to town. Gamagori hadn't seen anything like it in years. Everybody and nobody cut the ribbon. Yamasaki and Eguchi held it at the center, and outward from them were the mayor and various other corporate heavyweights and city officials. There were seven of them altogether, all wearing white gloves as is the Japanese custom on such occasions. They each scissored through at the appointed moment, each ending up with a snippet in his hands.

Yamasaki, blue-suited and elegant as always, briefly explained the syndicate and the Cup, first to a roomful of Japanese reporters, then from a dais to the assembled sponsors, suppliers, officials, and local notables; then came the mayor. They all spoke before the end—Eguchi, Ogimi, Kimura. Before the crew sailed, Yamasaki and Eguchi boarded the Twelves, uncorked some expensive champagne, and let the wind blow it over the bows until the bottles were empty.

Kensaku Nomoto; the professor from Osaka, was one of the syndicate's more important executives by the time Gamagori opened, and he was especially busy that day. During all the speeches, and after the boats had been towed out to sail, he made it a point to confer quietly with Yamasaki, Ogimi, and Gary Jobson, who had flown in for a few meetings in Tokyo before the ceremony. In separate conversations, the executive told them each the same thing: it was time to drop the Americans.

As he would often put it, the question was one of "East-West interface." It was more apparent than ever that Nippon Challenge couldn't go it alone. And he appreciated the contributions the American coaches had made. "But it was obvious to me that our first try with overseas members was not successful," Nomoto would recall. The problems ran from expense account disputes to schools for *gaijin* children who had accompanied their fathers to Japan. More sensitive, a few of the Americans were talking down to Japanese in the syndicate who occupied rather elevated positions in their own society. It amounted to the small change of such arrangements. Meshing with *gaijin*, however, is a delicate matter in Japan, an issue of *soto* and *uchi*, "outside" and "inside." The Americans, or any other foreigners, would always be *soto*, of course. But Nomoto lacked Kaoru Ogimi's tolerance and vision in such matters. To him, a foreigner had to be *soto* without so bluntly contradicting the Japanese way of doing things.

"From my point of view," he said, "the Americans are too frank and too straightforward and too aggressive for the Japanese. My judgment at the time was, the Kiwi people would be better fitted to our team."

Nomoto, by his own reckoning, had shocked Jobson when he delivered this assessment. Most of the others, who had quickly come to defer to the professor, simply nodded. Yamasaki had been troubled by reports of friction even during the Hamanako period. Ogimi—although he deferred to Nomoto not at all—said he'd try to work through contacts in New Zealand.

A month later Nomoto had his first contact, by telephone and facsimile, with a Kiwi named Roy Dickson. Then in his late-fifties, Dickson was by any measure among the most experienced yachtsmen in New Zealand. As skipper, tactician, or navigator, he had been racing internationally for New Zealand since 1951. He had coached New Zealand's Olympic team in the 1980 games, and he had just finished as sailing director of the country's first America's Cup Challenge.

Dickson, who had gray, close-cropped hair and deep-blue eyes, had already made an impression on a few of the Nippon Challenge people. During the '87 Citizen Cup, when Komatsu's team was standing alone and lost at the opening cocktail reception, the older man walked quietly over and spoke to Makoto Namba. "I'm Roy Dickson," he said simply. "Welcome to Auckland." Dickson was skippering another of the Stewart 34s, and the gesture made a lasting impression. "Other helmsmen, say, the Americans, would bark, 'Hey! How are ya?' " Namba once recounted. "It was a different feeling from him. He looked like a little old man. In Japan

we don't have many sailors his age. He seemed special. My grandfather is very similar to Mr. Roy."

Mr. Roy was on the compact side, but the comparison would
otherwise have stunned him. There wasn't much that was grandfatherly about Roy Dickson, not in the Western sense. In Japan,
however, older men are known mostly to be stubborn and difficult,
and Dickson would eventually prove to be both.

The comparison, in fact, would be made often: a month after
Nomoto's first telephone call to Auckland, Roy Dickson arrived for
the first of what was planned as a series of two-week training
sessions.

•   •   •

Just before Dickson arrived, in early June, Stu Argo took some of
the crew to Lulea, Sweden, for the Twelve-Meter World Championships. By the time the gun went off for the first race, they had spent
exactly forty days sailing the Twelves in Gamagori. Sweden was the
syndicate's first real test in the class, and Nippon Challenge was
going to watch it closely.

Gary Jobson had organized the Japanese entry. Through him the
syndicate leased a Twelve with a winged keel from America[2] and had
it modified in New York before shipping it across the Atlantic. The
keel was cut down, the wing angles changed, and sail area added—
all of which was supposed to improve boat speed. Instead, they
found in Lulea that they'd slowed the craft down and reduced the
skipper's control.

Altogether there were five Americans, five Japanese, and Robert
Fry. Jobson skippered, Komatsu navigated, and Stu Argo was starboard trimmer. Jobson could see the results of all the drilling Argo,
Stewart, and the other Americans had done. Afterward, he thought
crew work was the one bright surprise of the event. But Sweden did
not go well otherwise. The Japanese boat didn't seem too bad when
they lined it up to sail parallel with a few others during practice
sessions. Downwind, they were fine; but the speed deficiency became
apparent whenever they were tacking.

The races began on a promising note. Jobson had an excellent

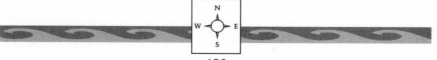

start in the first fleet race, but he was immediately faced with what he put down afterward to communications problems. The committee boat signaled that an entry had gone over early, and the Japanese crew fell immediately into confusion over it. Was it them? It wasn't, but nobody could call it with certainty, and Jobson went back to start again (the penalty for crossing early). First became last, and they stayed there the entire race.

The final fleet race was called the Midnight Sun because it began in the middle of the Swedish summer night. Robert Fry and a few others had worked through the previous night to drop the wings down on the keel to give the boat more angle when it sailed upwind. Things improved. Jobson was second around the first weather mark, and they dropped back only one position over the rest of the course, finishing third. It was enough, barely, to get them into the match-racing portion of the event.

The match races started well, too, but problems with crew work emerged again. They simply didn't have enough experience to handle the boat or the conditions. In the second match race the Japanese faced *White Crusader,* the British entry and another sluggish boat. Jobson beat them soundly at the start and it looked as if he would easily control the race. Then during one of the first upwind tacks, a line got twisted on the port-side winch, where Robert Fry was trimming. Fry had never handled an override before, and he grabbed the winch drum to reverse its direction.

"Let it keep winding," someone shouted.

But it was too late. Fry's finger got caught between the jib sheet and the winch drum and the pressure cut it straight through the bone.

"How bad is it?" Jobson shouted.

"You'll have to get me off," Fry called back.

Fry was transferred to the committee boat and then to a Swedish patrol vessel, which rushed him to the hospital. (The finger was saved.) But Jobson was forced out of the race. *White Crusader,* in any case, had already sailed past and led by many lengths.

Tatsu Yamasaki had been there from the beginning, along with Ken Nomoto and others from Tokyo and Gamagori. The mood had

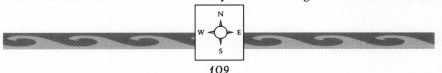

been bright during the preliminaries, when the *kaicho* had gone out to sail with Jobson and the crew. He liked what he saw. As the races wore on, however, Yamasaki fell into the deep, private silence familiar to those who knew him well. For more than a day, he spoke to no one. Only Taro Kimura, who arrived midway through the event, was able to revive Yamasaki's spirits, as he had often in the past.

"Even if we only want to put in a respectable showing for the America's Cup," Yamasaki pronounced as he emerged from his cocoon, "we'd better have one hell of a boat."

It was a fated judgment, one that would divide the syndicate to one degree or another until the end. To an important extent, the *kaicho* hadn't understood the challenge facing the Japanese, and he never really would. To him it didn't lie in finding or developing the right people, people who wanted to compete and win. Instead, he wanted to rely on money and things. And that set Yamasaki squarely against all that Kaoru Ogimi believed the challenge stood for.

Where Yamasaki's judgment in Sweden would lead wasn't clear, but the syndicate's direction was set. Jobson, indeed, remembered the moment as a turning point in the Nippon Challenge campaign.

"After that day in Sweden," the American said later, "technology was everything."

That was what Kensaku Nomoto, the scientist from Osaka, had been thinking all along.

CHAPTER VI

SENSEI

Kensaku Nomoto's route, in the summer of 1987, began in Malmö on the Swedish coast, led through the Danish archipelago, north to the deep, blue fjords of western Norway, and back to the Royal Yacht Club at Göteborg. *Haru-Ichiban II* had sailed from Malmö in May. When Nomoto docked at the Göteborg marina in the afternoon of September 20, Kohtaro Horiuchi was waiting for him.

It had been a long and satisfying trip, the beginning of the life Nomoto had planned for years. Whenever he wanted, which was often, he would tie up at a small Scandinavian port, head for the shipyard or library, and poke around in search of blueprints, texts, or records that shed light on the local shipbuilding tradition. Then he would photocopy, take notes, draw from originals. Northern Europe's rich maritime history had long been of special interest to Nomoto. After he finished there, when he decided he had gathered what he could, he would have *Haru-Ichiban II* cargoed home and do the same thing, sailing through the entire Japanese archipelago. It was Kensaku Nomoto's dream.

When retirement came that spring, Nomoto had two sign-off letters to write. He had kept his chair in the department of naval architecture at Osaka, and he had taught for four years by then at the World Maritime University, a United Nations institution dedicated to instructing Third World bureaucrats and shipbuilders in everything from harbor management to marine design. The years in Malmö, Nomoto thought, would be his final contribution to the profession.

By March, however, he had begun to hear regularly from friends, colleagues, and former students drawn into the design side of the Japanese challenge for the America's Cup. These letters were full of ideas, plans, experiments, and test preparations. Kohtaro Horiuchi, an old and close friend, was part of it. Together, they were preparing to build the nation's first Twelve-Meter yacht.

The first job offer had arrived just before Nomoto sailed. He had seen it coming, of course, but he was chagrined, nonetheless, when the letter from the syndicate's board reached him. He apologized profusely. He had retired, he said, and there was Scandinavia. He had been preparing to sail the local waters for several years and had thought about doing so for many more.

But that was only part of it. Nomoto's first response, which he kept to himself when he was invited to participate in the challenge, was somewhat more hardened. It's a bit too early, Nomoto said to himself. Yes, there are old acquaintances from the N.O.R.C. involved. But the America's Cup would reflect upon Japan, not just those on the local racing scene. Our knowledge of yachts is appreciably inferior when compared with North America and Western Europe. So are our technical standards in the field. We're simply not ready. And we shouldn't undertake something like this until we are.

Kensaku Nomoto and his wife, Nobuko, set sail as soon as they could after the academic year in Malmö ended.

Letters kept arriving over the summer. Mail from Tokyo would be waiting for him when he stopped at one of the ports on his itinerary, and more would have been forwarded from his successor in Malmö.

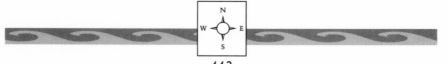

A note from Horiuchi came, saying he would be coming to Sweden that autumn. They should meet.

Nomoto admired the burly man from Yamaha marine. Adopting a bit of the slang he had picked up at the many international conferences he had attended over the years, Nomoto took pride in saying that Yamaha's marine side was "Horiuchi-*san*'s baby." The two men met in the mid-seventies, when Horiuchi was chairing a committee in the Japan Shipbuilding Industry Association. Every two months Nomoto would take a train up to Tokyo to work with Horiuchi on the technical standards applied to Japanese-made sailboats. Afterward they would drink together. A genuine fondness grew between them. To Horiuchi, Nomoto-*sensei* was "the boss in Japanese sailboat engineering."

Horiuchi had been busy that year. While Nomoto was finishing his academic duties, Horiuchi had gone to the Transport Ministry to discuss organizing a "hull form committee," as he called it, for Nippon Challenge. Hiraku Tanaka ran the ministry's Ship Research Institute, and he was another of Horiuchi's old friends. They started a working group together, Tanaka chaired it, and they went looking for others to join. There were professors from Tokyo University, Kanazawa Industrial University, and the National University of Yokohama. There were other Yamaha people. Tanaka brought in a naval architect named Mitsuhiro Abe, an old imperial navy man who ran a tank-testing facility at a Mitsui subsidiary called Akishima Laboratories.

Nomoto's name came up often. Everybody on the committee wanted to contribute, but what could they do? Where could they start? They had the facilities they would need—wind tunnels, testing tanks, computer gear. The universities were loaded with it, to say nothing of what industry could make available. But that was all dedicated to the construction of commercial vessels. "We had no testing apparatus whatever for sailboats," Horiuchi said. They needed a man in the middle, someone who understood the science they shared and knew how it could be turned to another purpose. When they got down to it, there was only one person.

After Nomoto declined the offer extended in May, Horiuchi,

Tanaka, and Abe decided that someone should confront the doctor directly. Horiuchi got Yamaha's permission to make the trip and he contacted Nomoto through the university in Malmö. Arrangements were made; ever after, Nomoto would be under the impression that Horiuchi was traveling in Europe on Yamaha business and that his visit to Göteborg was simply a stopover, the gesture of a friend.

It was actually an exercise in *kudoku*, or seduction, and Horiuchi was prepared to do whatever was necessary to get Nomoto on board. He remembered well what he had seen in Fremantle: building a boat was an enormous project; unless Japan pulled together the best shipbuilding know-how it had, Nippon Challenge would achieve nothing. Horiuchi knew all about Nomoto's lifetime dream, and he knew he would be asking the professor to give it up. But he also understood his friend well enough to aim his appeal where it would be most effective.

After he checked into his hotel on September 20, Horiuchi made his way to the marina and found Nomoto still aboard *Haru-Ichiban II*. The doctor was dressed as he always was while sailing—corduroys, a woolen sweater, and a heavy woolen cap—and he greeted Horiuchi with a warm, easy smile. Once on board, Horiuchi patiently admired the craft as Nomoto showed him the ship's cabin and the single-handed rigging he had designed. As the sun went down, the two men settled below deck.

"You know, this America's Cup challenge is a national affair," Horiuchi began. "And you know better than anyone that we haven't got the experience in designing boats in a class this large. We don't have any experience competing in regattas this size, either. The only chance for us—if we have a chance—is to build a boat fast enough to cover our lack of time on the water."

The doctor considered this and replied simply, "I agree." Then he added, "But Japan has advantages when it comes to ships. We have the hydrodynamics specialists and the research facilities. They are, of course, designed for commercial vessels. But basically they're the same. If we can adapt the technology, we might be able to produce a high-performance yacht to launch a challenge."

"But to do that we need people who know yachts and naval

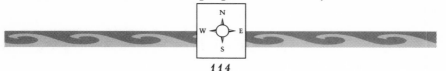

hydrodynamics," Horiuchi said, "someone who is familiar with the technical facilities."

Nomoto abruptly turned the conversation to ship designs he had just seen that went as far back as the Vikings. But he was thinking again about the implicit proposition that had been placed on the table. Horiuchi stayed late. He had no answer when he returned to his hotel; but he had done his job better than he thought he had.

"I decided to join that night," Nomoto said when he talked about the encounter. "Naturally, everyone has some love for his country. I was moved by what Horiuchi had to say. My fatherland was going to launch into a very new competition. Possibly, I decided, I might be able to contribute to some extent."

He would return to Tokyo in the first few days of 1988. He hadn't said yes yet. But as the autumn went on, Nomoto arranged to receive reports and drawings from Tokyo indicating the progress of the hull committee and the design group that was taking shape.

•   •   •

Hydrodynamics, simply defined, is the study of the forces exerted by water. The essential tools run from hammers, nails, glue, and marine varnish to electronically monitored testing tanks and advanced computers. Using wooden scale models, hydrodynamicists measure water flow, resistance, wave making, rolling, pitching, and all the other factors that add up to the interaction of water and a hull. The object, in the case of commercial vessels, is simple: to arrive at a design that carries the maximum load at the greatest speed using the minimum propulsion and consuming the least energy.

The Japanese were indeed masters at it. They had long dominated the International Towing Tank Congress, a scientific body founded in the 1930s. In the late eighties there were about thirty major tank-testing facilities worldwide, and almost half of them were in Japan. Nomoto could name all thirty, had seen most of them, and knew many of the scientists who operated them. In the industrial congress, he had represented Japan for more than a decade.

Testing yachts was another matter. The tank itself was the same.

But the equipment around it was different, as were the forces measured and the analysis of what scientists learned from the tank. The economics of yacht tests were vastly different, simply because there was no shipborne commerce to support the specialized application. It was an expensive proposition, and there were, accordingly, few facilities anywhere able to do it. One in Delft, Holland, was the most famous. Ben Lexcen, credited, after much dispute, with the winged keel on Alan Bond's *Australia II*, used the tank at Delft to conduct the first tests of his concept. Other facilities were in Copenhagen; Hoboken, New Jersey; Ottawa; Southampton, England; and Cambridge, Massachusetts. Japan had two—at Osaka University and at a merchant marine academy in Kobe—neither of which could be used to design a Twelve. In the industrial sector, Japan had none.

But advances were taking place on the scientific side in the autumn of 1987. Mitsui and the Ishikawajima-Harima Heavy Industries Company, leading concerns in the shipbuilding industry, were both official suppliers. Both operated advanced towing tanks to develop cargo vessel designs, and both saw, in the America's Cup campaign, an opportunity to expand into the marine-sports industry. It was a straight technology-transfer proposition, with one deviation from the traditional pattern: the outsider who would supply the new ideas was not a *gaijin* but Ken Nomoto.

The essential change that has to be made between tests of prop-driven commercial vessels and tests of sailboats involves the number of forces to be calculated and analyzed. In the case of commercial ships, there is only one important force, known as the fore-and-aft component. That simply means the amount of resistance the hull meets as its engines drive it forward. To test it, the model is pulled through the tank in a straight line. Why only one force? Because prop ships move in a straight line.

Sailboats, of course, don't. They advance through the sea by making headway, or forward speed, and also leeway. Leeway, or drift angle, is the sideways movement of a sailboat as it moves forward. What must be tested in a sailboat design is not only the fore-and-aft component but the leeway component, and what are

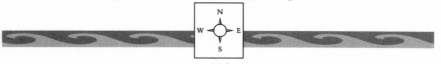

known as the heeling moment and the yawing moment. Heeling is the lateral inclination of a boat under sail. Yawing means turning. Anyone who has ever had trouble keeping a sailboat on course has coped with the yawing moment—the ship's proclivity to rotate sideways as if the mast were a vertical axis.

Mitsui and IHI began preparing tanks to test yachts while the doctor was still in Sweden. They followed his directions carefully by telephone, fax, and courier, and they sent him drawings of what they came up with every step of the way. Modifications were made. Late in 1987, still in Sweden, Nomoto thought the scientists at the two companies sounded more or less ready to test their first models.

In January 1988, when Nomoto had his first look, he found that they weren't. The new facilities could measure the fore-and-aft component, drift, heeling, and yawing well enough. But they measured them, in effect, all at once. The first readings, therefore, were inaccurate. It was a simple question of interference. "You have to think of crosstalk in a telephone conversation," Nomoto said after seeing the tanks. "We're communicating by phone, but someone else comes into our line. Suddenly we can't communicate clearly. You want to separate the lines, correct? That's what we wanted to do."

One morning later that month, Nomoto took a commuter train out to Akishima, where Mitsui's lab was located. He spent the day in consultation with Mitsuhiro Abe, a thin, agreeable man of Nomoto's age, and a younger scientist named Ryosuke Matsui. Matsui was tall, earnest, and unworn by the years of long hours his superior had kept. He had a bright, Boy Scout's smile. He was typical of those his age on the syndicate's technical staff: Matsui had an enthusiasm for Nippon Challenge that extended quite beyond his duties at the lab. He did a little dinghy sailing himself on weekends. He wanted to see Japan in the America's Cup. And he was a former student of Professor Nomoto.

When Nomoto trained back to Tokyo that evening, he was satisfied that Abe and Matsui would finally get the testing tank right. He had left them with a pile of sketches and technical drawings, and they had discussed the defects and the solutions in satisfactory detail.

Three weeks later, when Nomoto visited Akishima again, he found

that Abe and Matsui had rebuilt their equipment almost from scratch. And they had done it the way the *sensei* wanted it done.

That was important to Ken Nomoto. Among friends, he sometimes likened himself to a naval architect named Yuzuru Hiraga, a well-known vice-admiral in the imperial navy during the Second World War. Hiraga had built *Yamato* and its sister ship, *Musashi*, the largest battleships ever floated and the most famous in the Japanese fleet. In Japanese, *yuzuru* can also mean "accommodating" or "inclined to give in," but Hiraga became known in the service as Yuzurazu, which had the opposite meaning, "defiant" or "never gives in." The nickname suited Hiraga because he insisted that nobody who wasn't an engineer had any place in the design and construction process. "A naval constructor should take input from the officers who sail ships, but sometimes officers have stupid ideas," Nomoto once explained. "Yuzuru never backed down on this point. It's the architect's job to interpret what the officers want and build the best ships."

That was how Ken Nomoto saw his job, too, and he advanced the comparison between himself and Admiral Never Gives In often and with evident pride. He would design Nippon Challenge's boat his own way, and he had no intention of giving an inch so far as the men who would sail it were concerned.

•   •   •

In the end, it wouldn't matter much what mistakes the design people made when they first set out to build a Twelve. They learned from the exercise. In sheer scale alone, it was an enormous step forward for the Japanese. Three months after Nomoto's visits to Akishima, however, America's Cup circles started talking about "the Twelve-Meter era." It was thirty years long, and it was all but over.

The end of Twelve-Meter competition for the America's Cup is commonly identified with the fraught challenge issued in July 1987 by Sir Michael Fay, the New Zealand banker, to the San Diego Yacht Club. The tangled events that followed covered a race course and several New York courtrooms, and they ended only in April 1990. Sir Michael lost, and San Diego kept the Cup it won in Fremantle.

Competitive sailors around the world were appalled by the ungentle-manly spectacle that unfolded during those years. Even during the actual races in September 1988, designers and syndicate managers were meeting on shore to alter the rule that had allowed such a mess to take place.

In fact, the Twelve-Meter rule was ripe for change, and change had been under discussion ever since the Fremantle races proved to be the most popular America's Cup regatta in the long history of the event. Sir Michael was as much a catalyst as anything else, prompt-ing the Cup's organizers to advance from tinkering with a very old formula to inventing a new one.

Prior to the Second World War, America's Cup regattas were raced in huge and expensive craft called J-boats. Corinthian sailing, dominated by men of wealth and leisure, was at its apex, and the boats they sailed stretched to the maximum allowed by the Deed of Gift, the document by which George Schuyler, the last survivor among *America's* original owners, formally bequeathed the Cup to N.Y.Y.C.

The Deed of Gift stipulated that entries had to measure sixty to ninety feet at the waterline, and J-class yachts came in at the top end of that very simple rule. The last and most powerful J-boat, Harold S. Vanderbilt's *Ranger*, was a massive piece of machinery. It measured a hundred and thirty-five feet overall, eighty-seven feet at the waterline; it weighed a hundred and sixty-six tons and sailed under seven thousand five hundred square feet of cloth. *Ranger*'s defense of the America's Cup in 1937 would be the last by any boat for twenty-one years. Every J-class yacht save two was scrapped for metal during the war. When competition for the Cup was finally revived in 1958, the Twelve-Meter formula was used for the first time.

Competing nations had seen the prospect of returning to J-class racing prohibitively expensive given postwar economic conditions. New ideas ranged from an offshore race around Bermuda to com-petition in fourteen-foot dinghies. Instead, the N.Y.Y.C. sought to preserve the Cup's tradition of racing in the most advanced class afloat by making two amendments to the Deed of Gift: it reduced

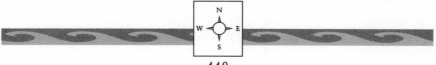

the minimum waterline length to forty-four feet and dropped the rule that challenging craft had to reach the regatta from their home ports under sail.

The Twelve-Meter rule fitted the times. The average waterline measurement was forty-five feet, a more manageable and affordable length; maximum sail area was roughly four thousand five hundred square feet. Twelves did represent the state of the art in competitive sailing, but the design rule under which they were built was not all that much younger than the America's Cup: the Twelve-Meter formula was devised in 1906, and it looked like this:

$$\frac{\text{length} + 2 \text{ x draft} + \sqrt{\text{sail area}} - \text{freeboard}}{2.37} = 12 \text{ meters}$$

Many appendices were attached to each component of the rule. Simply rendered, the equation forced the designer to balance a yacht's most important speed-producing factors with freeboard, the distance between the gunwale and the waterline. The rule generally produced deep, heavy boats of traditional shape. Some famous America's Cup victors had come out of this arithmetic: *Intrepid*, which was sponsored by Harold Vanderbilt and which defended for the N.Y.Y.C. in both 1967 and 1970, *Courageous*, which kept the Cup American in 1974 and 1977, and *Australia II*, which made more history than any other Twelve in the thirty years the class raced for the Cup.

But by 1983 it was a tired formula, unsuited to the kind of race organizers wanted after the tremendous worldwide interest generated by the Australian victory. The rule had been "appended, amended, and massaged so often over the years," as Tom Ehman put it, "that it began to look like a mess." Ehman, an accomplished sailor and a longtime member of the N.Y.Y.C. was asked to help rewrite the Twelve-Meter rule by the summer of 1988 to take into account new design techniques such as movable rigs and technological advances in such areas as materials. "Then along came Michael

Fay," Ehman said, "and out of that we began to think we ought to look at a brand-new boat."

Sir Michael stunned the world of competitive yacht racing by doing something eminently simple: he went back to the Deed of Gift. The changes in the deed to allow for Twelve-Meter racing had not altered the original document but in a few details. There were rules for measurement prior to the races, and others covering masts and the timing of challenges, but little else by way of restrictions. There were no mathematical formulas. A paragraph in the middle began:

> The Club challenging for the Cup . . . may, by mutual consent, make any arrangement satisfactory to both as in dates, courses, number of trials, rules, and sailing regulations, and any and all other conditions of the match. . . .

Sir Michael's challenge, advanced in the name of the Mercury Bay Boating Club, called for a one-to-one match with the San Diego Yacht Club "outside class or rating rules." The M.B.B.C. was a curious animal. Its clubhouse consisted of an old Ford Zephyr parked at a beach outside of Auckland. That, however, was enough. Sir Michael had flung mud at the clear trend among Cup competitors—there were more challengers in Fremantle (thirteen) than in any previous America's Cup race—but he was within the rule. The S.D.Y.C. didn't think so, but the New York Supreme Court, which has jurisdiction over Cup disputes, upheld Fay's challenge.

They raced off Point Loma in San Diego, a best-of-three series, on September 7 and 9, 1988. Sir Michael came with a hundred-and-thirty-two-foot yacht, the largest racer built in more than half a century. But the Mercury Bay entry was beaten flatly by the S.D.Y.C., which floated a sixty-foot catamaran. *Stars & Stripes* was so light that Dennis Conner, who tended toward the plumpish, lost thirty-five pounds to skipper it. Conner's multihull finished twenty-one minutes in front of *New Zealand* in the first race and eighteen minutes ahead in the second.

It was Fay's turn with the attorneys. He claimed the use of a catamaran was illegal and won his case in March 1989. Then he lost

it on San Diego's appeal, and he lost his own appeal after that. "If the America's Cup has lived on controversy, then it's never been more alive," Fay famously asserted just before the races. He was right in a perverse sort of way, but that was not how others saw it. "It was a terrible shame," Kaoru Ogimi remembered. "We all felt the whole America's Cup tradition was suddenly in danger of falling apart."

Ogimi attended the first meeting called to shore up the America's Cup scene by fundamentally transforming its rules. So did Tatsu Yamasaki, Kensaku Nomoto, and two others from the management side of Nippon Challenge. They had all flown over from Tokyo to watch the bitter twenty-seventh Cup event in the autumn of 1988 and to see where the competition was headed. They joined an ad hoc group, comprised of yachting figures of many nationalities. During the sessions, the world's leading yacht designers joined others who advanced a few rough proposals for a new design rule.

The more important sessions took place a month later in Southampton, England. For four days syndicate managers met in one room and designers in another. They worked rigorously, submitting each day's advances to overnight computer analysis and reviewing the results the following morning. "This was truly design by committee," Ehman recounted. "It's amazing we didn't come out with a camel."

The new rule, still incomplete but more detailed than an outline, was presented to a group of America's Cup challengers in London a month later. Four months after that, in March 1989, the final version was unveiled in Geneva, the city of diplomacy:

$$\frac{\text{length} + 1.25 \times \sqrt{\text{sail area}} - 9.8 \times \sqrt[3]{\text{displacement}}}{0.388} \leq 42 \text{ meters}$$

What did it mean? In principle it presented designers with a series of trade-offs, as the Twelve-Meter rule did. Put another way, it imposed costs on the main speed-producing factors and gave credit for the most important resistance factor. Build a heavy boat, and

you get length and lots of sail in return; go with a light one, and it will have to be either short or small in sail area to satisfy the math. In effect, the International America's Cup Class formula produced a rating chart with certain extreme choices at either end.

A sixteen-ton yacht would be 21.3 meters long with a sail area of 254 square meters.

A twenty-five-ton yacht would be just over 22.5 meters in length with 344 square meters of sail above it.

One could design beyond these extremities; but the gains dropped dramatically. The design committee also included "mathematical closing functions," caps in each speed-enhancing category: go beyond the range targeted by the rule's authors, and the formula added heavy penalties to the shrinking gains.

The rule worked much as others did: the trick for designers, in essence, was to beat it. But the new class allowed designers significantly more latitude than the old rule, and boats built to it would be far more dramatic to watch than the Twelves. They would have a maximum measured length of seventy-five feet, compared with sixty-five by the Twelve-Meter rule. They would be deeper: the draft would be thirteen feet, compared to nine feet on a Twelve. And they would have masts of up to one hundred ten feet above the deck, compared with eighty-six feet in the old class.

Yet they would be lighter, at thirty-seven thousand pounds, by almost ten tons. And they would have immense sail area: seven thousand five hundred square feet with a spinnaker up, equal to the vast expanses of most J-class yachts and forty percent more than Twelves carried. All of these elements together were intended to maximize power and speed. The I.A.C.C. boats would be wafer-thin on the water yet driven by sails that seemed as high as cathedral towers.

What the design committee did not want to maximize was the cost of building an I.A.C.C. yacht. Numerous limitations were accordingly attached to the new rule. Carbon fiber was required in the hulls and masts, for instance, but the grades used were strictly regulated. Autoclaves, high-temperature ovens that produce the most durable carbon fiber, were allowed in the production of spars but not of a hull. The reasoning was simple: any nation capable of building a furnace large enough to bake an I.A.C.C. hull at high temperature would overpower competitors simply by virtue of its wealth.

"Different people argued for different things," Tom Ehman recalled of the rule-formulation process. "Countries with a lot of experience with carbon fiber fought for an advantage there; the Americans were good at wings and sails, the French, the same thing. But everybody wanted a good design. We wanted a boat on the leading edge of technology. The Twelves were jet age—they used aluminum masts, for instance—and we wanted space age."

They also wanted certain financial constraints. "Designers will always come up with something more than the owners can afford," Ehman said. "It was never articulated, but some people felt that if the formula produced an inexpensive boat there'd be too many challengers—twice as many as in the '87 race."

The rule, in the end, was only a technical certificate attached to a much larger graduation ceremony for the America's Cup. And it was Alan Bond, not Sir Michael, who set in motion the real transformation of the event.

Red Smith, the eloquent New York sports columnist, once remarked that watching an America's Cup regatta was like watching the grass grow. The drama and the art of sailing in the sport's greatest event were intricate and stirring—anyone who had ever been in one or seen one close enough knew that. But you could see little of the excitement even if you were lucky enough to be on a spectator craft, and you could rarely see any of it on television.

People wanted to change that after '83, and they wanted to change it still more after Fremantle. There was a lot of money waiting to go into the America's Cup once it was freed from the N.Y.Y.C.'s staid grip—not just from yachtsmen interested in the yachts themselves, but from television and corporate sponsorships. There were twenty challenges, from fifteen nations, after the new rule was announced and the new deadline closed in May 1990. ESPN, which had covered the Fremantle races more thoroughly than any broadcaster had ever covered a sailing event, committed itself to an even greater effort for the first Cup regatta in the new class. San Diego braced for what civic planners started to term "The Year of the America's Cup."

To an extent this transformation only crystallized what was already in train in the wider world of sailing. Where sailors felt it most was in the emerging divide between amateurs and professionals. Sailors weren't golfers or tennis players—the number of yachtsmen who had grown wealthy on the water could be counted on the fingers of two hands. But the age of the dedicated amateur was ending, for better or worse. Competition was getting too tough.

Was all this good for the sport? Asking that of any sailor was like posing a simple procedural question to a computer maniac: you'd usually be stuck for hours. There were too many sides to the issues, and too many points of view on each. But it was decidedly good for the Japanese. The internationalization of America's Cup crews— another feature of the dawning era—would prove crucial to their ability to learn in the traditional way and to participate at the same time. Beyond that, the new look would underscore the logic of their presence in San Diego. "The America's Cup has always been about shifting cultural balances, strengths and weaknesses," Tom Ehman said. "After Fremantle, you have to wonder, is this part of some definite shift to the Pacific Rim?"

The delay caused by the Michael Fay flap pushed the twenty-eighth America's Cup back a year, to 1992. That, too, was good for the Japanese. They had the money, and they had learned enough by then to know they needed the year.

"This is your window," Roy Dickson advised Yamasaki in one of their early meetings. "This is the first time this class of yacht will be raced, and it has to be the easiest time to win. No one country's team is any better than another. Nobody has a jump start."

•   •   •

Just inside the gated entrance to Akishima Laboratories, forty-five minutes from Tokyo Station, stands a vaguely academic-looking building that houses executive offices and drafting studios. Behind

it, and connected by a closed passageway, is a long concrete edifice of two stories on which a sign reads, SECURITY FIRST. There are few windows or doors; it looks like it might turn out machine-tooled industrial components or heavy-duty electric motors. In fact, its only products are long sheets of graph paper that resemble electrocardiograms.

If the first Japanese boat in the new America's Cup class had a single birthplace, it was in the towing tank housed in the back building at Akishima Labs. It was a brief gestation. Ken Nomoto was just back from the technical meetings in Southampton when, on October 20, 1988, he sent Akishima a few hull lines that described the design team's idea of a basic I.A.C.C. boat. What the lab produced in the final days of the following March were performance reports indicating precisely what *Nippon*, as the Japanese boat would be named, should look like.

The room where these results were achieved was long, dim, and cold and had a tank at its center that was three hundred feet in length, fifteen feet wide, and just over six feet deep. At one end was a platform loaded with computer equipment, a control board, and room enough for two technicians to sit. Beneath that, and connected by many wires, was an overhead carriage that moved boat models through the tank. It was suspended over the water on tracks laid on either side. All along the walkway that ran the length of the tank were wooden models about four feet long. But for the many lines drawn on them, they looked like oversized bathtub toys. Most of them represented cargo vessels, but a few were recognizable as miniatures of keeled yachts.

"These," Ryosuke Matsui said one day, "are the first sailboats we ever tested in here." They were models of Twelves.

At Ken Nomoto's suggestion, Matsui had been placed directly in charge of the experiments run through most of the 1988–89 winter. Before the *sensei* arrived, Abe and Matsui had conducted two types of tests on the Twelve-Meter models. One was a simple procedure called an upright resistance test. In it, a boat was towed straight through the tank so that its performance when broad-reaching or running downwind—when the leeway component is minimal—could

be observed. It also indicated what sailors refer to as VMG, or velocity made good, meaning the notional speed a boat would achieve if it could somehow sail straight upwind without tacking.

The second test was called heel-free. It was also known as a free-sailing test. Because the towing carriage is attached to a point on the mast called the center of effort, the model adopts its natural heel angle, and the overall performance of the hull concept can be judged.

Nomoto had instructed Matsui to add another set of tests called heel-restraint, or semicaptive tests. First attempted in 1936, these experiments were two decades older than heel-free tests. But they were more complex, and they didn't come easily to Matsui. Heel-restraint tests effectively eliminated Nomoto's "crosstalk" by fixing the important movements a yacht makes under sail and then measuring each separately. Instead of towing the yacht by the mast, the carriage is attached directly to the hull. The tests tell you, in effect, one thing at a time without concern for the overall performance.

"It's not that the heel-restraint tests are more difficult—in fact, they're easier than the heel-free tests—but they take more time because they require tows to be repeated over and over at different settings," Matsui said. "A heel-free test will give you a certain heel angle, but it won't tell you *why* the model sailed that way. That's not part of the output. In the heel-restraint test, there are many inputs—settings—and many separate outputs, so you can understand the "why."

"You can look at it this way," Matsui concluded. "Each method has what we call test points. The heel-free test has sixteen and the heel-restraint test sixty-four."

Computers had added vast new steps to the tank-testing procedure. The information Matsui collected was first added to other data on hull resistance obtained from exercises in CFD, or computational fluid dynamics. CFD data on keels, wave-making, and other underwater factors were then combined with information obtained through wind tunnel tests conducted on various models of sails. Computers made it possible to combine the results because they could, in effect, calculate the equilibrium between two separate disciplines: how the hull performed in water (hydrodynamics) and how it sailed in wind (aerodynamics).

The program that combines these sciences is called a VPP, or velocity prediction program, and every advanced yacht designer has one for each of his models. It begins with the dimensions of the design and the results of tank and wind tunnel tests. Added to these on the input side are wind speeds and wind directions. The VPP produces a semicircular chart, called a polar diagram, that shows the speed a yacht should attain under various conditions and the heading at which it should sail to reach that speed. Once devised, the polar diagram becomes a basic piece of equipment for a yacht's navigator.

Nomoto-*sensei*'s VPP, crucial to the syndicate's understanding of what it was building, would be in development for many months after Akishima Labs completed work in the cold, concrete building at the edge of Tokyo. But Matsui's experiments produced a hull concept—basically, where *Nippon* would fall on the I.A.C.C. rating chart—that the VPP would eventually confirm. The tank tests were the key element. Indeed, they had begun to attract interest among other sailing syndicates even before they were finished. In early 1989 the lab received a letter from an Australian group then planning a challenge. In it the syndicate asked for a list of the charges the lab would attach to a requested set of tests. Akishima's response included these figures:

96 drag and lateral-force measurements;
8 speeds x 3 heel angles x 4 yaw angles;
Upright tests: 15 test points.

Then it read:

Testing fee: ± $60,000;
Model building: $55,000, incl. $15,000 for keel model;
Dynamometer development: ± $30,000.

For good measure, Akishima rounded up its estimate to a hundred and fifty thousand dollars.

It was enough to scare the Aussies away, which was part of the point. Akishima wanted outside business, but not with Nippon Challenge's competitors. The exchange did, however, serve to locate Japan on the spending curve. While little of what Japanese industry did for Tatsu Yamasaki and his syndicate was free, much of it was subsidized, often heavily. By the time Akishima finished its tests, the syndicate's commitment had risen to roughly thirty-three million dollars. But even Yamasaki could only guess the commercial value of what he would get in the course of spending that amount.

Such was the case with Matsui's tank tests. Akishima Labs usually built three to five models before making final the design of a cargo vessel. For *Nippon* it built twenty-two. At roughly fifteen thousand dollars each, that meant a third of a million dollars' worth of precisely measured wood. Each testing configuration, including models, cost a hundred and fifty thousand dollars, and Akishima ran forty of them.

Nippon Challenge paid a fraction of the figure, but it did six million dollars' worth of tank tests before arriving at *Nippon*'s final lines.

. . .

Kohtaro Horiuchi had already enunciated the strategy during his evening on board *Haru-Ichiban II*. And for the eighteen months it took to design and build the first *Nippon*, Ken Nomoto would repeat it often.

"Our policy is to cover our lack of design and building experience by making full use of advanced hydrodynamics expertise and advanced facilities," Nomoto would say. It was like a creed to him. He called it "the basic principle."

The marriage of science and the America's Cup was an old one, and although the relationship was rocky, the *sensei*'s emphasis did not seem misplaced. The first Cup contender to be tank-tested was a British challenger called *Shamrock III* which raced in 1903. Those tests measured only water resistance in upright and designated heeled positions. Harold Vanderbilt's J-class *Ranger* sailed in 1937 after scientists added the leeway component so that upwind performance could be estimated. Eight succeeding defenders were tested similarly at the Stevens Institute of Technology, an engineering school across the Hudson from Manhattan.

Mariner, a yacht drawn by an innovative designer named Britton Chance, helped change all that. *Mariner* was built by a New York syndicate to compete for the right to defend the Cup in 1974. It had a lot going for it. Chance was a respected architect. The crew included Ted Turner, then reaching his height as a yachtsman, and Dennis Conner, who was rising fast. But Chance produced a peculiar-looking craft that proved a dog as soon as it was launched. Gone were the traditional lines typical of Twelves. *Mariner* had a thick, U-shaped bow, a radically shortened keel, and a chine—the line where the sides of a boat intersect with the bottom—that ran high along the top of the hull from the middle of the boat back. Its stern—blunt, squared off, and stepped—was something no one had ever seen on a Twelve.

Mariner was an Edsel. It was trounced all through the '74 defender trials and judged afterward one of the slowest Twelves then on the water. It had ripped the syndicate apart with internal dissension. *Mariner* prompted one of Turner's best-known lines in yachting circles. "Jesus, Brit," the profane Southerner complained during the campaign, "even a turd is pointed at both ends." The lasting lesson was more subtle. *Mariner*'s lines reflected the most extensive use of tanks and related equipment ever brought to bear in a yacht's design. Chance had put too much faith in theory and lab experiments; he put science alone on the water.

Through the rest of the seventies and into the eighties, the pendulum swung the other way. The tendency among Cup defenders was to deemphasize the tank in favor of what one could learn in actual performance on the water that would be sailed. Intuition, experience, art, and feel were the ascendant values among designers. The trend reached its peak in 1983, when *Liberty* defended the Cup off Newport. No tank tests at all were used in *Liberty*'s design. But *Liberty* lost, and it lost to *Australia II*, a yacht that had derived a radical new concept in keel configurations from the calm waters of the tank.

In '87, every challenger in Fremantle carried a winged keel, and every boat there had models behind it that had undergone extensive tow tests and CFD calculations. Testing methods had improved to the point where simulations using larger models could come closer than ever to matching precise sailing conditions. Yacht testing was becoming an industry.

All this added to Ken Nomoto's confidence in "the basic principle." He was deeply satisfied with the results he got from Akishima in early 1989, and he went forward without hesitation in the direction they suggested. On March 28 the design committee drew *Nippon*'s basic lines. Things happened quickly after that. Detailed construction plans, deck layout, sail plan, rigging, fittings, and hardware design were all made final that spring and summer. "We had confirmed that our scientific studies were correct," Nomoto remarked proudly. "We knew we were on the right track."

The *sensei's* track led him above the midway point on the I.A.C.C. rating chart, but it didn't put him at its top end. He would build a relatively heavy boat with a wide beam and lots of sail. Underneath, he was tending toward an unusual configuration, and by early autumn that, too, was ready to be built. The Kobe Steel Corporation, one of Japan's "Big Five" steel producers, had never made yacht appendages before, but it would meet Nippon Challenge's needs free of charge. What Nomoto ordered was a conventional keel strut of medium length with a heavy bulb at the end of it; then he added a nearly untried feature of modern yacht design: a forward rudder.

Forward rudders had occasionally been used in large cargo vessels, which was why Nomoto was familiar with them. And they had been tested on yachts from time to time since the early seventies. But the forward canard, as such devices are also called, had had only one serious outing in a full-sized racer, and that was a qualified failure. It was designed in 1986 by an American syndicate contending for the right to sail against the Australians the following year. The Twelve that carried the canard showed promise; but the steering mechanism proved complex and difficult, and the rough waters off

Western Australia frequently forced the bow rudder out of the water. The essential problem was control.

Ken Nomoto contended that the Americans had left out half of the equation. Forward canards are essentially a borrowing from the flaps on airplane wings. They have two basic functions: one, a dynamic function, is to improve maneuverability; the other, a static function, is to increase speed and lift. Lift, in the context of sailing, is the boat's ability to sail at a heading closer to the wind.

"The Americans made a great effort," Nomoto said in explaining his own decision. "But they emphasized the dynamic part, so control was a problem. A forward rudder *can* make quite a big contribution to static performance. Our idea to adopt a forward rudder was based on both principles. Most of the towing tank experiments as far as design was concerned were to test static performance. I think we perfected it."

By the time Nomoto reached these conclusions, Bruce Farr & Associates had begun offering a kind of generic I.A.C.C. design to any syndicate interested in buying it. Cup rules stipulate, of course, that designs must be indigenous, but the Farr lines were offered as a point of reference. Farr himself, a New Zealander who operated from Annapolis, Maryland, would eventually design exclusively for the Kiwi syndicate. As one of the world's leading yacht designers, however, his earliest thoughts on the I.A.C.C. formula would be of interest to any less experienced yacht designer who felt he was firing in the dark—as everyone working in the new class was.

Nomoto was less than captivated when Farr first offered the reference design to Nippon Challenge. In fact, it was Yamasaki who eventually urged the *sensei* to make the purchase—Yamasaki and Gary Jobson. When Nomoto made his first of several visits to Jobson, who also lived and worked in Annapolis, the professor showed no interest in even meeting Farr. "I practically had to drag the doctor to Farr's office and push him through the door," he recounted.

That was in March 1989, a week before Akishima completed its tow tests. Things changed through the spring and summer. Late in May, Nippon Challenge reached an agreement with Farr, and in July the lines arrived from Annapolis. Nomoto was keen by then. Tank tests normally require two to three months of preparation; building a model takes a month or more, and then there is equipment to prepare and a testing schedule to fix. This time the *sensei* faxed Abe and Matsui to ask that an urgent set of tests be arranged, and he carried the Farr lines out to Akishima himself the following week.

In mid-September, a month after his message to Akishima Labs, Nomoto had his result. Farr had been traveling regularly between Annapolis and Tokyo by that time, and a few weeks later he made his final trip. The *sensei* was no longer hesitant in the Kiwi's presence. He waited patiently for Farr to ask about the results and, when he did, Nomoto simply smiled. Farr did too.

"Okay, how much faster is your design?" Farr finally inquired.

It wasn't an enormous difference, Nomoto recounted later. "But ours was appreciably faster than the model built from the reference design."

The *sensei* had taken his first look outside, and the superiority of what he had done was there to be read.

"I've spent nearly a lifetime in towing tanks, so I'm quite confident in them," he said once. "Of course, you cannot be one hundred percent confident in them, but then you cannot be one hundred percent confident in anything."

• • •

That turned out to be a wise perspective as *Nippon* advanced toward completion. In fact, many of the apparent advantages Japan enjoyed when Nippon Challenge got under way were proving less beneficial as time went on. Japan's capacity in supercomputers was second only to that of the United States; it produced five thousand tons of carbon fiber yearly, almost two thirds of world output. These were looked upon as secret weapons for the Japanese, at home and abroad. Would they make the difference they were expected to make? Would "the basic principle," broadly defined, apply?

Carbon fiber, plastic reinforced with resin and combined with carbon, was developed in Japan, with government support, in the 1960s. Two decades later, Japan's output so far outstripped applications that a global glut, a supply overhang of some sixty-four percent, loomed in the market. Carbon fiber's strength seems a miracle when its weight is compared with the materials—aluminum, steel—that it replaces. Yet manufacturers were scrambling to downsize applications, from high-technology industrial products to tennis rackets and umbrella shafts, to get demand moving so that they could recover research and capital expenditures.

Virtually all of Japan's carbon fiber capacity is at the high end of the industry—in aerospace, for example. It can cure fiber at a hundred and thirty degrees Centigrade or at a hundred and eighty degrees, the temperatures that produce the strongest grades of product. That is done in small, expensive autoclaves that can withstand the high pressures that high-quality fiber also required. Usually these furnaces are five or six meters long and roughly two meters wide. The Mitsubishi Rayon Company can build airplane wings in them because, like traditional wings, they are built in panels.

The new I.A.C.C. rules limited both the temperature and the atmospheric pressure at which the hull and mast could be cured. For the hull the maximum allowed was ninety degrees; for the mast, a hundred and twenty degrees. At those temperatures, the hull could be hardened in not much more than a room closed off with heavy plastic curtains, and the mast would need a less expensive autoclave. In effect, this put the industry on which Nippon Challenge would depend back to square one. Some Japanese producers had worked with the fiber in those ranges, but they had never built anything as large as a boat or a mast.

The carbon fiber of which *Nippon* was to be made came in sections called pre-impregnated panels, or PPP. Japan didn't make them, but the America's Cup rule allowed competitors to import materials so long as they designed and built their boats themselves. "Prepreg" panels are long rolls of carbon fiber already saturated with epoxy resin so that they are ready to be shaped. Yamaha bought its supply from a British company known as the SPS Company, whose initials stood for Structural Polymer Systems. By the time the panels arrived at the factory where the boat was to be built, Yamaha had already learned from SPS how to refrigerate the material until it was applied to a mold, how to construct the room in which the fiber would be hardened, and how the panels should be layered so that the grain ran diagonally across the hull in the direction of the greatest stress. The arrangement fit the Japanese situation perfectly: while Yamaha hadn't time to learn the intricacies of producing PPP, its factory would learn to handle it and, when the moment came, shape it into a hull.

•   •   •

Arai, a small coastal town in Shizuoka Prefecture two hours south of Tokyo, is actually in the middle of motorcycle country. It is fifteen minutes by commuter rail or car from Yamaha's Hamamatsu head-quarters, and all around it the big names in Japanese motorcycles—Honda, Suzuki, and Yamaha itself—had built massive production plants in the fifties and sixties. Later on, Yamaha chose Arai as the site of the marine division's technical and design center. It had a small factory there, too, which produced simple dinghies, custom sailboats, and swimming pools. Arai had one other important feature: it was a few miles from Gamagori.

The man in Arai who received *Nippon*'s lines in early September and oversaw its construction was named Akira Kubota. He was in his mid-forties and dressed every day in a light blue technician's jacket with his name and the Yamaha insignia on the breast. Kubota had never before taken on a project of *Nippon*'s magnitude, but he brought the zeal of a diligent student to the task. "Yamaha doesn't consider this an especially complicated project," he said. "We've been through a lot of other difficult experiences. We had even used pre-preg before, but on much smaller boats—single sculls. The difficulty with the America's Cup job was meeting the standards. In each detail—for example, weight control—we had to meet demands from the designer team. That applied to every component, and it meant we had a tough target to meet."

Construction of a wooden mold began on September 20, and in November Kubota's technicians started the lamination process. To accomplish it, the refashioned a single-room factory that was roughly thirty yards square and fifteen yards high. About a third of

it was sectioned off by plastic curtains. A hundred and fifty small heating ducts, like hair dryers, were put into both the ceiling and the walls.

They had sixteen hours to do the job once they took the panels out of the refrigerated warehouse: apply the pre-preg laminate to the mold and apply a plastic called Nomex, a honeycomb-shaped core about an inch thick, to the panels to achieve the required strength. That happened at room temperature; then it went into the room lined with plastic, and the hair dryers were turned on.

There were no serious hitches. After the hull was finished, the deck frame was laminated, fitted with hardware, and joined to the boat. It would be ready for transport to Gamagori by March 1990, well in time to be fitted with appendages and sail the following month.

Kubota knew little about other segments of the project. He was peripherally involved in the design phase, and when *Nippon* left for Gamagori the undertaking was more or less out of his hands.

He usually had difficulty stepping back far enough from what he had done to understand the larger meaning of it. But not always. "Basically we've introduced a new production process at this factory," Kubota said one morning. "We can't say if these technologies can be used immediately for commercial purposes. The whole thing is still too expensive. But we expect to incorporate what we've learned in mass production within"—he hesitated—"we can say, within several years."

The hull had gone smoothly enough, but what of *Nippon*'s spars? They would not be built with anything like the same ease. It was not a matter of supplying the fiber but of curing it in one piece. *Nippon*'s mast would be a hundred and fourteen feet—a hundred and six feet above the deck—and no manufacturer had an autoclave that even approached that size. Through much of 1988, the syndicate couldn't even get bids. When Nomoto finally did, they ran to thirty million yen, about two million dollars, because they included R & D, a mast mold, and an enormous investment in a furnace.

Roy Dickson had helped negotiate a contract with Southern Spars, a New Zealand company, for the delivery of three carbon

fiber masts in the interim, but the delay in developing an indigenous spar program drove him nearly crazy. "No one was building composite spars in Japan at the time, which was exactly why I recommended from day one that they develop their own program," Dickson snapped later. "Technology was Japan's number one strength, and I made a firm determination to use it."

Mitsubishi Rayon finally took the job and began work in July 1990 on an autoclave a hundred and twenty-five feet long. It was finished in November, and Mitsubishi immediately began building a mast mold. Once the piece was completed, another nightmare ensued. How would they ship it? The longest rail car in Japan was a little more than seventy feet, and a truck big enough to carry *Nippon*'s spar would be illegal on Japanese highways. "We decided to rely on purely human power," joked Takaaki Nakagawa, the Mitsubishi Rayon executive who headed the project.

It resembled a scene from an *ukiyo-e* print. The factory crew started on foot at midnight, March 8, from the plant in Toyohashi. It was fifteen kilometers to Nagoya, the port from which the mast would be shipped, and they delivered the piece, wrapped in plastic and crated, at five the following morning. Nippon Challenge's crew wouldn't sail with a Japanese-made spar until it was in San Diego in April 1991, by which time the first races in the new class were hard upon them.

•　　•　　•

Most of the time Japan's boat was known not as *Nippon* but by its official designation, *J-3*, which meant it was built in Japan and was the third I.A.C.C. yacht to be officially measured and launched. At the factory in Arai, I once asked Akira Kubota who designed it.

"In the contract between Yamaha and Nippon Challenge, we agreed it's confidential who did what in the group," Kubota replied.

"Why?"

"Because it's in the contract."

"Yes, but why is it in the contract?"

"We agreed to call it a team project, and everyone takes responsibility for each piece of work."

"Can we call this a Yamaha design?"

"I'm not in a position to answer that."

Ken Nomoto was eventually more forthcoming. "I cannot tell you who designed the boat," he said one afternoon in Tokyo. "Our system is different from the normal procedure. Normally one chief designer is responsible—Bruce Farr, for example. But we gathered a number of scientists, engineers, some boat people from Yamaha, some independents, and formed a design team. I was a coordinator, not a designer. For example, the way we drew the lines. In the normal way, Bruce Farr would draw the lines representing the hull. But we asked one of the Yamaha designers to draw the lines under such and such conditions. I would say, 'Length twenty-two meters.' Then I would ask for lines with another set of specs. All those lines went to the towing tank, and we chose the optimum combination. This was based on calculations by scientists, not designers, using computers and tank tests. Out of that we got lines, not by one designer but by a group."

Many, indeed, were in the group. There were the Yamaha people and a few independent designers. There were the consultants— Bruce Farr and Southern Spars—and the legion of supporters in the universities and companies involved.

There were also those inanimate but essential advisers, the super-computers. Nippon Challenge's CFD calculations were heavily dependent on them, and within the design group the argument was advanced that computer calculations could have been more valuable than all the work in the towing tank. In the end, Japan's CFD didn't prove to be more than "a technology under development," as Kohtaro Horiuchi delicately put it, because they didn't know how to apply the immense computer capacity they had.

"Maybe in the future we can replace the towing tank with computer-based hydrodynamics," the *sensei* reflected at the end. "But not at the moment. I had no illusions about the advantages of supercomputers and numerical science, but some of the younger scientists were disappointed."

They should have been. The syndicate logged roughly one hundred and fifty hours on supercomputers before *J-3* was launched.

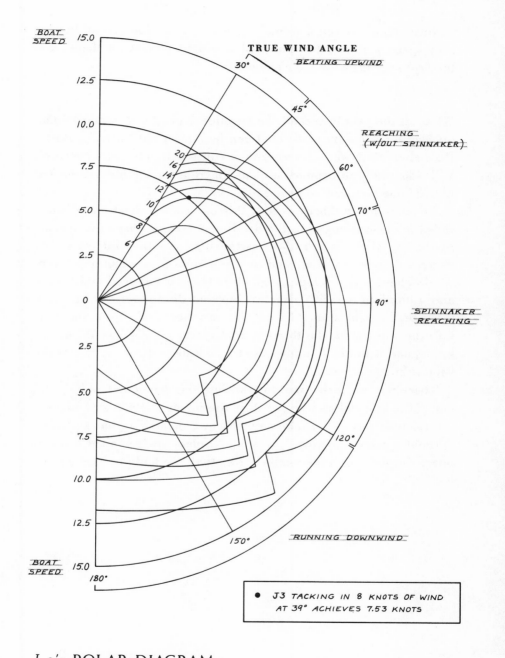

BOAT SPEED

TRUE WIND ANGLE

30°

45°

60°

70°

90°

120°

150°

180°

BEATING UPWIND

REACHING
(W/OUT SPINNAKER)

SPINNAKER
REACHING

RUNNING DOWNWIND

BOAT SPEED

15.0
12.5
10.0
7.5
5.0
2.5
0
2.5
5.0
7.5
10.0
12.5
15.0

20
16
14
12
10
8
6

● J3 TACKING IN 8 KNOTS OF WIND
AT 39° ACHIEVES 7.53 KNOTS

J-3's POLAR DIAGRAM

At three hundred yen a second—just over a million yen an hour—
they spent a million two hundred thousand dollars on them. And
they got very little for their money.

•   •   •

What all the people and all the machinery produced would remain
unclear for some time. No boat can be known until it sails. But in
December 1989, while *J-3* was under construction in Arai, Nomoto's
VPP was ready to produce a polar diagram for the boat. It looked
like the one pictured on page 139.

As other polar diagrams did, this one showed boat speed when
sailed at various angles to the wind, and various true wind speeds.
At the top of the graph, *J-3* was tacking; on either side of ninety
degrees, it was reaching, and at the bottom it was running downwind. There was a computer glitch between a hundred and twenty
and a hundred and fifty degrees, but that didn't alter the essential
message. In eight knots of wind, for instance, *J-3*'s optimum angle
into the wind would be thirty-nine degrees. Its VMG would be 5.6
knots, and it would actually sail at 7.53 knots, almost as fast as the
wind itself.

There was an easier way to translate this particular polar, and
one of the first sailors who saw it, in the spring of 1990, gave as good
a version as any. "You take one look at a polar like that and your
adrenalin starts running," he said. "Unless you've sailed a maxi-
boat, you just don't see numbers like that. We had a rocket on our
hands."

PART II

J

I

B

I

N

G

ROY-SAN

Among the first things Roy Dickson did when he arrived in Gamagori in mid-1988 was draw a pyramid with a large dot at the apex, an image as simple as a child's crayon sketch. Then he handed it to his new employers. "Without the proper attitude," he said, pointing to his dot, "you'll never get there."

That was Roy-*san*. He could smile easily, but he would also fix his light-blue eyes intently on whomever he was speaking to. There were no side doors in a conversation with Roy Dickson. His compact frame exuded a kind of frenetic energy, and he applied it to reducing everything to its least common denominator.

Dickson would repeat the pyramid exercise over and over during his time in Gamagori. "If getting to the top were easy," he would assert, "everyone would be there." Then he would say, "There are winners, there's a big bunch in the middle, and there are losers. You can see that in any organization you care to look at." Or he would tick off a list that had evolved over years into his own barren-rock theory: fund raising, direction, management, design, construction, sailmaking, spars and rigging, maintenance, team welfare.

"Victories are decided by crews racing yachts on the water," Dickson would conclude. "But without all the other elements you're not going to win. Others will have these things."

Dickson was the kind of sailor Kaoru Ogimi had been trying to prepare the syndicate for. He was all business in the business of winning yacht races, a man of straight lines and squared corners. Like Ogimi, Dickson understood the place of money and technology in a campaign, but he also understood that both were useless without committed people. But Ogimi had never gotten through to the *kaicho* with regard to the latter point. The two men, Dickson and Ogimi, grew to respect one another quickly after they met; but Ogimi was rarely at the sailing camp to back the Kiwi up. Dickson on his own in Gamagori was certain to precipitate a showdown, although neither he nor his Japanese hosts recognized that at the time.

To Ken Nomoto, who was still managing the sailing camp, Dickson seemed the man he wanted from the first time they met. Nomoto had structured the part-time arrangement—Dickson would spend two weeks in Gamagori and a month at home—to avoid conflicts stemming from what he termed "the cultural gap." And Dickson had shown Nomoto a clear understanding of that gap as soon as he got off the plane from Auckland. Together they overnighted in Tokyo and took a *shinkansen* to Gamagori the next day. It was June 19. During the ride, Roy was the one who brought the subject up. Nomoto said, "It's not possible to transplant American pine onto Japanese soil. Nor kiwi trees." Dickson agreed, and they chatted amiably. To Nomoto it was a question of recognizing and respecting differences. And from that would come what the Japanese fondly call "mutual understanding."

Dickson's understanding deepened quickly. Before his first visit was over he was writing a paper he called "S.W.O.T.," which stood for strengths, weaknesses, opportunities, and threats. It was four pages long and consisted of four handwritten lists. This was the syndicate's first taste of the Dickson management method. His line of logic never varied: set the long-term strategic goal; divide it into short-term goals with fixed schedules; identify the tasks involved, find the best person to execute each task. S.W.O.T.'s entries ranged from "very best gear available" to "possible lack of focus" to "identify method of measuring performance" to "risk of time being wasted."

Dickson wasted not an hour. He was training sailors on Mikawa Bay two days after his arrival, and he divided the enterprise into several parts. There was basic technique, there was seamanship, and there was handling the Twelves. Dickson saw no point in splashing around in shallow water. Under the second heading came practice on the Yamaha 30s in what he called "semisurvival conditions," which meant sailing in thirty-five to forty knots of wind. Then there were the Twelves, boats that, as *KZ-3* and *KZ-5*, Dickson had more or less lived with during the Kiwi campaign. Dickson loved Twelve-Meter racing. Much later he would judge the class superior to the new I.A.C.C. yachts. When he first sailed on the Twelves at Gamagori, however, he concluded that the Japanese were dangerous on them in anything above twelve knots of breeze. It was, he said, "a hell of a place to start."

His own days were lengthy, and he expected everyone else to keep the same hours. Assembly at the camp for an hour of exercise was at six-thirty. They breakfasted for half an hour and held a morning briefing at eight. Then came an hour or so of fitting out the boat—checking equipment, loading sails, completing repairs begun the previous day. Dock-out was at nine-thirty. They lunched on board and started in at five. By six-thirty they were reviewing videotapes of that day's practice. Then came an evening debriefing. With Roy in charge, that could last up to an hour and a half. Then dinner in the camp mess; then home.

Out in the bay, there were five routines laid out in a kind of progression. One Japanese coach, Yoichi Takemura, remembered it as if he'd learned it by rote, which he more or less had. The first exercises were free practice, "sailing wherever, without a theme," as Takemura put it. Next came straight-line sailing, two boats moving parallel to one another. Tacking and jibing practice was a long series

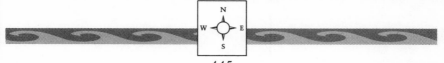

of two-boat tacks upwind and another of jibes downwind, each series made up of maneuvers conducted at two-minute intervals. Drill practice consisted of five different maneuvers around marks. Last came racing practice, which took up more of their days as time went on. It was a compact set of exercises, but it took in everything a sailor needed to know.

In the beginning, during the seasickness and men-overboard days, Dickson wouldn't let the Twelves near one another. After a time he floated boat fenders on long lines behind them, and when they raced together or spent an afternoon tacking, they were allowed no closer than the rubber floats. Gradually Dickson shortened the lines until, after many months, he removed them. A year after he arrived, Dickson announced a program called "Wind It Up"—not in the sense of "finish it off," but, as in a watch, "tighten the spring." "Wind It Up" became the campaign's first-year goal. One of its chief objectives, as Dickson often repeated, was "to sail the Twelves competently and confidently in twenty-five knots of wind." That was a powerful blow by any sailor's standards. But they accomplished it before the end of the autumn sailing season.

They were on a steep upward curve, and they were advancing along it with the help of some of the best sailors in New Zealand. Joey Allen, Warwick Fleury, Brian Philamore, Dave Clark—these were well-known sailors at home, some of them among the most competent people in the sport. In the spring of 1989, Roy would import a very special young Kiwi to assist, a champion match racer named Chris Dickson, the second of his four sons.

To the Japanese, executives and crew alike, it seemed as though they'd found what they were looking for when they set out to enlist skilled *gaijin*. Roy Dickson was teaching more than simply technique. They were learning that sailing was *shisei*, attitude, "an approach to life," as one of the grinders put it. Jin said, "When we started it was nine to five. You did the work and went home. Roy-*san* taught us that there is no nine to five. If there's work, you stay and do it. That's *shisei*."

Roy-*san*, it seemed, was getting through. This was learning from abroad the way the Japanese had always wanted it. Even Ogimi, the

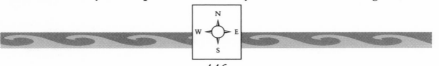

strictest judge the campaign had, was heartened by the progress Roy was making. The Kiwi seemed, after only a few trips to Japan, to bring a certain unity to the syndicate, a desire to learn to compete, that had been sorely lacking before his arrival. "Drill hard," Dickson told his sailors, "and the race itself will be no more than a formality."

Roy Dickson paid five visits to Gamagori as an intermittent coach. Yamasaki, off in Tokyo running S & B and rarely at the camp, saw him at board meetings and liked the Kiwi as much as Ken Nomoto did. It wasn't long, in fact, before the coach and the *kaicho* counted each other friends. By the end of the year the Dicksons, Roy and his lively wife, Marilyn, were exchanging gifts with Tatsu and Ayako Yamasaki.

Dickson had sailed all his life as an amateur, and it was understood at Gamagori that he was proud of having stayed that way while achieving the international status he then enjoyed. Home from Japan, he had retired from the engineering firm where he had spent much of his career as a surveyor. In a little less than a year, though, he was invited to direct the Gamagori camp full time. Everyone knew he could handle it; everyone was comfortable with a *gaijin* of Roy's sympathies in charge. Not even Nomoto-*sensei*, who was never cut out to be a manager, objected with much conviction. He wanted to see through his tank tests in Tokyo anyway.

Dickson accepted the offer. Marilyn would come, and in the evenings they would often have a few of "the boys" in to sit on the floor, drink Coke, and talk about lives so different from any the Dicksons could imagine. Roy's would be a difficult and delicate job, one that immediately cast him as a man in the middle. He had long since seen clearly where the Japanese were—they were still next to nowhere. They were measuring progress against themselves and coming away satisfied. You could look at it that way and say the glass was half full. But Dickson knew that the world into which they were seeking admission, the world of international sailing competition, was one they were still almost entirely unprepared for. The glass was half empty at best. Neither his employers nor his charges had

caught much more than a glimpse of that world. Briefly defined, Dickson's job was to introduce them to it.

Dickson saw it that way, but he put it differently. He had gained a wider picture of things by the time he signed on as sailing director. Around the camp he always talked about crew drills and hardware and race results. But he thought about psychology and method. "I saw it as my task to tackle the problems of motivation, commitment, and responsibility," he said. "And as I looked at these problems, I began to realize that I was looking at a national philosophy, one country's way of doing things."

•　　•　　•

Roy Dickson derived his sense of order and discipline from his days in the New Zealand army. In a way, that was his stamp. Even in New Zealand, sailors found him, at times, rigorous to an extreme and about as flexible as a drill sergeant. Around Gamagori, he was like a visitor from another universe. Roy bore a foreign set of truths; few Japanese other than Kaoru Ogimi understood them. But he was hardly the originator of the psychology that, by definition, pervades any sailing camp seriously bent on a win.

Roy Dickson understood the lessons of Cups past. Even before he went full time in Gamagori he began to range around Nippon Challenge, poking into every corner of the organization, up and down it, like an officer on an inspection tour. Inevitably, his yardstick was the Kiwi campaign for the Fremantle races. Often during his time in Gamagori, Dickson would think back to the months of preparation in Auckland, when he as sailing director, Laurent Esquier as project manager, and Michael Fay would confer almost hourly on the next step for the crew, the next sailmaker to draft, the next technical move to try. The three of them complemented one another, and they expected everyone to be as switched-on as they were. They had more or less invented the military style in yachting campaigns, and like generals and field marshalls they expected the best. "We measured people on an international scale, not a local scale," Dickson remembered. "I've never understood anyone who wanted to be a big fish in a small pond."

He was in one, though. *Wakon yosai*, foremost among the old Meiji credenda, is never used in conversation anymore. But "Japanese spirit, Western things" would have been an apt way to describe the state of affairs the Kiwi encountered. There were the Twelves he loved, there was money to buy in the gear he wanted, and a new boat was on the way. Then there were the people managing the things, people who lived in a world of Confucian hierarchy, and for whom the delicate matters of *nemawashi* and consensus were paramount. There were fiefdoms; everyone was either *soto* or *uchi*, on everyone else's list. One spoke indirectly and prepared in secret. One presented *omote*, a face to others, while true thinking, *ura*, was withheld. Japan was not preparing to race for the America's Cup so much as to dominate the event at some distant point in the future. Dickson was mystified. There didn't seem to be any leadership, any passion for victory. "Where is the direction coming from?" Dickson began to ask. "Show me the management. Show me the people who are ready to compete."

For the first time, it occurred to Roy Dickson that he did not know where he was. Show me, Dickson may as well have demanded, the world into which I have stepped. Under different circumstances, Kaoru Ogimi could have helped him out. Ogimi understood that the Japanese disliked competition, didn't understand it, and had a thousand ways of avoiding it among themselves. He knew, too, that sooner or later they would either have to leave all that behind or the campaign would find itself in trouble. Ogimi had two sets of eyes; he could have emerged as one of Nippon Challenge's greatest assets. But Ogimi had been rendered, if not quite powerless, a secondary figure in the syndicate, and he was in no position to guide Dickson through the maze.

Roy-san could see things only one way. And it hadn't taken him long to bring Nippon Challenge face to face with the conflict Ogimi had foreseen. The question to be resolved, Dickson figured, was the object of the exercise. Everything else would follow. What were the Japanese trying to do? Did they want to win, or were they only out to demonstrate the superiority of their way of doing things? In any other campaign, it wouldn't have occurred to him to ask. But he

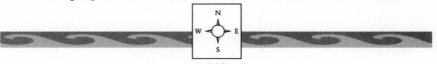

began to recognize that few on Nippon Challenge's swelling list of employees had joined the campaign to carry home the Cup. The spirit of *gambatte* pervaded the entire campaign: if we don't win this time there's always the next time, and the time after that. "Too many don't know what a commitment to Nippon Challenge means," Dickson complained. "Too many are just along for the ride."

Even at Dickson's proximity, it was hard to see into the people around him. Given the Japanese habit of preparing in seclusion, he couldn't make out their intentions, either individually or as a group. But he had been given a large clue at the very beginning. The syndicate slogan, when Dickson arrived, was "Challenge the Cup." The notion that that wasn't enough would vex the Japanese to the very end, but Dickson wanted no part of an exercise in good effort. "Winning in the *long term* is of no interest to me," he announced. "To me it's completely irresponsible to spend other people's money if this is just a learning experience."

One of Tatsu Yamasaki's most valued assistants in Tokyo, Emili Miura, fixed the why-we-are-here problem simply enough by getting a team song drafted, complete with Olympian reference, and hiring a young composer to set it to music. Once introduced, "Win the Cup" would crackle through outdoor speakers in Gamagori and San Diego until the campaign ended. The song was sung in Japanese, of course, but the title line, which became the new campaign objective, was rendered in English throughout:

Win the Cup!
This boat carries our hopes and dreams.
Into history we sail.

Our pioneering spirits and this boat are our proud commemoration.
Dignified we stand on this boat,
Anticipating tomorrow's rainbow.

Win the Cup!
This boat carries our hopes and dreams.
We sail with those into eternity.

Win the Cup!
This boat carries our hopes and dreams.
Into history we sail.

The silver grail that shines with inspiration
Infuses us with fighting spirit.
O Goddess Hera,
Please send your blessing to this boat
And guide us to your way.

A fine sentiment. But songs were the least of Dickson's concerns, given the list of shortcomings he was gathering. A song could not change attitudes, least of all Tatsu Yamasaki's.

Among the most serious weaknesses he saw was in the thick layers of middle management draped over the operation in both Gamagori and Tokyo. Indeed, as time went on he began to suspect that, for Yamaha, S & B, and many other companies involved, the syndicate was something of a dumping ground for mediocre performers. Yoichi Takemura, the sailing coach when Dickson arrived, was an S & B man who had looked after a children's sports club Yamasaki had started. "Nice guy," Dickson said of Takemura in clipped tones, "but he made no contribution whatever. He was filling in time."

Typical of the breed was a front-office manager at the sailing camp named Hidemichi Onozawa. Ono, as he was familiarly called, was a tall, pear-shaped fellow who was kind, above all, and unfailingly obliging. He exemplified the meaning of *gambatte* in all its nuances; he was always there, and he could always be counted on to get a job done. But Ono showed as clearly as anyone else that *gambatte* was in essence the way of the uninspired. Duty to the process always came first. In Ono's hands a job got done—providing an unexceptional performance was sufficient and self-motivation uncalled for. Once, as Dickson's frustration was rising like sap, he pulled Ono aside in the office shed at Gamagori and asked him point-blank, "What are your priorities?" It wasn't intended as a hostile question; Dickson wanted merely to understand the people around him.

Ono replied matter-of-factly and in order. "They're to myself,

my workmates, my family, and Nippon Challenge," he said. It was a moment of recognition for Dickson that he would carry with him to the end of his days with the Japanese.

Though he failed to list his employer, Ono was a Yamaha man. Others at the base camp felt more strongly about such affiliations. Yamaha began to draw a corporate circle around its people—or they around themselves—and in time one was either Yamaha or not. Dickson, Kaoru Ogimi, and others later ranked the company's multiple roles in Nippon Challenge one of the syndicate's biggest mistakes: it was taking lessons copiously from its *gaijin* instructors, as it had for a century, and it was a lead sponsor. "You can't design the boat, build it, and be a sponsor and supplier all at the same time," Ogimi said. The split in interests was visible even among the crew members, but where it took its greatest toll was on the technical side.

Japan had no wealth of independent yacht designers, but there were a few. Chief among them was a quiet man named Ichiro Yokoyama. He was balding, diffident, and had a reserve that led strangers to assume he was simply ineffectual. He wasn't. Yokoyama's father, Akira, was one of the first yacht designers in Japan to make a living at the trade. Akira was a postwar pioneer. He had, in fact, designed *Mermaid*, the nineteen-foot sloop Kenichi Horie sailed solo across the Pacific in 1962. "My playground was my father's boatyard," Ichiro remembered of his childhood near the harbor in Yokohama. After university, Ichiro Yokoyama spent ten years in the Yamaha marine division; then he went independent.

There were others like Yokoyama on the technical team, but as Dickson gradually discovered, they were strictly out of the loop so far as Yamaha was concerned. Yokoyama seemed to be a particular object of Yamaha's phobia because he had once been with the company. The circumscription left the technical program in the hands of people with the least experience. "One or two on the outer edge had some knowledge of international yacht racing," Dickson recounted. "Those inside, responsible for forming initial concepts and then budgeting them, were making their decisions with no understanding of what they were doing. They had appointed designers who had no idea of the tasks, how long they would take, or whether they were getting value for money."

• • •

By May 1989, Dickson was focused sharply on the electronics systems that were to accompany the new boat. It was, he had reckoned at the outset, one of the areas where the Japanese were unassailably strong. But the technical people were missing one deadline after another. Dickson had especially wanted various testing and monitoring systems mounted on the Twelves well before the new boat arrived. It was apparent by then that the Twelve-Meters wouldn't sail in San Diego, but he wanted the kinks ironed out so that the systems could be installed, up and running, as soon as the new A.C. boat rolled out of the shed.

Yachting technology, largely because of hypercompetitive campaigns such as the America's Cup, moves quickly. The cutting edge is usually right over a technical director's shoulder, and electronics has moved as quickly as any other segment of a campaign. It covers a range of equipment used both on the boat and off. Most basic are the on-board instruments—compasses and digitalized meters that read out wind and boat speed, wind angles, wind direction, and the like. Also on the decks of many advanced racers are tactical computer systems that show the afterguard everything from the location of opponents to laylines and the distance to the next mark.

Then comes the task of moving data off the boat so that it can be used to measure performance. Telemetric equipment transmits raw data to the tender, the cabin cruiser that follows the yacht, where computers can record it in graph and numerical forms and then analyze it. Sail vision is another dimension of a race campaign. Teams have produced and studied sail images as long as there have been tenders and cameras that could be carried on them. A photographer would shoot pictures of the sails, which were later used to judge the efficiency of the basic sail concept. Roy Dickson was familiar with sail vision programs that consisted of tiny cameras mounted on the mast, from which streams of images were sent, along with everything else, back to the tender.

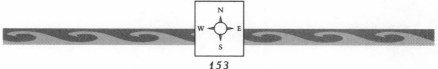

By the late eighties state-of-the-art telemetry could record and present data in real time. On the sail vision side, real-time programs were first used during the '87 Cup in Perth. These were powerful assets, particularly in a two-boat program. Say a testing day is devoted to calculating the performance of two different keels. A usable test requires that everything else about the two boats be equal. Way back in the early eighties, skippers could determine only overnight whether two boats were sailing in the same wind, or at the same angle, or if sails were similarly trimmed. With the latest equipment, there could be constant correction. "Tender to *J-3*. Trim on your mainsheet, please. You're slightly easier than *J-5*."

Dickson wanted those advantages. And as the months slipped by, he reckoned the campaign was running out of time if it was going to enjoy them. "I recommended the syndicate do what Japan does best," Dickson said later, "import the technology and then use Japanese expertise to improve it." What he had in mind was the system built for *KZ-7*. Richard Morris, who had run the *KZ-7* testing program in Fremantle, had even agreed to spend a few weeks in Gamagori showing the Japanese how the system worked and, as one of the Kiwis there put it, "answering questions the Japanese technicians didn't know enough to ask yet."

Six more months passed before Dickson got a straight answer—a no—and it came from a Yamaha man named Yoshihiro Nagami. Nagami was young, wiry of build, and was said to have a line straight into senior management at the Yamaha headquarters building in Hamamatsu. Nagami had never sailed, but he managed to exude unusual self-confidence nonetheless.

"We don't have the resources," Nagami finally told Dickson. "Anyway, all we need are two computer engineers for two months."

Certain decisions within the syndicate—a mounting number of them, usually those of greatest importance—were disappearing from Roy Dickson's view. Dickson never knew what happened to the campaign's electronics systems. Nothing was ready in time to mount on the Twelves. When the A.C. boat first sailed, there was nothing to put on it either. One of the sailors said, "We kept hearing they

were working on it, but it was always as if they had started yesterday."

Some of the telemetry gear eventually arrived. They never got a tactical computer system, and the sail vision program, on which the syndicate spent a hundred thousand dollars, never got beyond an old Canon 35.

Dickson had come up against another of the many walls bordering his maze. Those around him were unable to admit that anything at all might be beyond them. Saving face, they preferred to labor away in silence, missing some schedules and ignoring others. Responsibility, key to Dickson's method, was so diffuse that no individual could be held accountable for anything.

Roy Dickson had bought into the familiar mythology draped around the Japanese economic "miracle"—the *samurai* spirit, the feats of technological derring-do, the white-coated armies that never slept. These were half-truths at best. Long hours may be a reality for many Japanese wage-earners, but corporate power in Japan flows less from an inspired work force then from advantages derived from the nation's economic and political structure. Nonetheless, the popular myths were partly what brought Roy Dickson to Japan.

Now he began to reconsider. In international athletics, the Japanese had failed singularly, especially in team sports, since the Tokyo Olympics. What was it that had led to the nation's success in business and industry? he wondered. Dickson began to watch trade talks, arguments about rice imports, the range of issues on the table between Japan and its commercial partners. He especially liked a series of negotiations between Tokyo and Washington called the Structural Impediments Initiative, or S.I.I. The Japanese promised many things in the course of the S.I.I. talks. But what the Japanese said and what they did, Dickson saw, were often very different.

"The Japanese were very clever in the areas where they excelled," Dickson concluded. "There was the social structure they kept in place, and the low level of expectations at which they managed to keep the bulk of the people. They had protectionist policies, a large reservoir of cheap capital, and a way of joint venturing that shut

others out. They took excessive manpower as an inbuilt cost and wrote it off."

Dickson was no deep thinker in such matters, and his thesis was hardly original. But he had an unusual perspective. He wasn't at a distance, like almost all other *gaijin*, trying to peel off endless layers of the onion. Along with the handful of young coaches and sailors he had brought with him, Dickson was looking from the inside out. From where he stood, Gamagori began to look more and more like Japan in miniature. Here, indeed, was the cultured irresponsibility of which the nation's critics often spoke. And it suggested that Japan was very far from learning to compete, despite all the talk to the contrary one heard in the late 1980s. This presented Dickson with an unusual problem. Nobody ever won the America's Cup by negotiating for it. And nobody ever won it without first wanting to win it.

Little by little, the early success faded and it began to look as though Roy Dickson was losing the battle he had been hired to fight. The Japanese would do to him what they had done to Kaoru Ogimi: they would take what they wanted and leave the rest. Then they would do things their way.

"It seems to me," Roy-*san* said one day, "that all of what I see in Japan has produced a race of people who can't compete on a level playing field. And you can't buy an uneven playing field, not in sailing."

• • •

America's Cup races are rarely pleasant experiences for those participating in them. They are unusually rigorous. Schedules are tight; jobs often do not get done to the satisfaction of the shore crew or the more meticulous sailors. Campaigns are managed and boats sailed by men with egos the size of spinnakers and of roughly the same characteristics—they bulge when there's wind behind them. "Doing an America's Cup," as the expression goes, is one of those things a lot of people swear halfway through they will never trouble themselves with again.

Ego isn't normally a problem among the Japanese. By the first few weeks of 1989, however, Kazunori Komatsu's opinion of himself

as a skipper was veering out of control. Over the previous year he had been absent frequently from Gamagori while training for the '88 summer Olympics in Seoul. After his return, however, the syndicate was increasingly divided as to whether he should remain.

Tatsu Yamasaki had been hearing reports of trouble for months, and he would occasionally train to Gamagori to conduct private interviews with crew members whose judgment he had come to trust. What he learned was not encouraging. It was the same old story: cruelty, unreasonable demands, unnecessary discipline. Komatsu, who had sailed with tillers throughout his career, rarely with wheels, had learned much during his stint as navigator in Sweden; but he shared nothing of the experience with Makoto Namba, Robert Fry, or anyone else among the senior crew whom he judged a threat to his primacy. That was typical; Komatsu was empire-building. As Ken Nomoto saw it, the skipper had brought the camp "to a point of crisis." Lines of loyalty were a tangled mess. He was detested by the staff and the senior crew, the original Hamanako crowd, and he detested them all in return. The later recruits still admired him and were therefore united against all those who felt otherwise.

Meetings Nomoto and Yamasaki held with Komatsu in late January were inconclusive. The *kaicho*, who had, after all, known Komatsu for years, was against firing him; the *sensei*, much closer to the scene in the sailing camp, saw it as a question of sacrificing Komatsu or sacrificing all the rest.

The end was abrupt and awkward. A reception had been scheduled for the last day of January at the Imperial Hotel, during which the crew was to be presented to the press for the first time. An hour before it started, Komatsu, who was to do the introductions, announced that he was quitting and walked off. There could hardly have been a syndicate manager in the Cup's history who wasn't familiar with moments when the mess inside had to be contained. The task fell, this time, to a young Yamaha man named Tetsuro Nabata, an engaging fellow who helped run Nippon Challenge's PR office. As Komatsu stormed out, Nabata grabbed Makoto Namba and began to drill him in the grosser points of the exercise. Namba, diffident as always and quaking with nerves, handled himself well

enough on stage to throw the local press off the scent of trouble. It was his first act as Nippon Challenge's team captain and skipper.

Namba slipped quietly into the top spot. Chris Dickson, the whiz kid who was shortly to begin his periodic coaching visits, would drill Namba day in, day out for weeks at a stretch in racing technique. There was blackboard work, hours with the younger Dickson's tactics books, and there were exhausting sessions out on one of the Yamaha 30s. Chris exposed Namba to everything he knew, which was considerable: game plans, moves, countermoves—what could legitimately be called the theory of match racing.

Namba improved. In September 1989 he won the Danish Cup finals in Copenhagen against the Frenchman Marc Bouet in two straight races. When he got home he went straight to a sponsors' party at the Imperial, trophy in hand.

"This wasn't luck," Namba declared to the audience of executives. "This was practice, a good afterguard, and confidence going into the race." In time Namba would rank seventh on the world match-race circuit. He had few firsts but—*Gambatte!*—he developed a steady run of thirds, fourths, and fifths. Chris Dickson would look proudly upon that record as a measure of his own handiwork.

Namba was skipper apparent. Was he the man, though, to sail *Nippon* in the America's Cup?

Much is made in sailing circles, as in many sports, of "the killer instinct." The adages are many: a race is never over until it's over; never leave an opponent for dead until you're over the finish line; no skipper will win without a streak of naked aggression. Dennis Conner, more than any other sailor, has sought to elevate a taste for blood to a kind of mythic attribute. There's a measure of hokum in there, as any honest yachtsman will tell you. But drive and desire, it can be argued, are especially important in yacht racing because the helmsman's task is unusually complex and the demands on his concentration extreme.

Coaches and managers had been looking for these qualities in Makoto Namba from the start. But they were elusive. Kaoru Ogimi, never a mincer of words, was emphatic. "Namba's hopeless," he would say whenever the subject came up. Roy Dickson was inclined

toward the same opinion. Stu Argo, who left the syndicate after the Twelve-Meter Worlds in Sweden, had been through the same exercises with Namba as the younger Dickson, though at a more elementary level. "Namba was the perfect company man—very polite, never steps on toes, knows who's in charge," Argo said. "We spent a lot of time on technique—steering, timing, calling sail changes—and he had a fairly good grasp of what I was trying to teach him. Over five months, I could see the knowledge was there. But where was the aggression? After a while we just wanted to make him mad. But it was like trying to get a Japanese to say no. You can't do it. How often did we have to maul him on the water? How long did we have to humiliate him? A few times we got him going. He would come to the recognition, this is the wrong attitude."

Namba commanded respect, whatever his limitations. But he never left behind the mentality that he, as a *nihonjin*, a Japanese person, had brought to Gamagori with him. A visiting *gaijin* once asked, "Namba-*san*, who are the best crew members, the ones who have excelled?" Namba couldn't answer. Singling people out, for either achievement or criticism, was simply not in him. He saw Nippon Challenge as a replica of the promotion system in a Japanese company.

"We've all advanced evenly," Namba replied. "We're all at the same level. Nobody's any better than anybody else."

• • •

That was not quite so. Others were having their epiphanies.

In the spring of 1989, Roy Dickson invited a friend named Jim Blair to Gamagori. Blair, a burly Scot of fifty-five, had arrived in Auckland in 1962 with a pregnant wife, fifteen pounds sterling, and a new job as a high school gym instructor. By the late eighties he was a noted specialist in the science of sports physiology. He had coached the New Zealand team for the Whitbread Round-the-World race in 1984, an Admiral's Cup entry from Auckland after that, and then the Fay campaign in Fremantle. He was the trainer for the All Blacks, New Zealand's world-class rugby team. Blair came across as simple, honest, and steady as a rock. His brogue was thick, and his

sentences all ended in an upturn, as if each were modestly put forward as a question. He had a paunch, a receding hairline, and he smoked heavily, but that fooled no one. Blair was keenly intelligent about what he did, and he did it by combining a knowledge of muscles with a capacity to understand the man within them.

Blair would stay with Nippon Challenge—he held two-week sessions every two months—until the final months before the America's Cup race. What he saw from beginning to end was as good a measure as any of the progress the crew would make.

Three things troubled Blair on his first visit. He thought the gym equipment was wrong. (He couldn't change it, so he changed each sailor's workout routine on it.) He thought Roy Dickson's regimen—monotonous and running twelve to fourteen hours a day—was threatening team motivation. (He couldn't change that either.) He also saw that the crew, in the gym and on the water, was "staying within a comfort zone," as he put it.

"Westerners, especially Western sporting men, tend to attack physical preparation aggressively," Blair explained. "This didn't seem to come naturally to the Japanese."

It was the attitude problem. But Blair differed from Roy Dickson in one important respect: as he saw it, that was another thing he couldn't change. "You don't change attitudes," Blair would say. "They're there. It's up to people to change their own attitudes. If you give them enough opportunities to perform, the attitude will come out. If it's the correct one, they'll win; if it isn't, they'll fail."

They liked Blair at Gamagori. Early on he had thought through his own approach, and it showed. Do I have to understand the Japanese as Japanese to reach my objective? he asked himself. Or do I treat them as I would any other human beings? Do I treat differences between us as individual differences or as cultural differences? Blair thought it would take too long to understand what was in front of him as a cultural phenomenon. "I decided to treat them as individuals," he recalled later. "Differences in facial features are only that. What's inside is the same physiology."

For most of the crew, Blair found, the America's Cup was still a story, as he called it, something far away in space and time. It was a

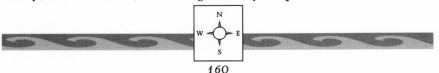

hard wall to break through. Blair would finish a morning workout and say, "Good session, men," and someone would say afterward, "Yes, Jim-*san*, because you're here." Most of the crew were still smoking when Blair arrived. He didn't tell them to quit, but he took it as important when they did so on their own.

"They found it difficult to see what I was concerned about," Blair said. "It was like trying to describe cricket to an American. I had to change the quality of the goals they set for themselves, but it's difficult to explain the standards needed when they have nothing to compare them with. Then your exhortations are misconstrued. For a long time, they thought I only wanted them to get better."

There were moments, nonetheless, when they learned to reach inside. Jin's had come during the '88 Citizen Cup, at which the Japanese again placed last. They had chartered a Stewart well in advance, and they practiced a week straight before the event. They were Jin's first races, and he was at the bow. One afternoon, in a fresh breeze and choppy seas, Jin grabbed an unshackled foreguy while raising a spinnaker and went over the leeward side. The plunge into the cold waters off Auckland was like a mental awakening. We can't win these races because we aren't giving it a hundred percent, he thought as he climbed back on board.

"That became my object," Jin said later. "Racing wasn't even about winning or losing after that. It was about giving it everything I had."

Sailing the Twelves with Roy Dickson meant specializing. It was a simple process. Namba, Robert Fry, and Ryozo Tanaka, another of the senior crew, would interview each crewman in the briefing room at Gamagori. They would listen to preferences and conform to them as best they could. Sometimes it worked and sometimes not. Yoshia Sasaki, a twenty-six-year-old with the build of a Notre Dame tackle, was a grinder from day one—no debate on either side of the interview table. Jin started at the bow but ended up the pitman; Ken Hara was headsail trimmer for a year before the interviews and wanted to stay where he was. But they urged him to take the bow, which he did. It was where he would remain until the America's Cup was raced. Specialization was unusual to the Japanese. But any boat as large as a Twelve or the new A.C. yachts required sailors to know one job better than they knew any other. In Gamagori, matching a man to a job became part of the larger process of individuation.

No position on a yacht can be occupied successfully by anyone without a quick mind and, in all but a few cases, an athletic build. But there are tasks that can be taught and those that can't. Out front is the bowman, who is visible and vulnerable and whose mistakes are immediately apparent; if someone's going overboard, it's likely to be he. The bowman works all the lines and clips involved in getting sails up and down; he handles the spinnaker pole, helps haul sails up from below, feeds them up as they're raised, and pulls them in when they're dropped. He's shouting orders a lot of the time, but he's a scout more than a director. He needs to be muscular but compact, steady, aggressive, and well organized.

Behind him is the mastman, who helps on the bow and handles the sails below deck. Then comes the pitman, also called the keyboards man because he sits in front of a dozen controls behind the mast. He manages the winches and the lines the bowman uses to raise and lower sails and poles. A pitman must be organized and agile; he is the coordinator, in effect, between the bow of the boat and the afterguard. Next back are the winch grinders, six of them on an A.C. boat. They ease or tighten all the lines and rigging—the spinnaker and gennaker sheets, the mainsheet, the runner backstays. Grinders need powerful arms and shoulders, but they also need to understand sails well enough to apply their strength properly: how fast or gradually should a line be eased or trimmed, and exactly when? A good grinder knows.

What remains are the sail trimmers and the afterguard—the helmsman, tactician, and navigator. By any yachtsman's reckoning, these are the jobs that can be understood but never taught. It amounts to possessing a full knowledge of the boat, the appendages, the sails, the rigging, and knowing the principles by which they work well enough to draw from them a sense of the yacht as a unified machine. Experienced sailors can never avoid the word "feel" when they are talking about these positions. And feel can come from only one thing. "Experience was the deficiency I could do very little

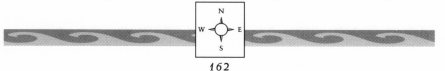

about," Roy Dickson once said. "Essentially I was trying to give them four decades of experience in a couple of years."

His son Chris put it this way: "The physical jobs can be learned in one-two-three fashion. It takes work to be the best, but you can bring the right person to a competent level quickly on any given boat. The technical areas are different. They need years. A trimmer needs to understand racing, sailmaking, design, and the physics of the boat—lift, drag, leeway, heeling, pitching, wind angles. Give me a mastman on a Twelve and I'll have him doing a good job, on that particular boat, in two months. A trimmer? I'll want two years just to get to first base, three or four or five to get to a reasonable level, and probably ten to reach world standard. It's the difference between a train driver and a top surgeon. Both deal in human lives. But you can teach only one relatively quickly. You can't teach a surgeon by using pictures in a book."

•　　•　　•

Most of the syndicate's executives and sailors took it for granted that Japan could produce bowmen, mastmen, pitmen, and grinders of adequate proficiency. Trimmers would be another matter, but the campaign would produce them sooner or later, too. A helmsman? The rest of the afterguard? Kazunori Komatsu, the terror of Mikawa Bay, had allowed Nippon Challenge to avoid the issue. But by the end of 1989, it could no longer be skirted.

"What about Namba-*san*?" someone once asked Ken Hara.

"Good question," Hara chuckled. "What about Namba-*san*?"

"Can he do it, Ken?"

Hara didn't even pause to think. "He's got the technical ability, but he's not the kind of person who can skipper. A skipper has to make a hundred people work as one. Namba-*san* hasn't got that kind of ability."

"Is there someone else in Japan who has it?"

Hara frowned. "We have to make that kind of person," he replied.

Makoto Namba lasted a year as helmsman. Ken Nomoto liked to think the decision to replace him had mostly to do with his boat. Until *Nippon* began to materialize, the *sensei* would explain, the

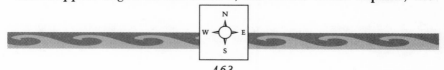

syndicate's goal had really remained making the semifinals in San Diego, the top four. Then they found *Nippon* to be something other than a plaything. Nomoto's VPP showed they had a winner, and that required them to do more than write a song with a goddess, a rainbow, and lots of glory foretold in it.

That was Nomoto's story, but no one else who heard it really believed it. Some sailors laughed when told that version of events. Replacing Namba-*san*, they said, really had nothing to do with the boat.

What it came down to was far simpler. Ken Hara had said it perfectly. Namba-*san*, whatever his higher qualities, didn't have what it took. Nor did anyone else in Gamagori, or anyone else Nippon Challenge could think of who hadn't yet joined the syndicate. It looked as if the campaign had come to see things the way Roy Dickson did, or Kaoru Ogimi. If they were going to try to win they had to have the right people, and getting the right people in the afterguard meant hiring *gaijin*. Even Nomoto, a master of Japanese understatement, acknowledged that.

"Sometimes it's difficult to operate the boat, navigate, and judge weather and opponents' tactics," he said one day. "Our boys aren't top class on these points. And that's all that's missing."

Nomoto was vigorously opposed to the decision, nonetheless. To him, it was the most critical turning point in the entire campaign. If winning meant putting *gaijin* at the top of the hierarchy, then winning had to be forgone. There would be the next time. Nomoto's respect for the *kaicho* kept him from making his case directly. But he counseled extreme caution. "I'm no fanatic patriot," he advised Yamasaki, "but you can't change people overnight. What about the harmony and integrity of the team? What about the cultural gap?"

Tatsu Yamasaki's attitude had never been very clear. He had dreamt of winning, but then he thought challenging was enough. He had sought the right people, but when he saw his recruits on the water in Sweden, he gave up and went for a technological solution. Now he shifted his ground again. Over the months, Roy-*san* had shown him what it meant to lead and what it meant to want to win. He finally seemed to get the point. Whatever had to be done would

be done, even if it meant hiring a *gaijin* skipper. The commitment
was huge, but Yamasaki would make it. And behind him stood
Hideto Eguchi, the gray, soft-spoken Yamaha president. Eguchi
rarely tipped his hand in Nippon Challenge matters, but he did this
time. He had seen too many motorcycle races not to understand that
gaijin knew best how to get all that could be had out of Japanese
machines.

Eguchi made no apologies for his point of view. "We were satisfied—almost astonished—at the progress of the crew," he said one
day in his Hamamatsu office. "But there were two years left. It was
time to find foreigners to do the things we couldn't."

It was a complex judgment. Others felt roughly the way Kazunori
Komatsu did after *Magician V*'s victory in '78. Komatsu had faded
back into the woodwork at Yamaha, resuming his old job as a test
pilot and match-racing whenever he could. But he burned with
bitterness for years after his departure from Nippon Challenge.
"The pleasure of sport lies in teams from different environments
and cultures competing under the same rules," he said once. "National identity is important. Some people say, 'There are no borders
in sports.' I have to agree, in the end; but if we don't maintain our
differences, as we do in the Olympics, we'll see the wealthiest team
always winning. Is that what we want?"

Many beside the Japanese would ask that question in the course
of the twenty-eighth America's Cup. But there was no time to ask it
in Gamagori as 1990 approached. So long as a two-year residency
rule was met, syndicates could hire whatever crew they wanted. The
challenger series was scheduled to begin in early 1992; Tatsu Yamasaki had a few weeks to hire the right skipper. And he had made up
his mind to find one who could sail *Nippon* across the finish line
first.

●　　●　　●

A number of names were mentioned, chief among them Gary Jobson.
Jobson quickly declined, but with his help the board narrowed the
list to five and then to two. John Bertrand, an American of no
relation to the champion who sailed *Australia II* to victory in 1983,

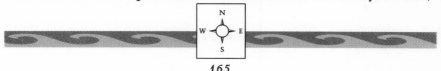

was Jobson's choice. The other was Chris Dickson. Pa Dickson was fair and pushed his son forward not at all. Bertrand had his supporters—Eguchi was among them—but he priced himself out of the running. He had yen signs in his eyes, and they were simply too visible. He went to Tokyo with an elaborate presentation, but he wanted too much money and too many Americans hired along with him.

Chris Dickson had no satin robe to shrug off when he arrived to skipper *Nippon* in February 1990. But he may as well have. He had been at the top as many years as he was eligible to compete: New Zealand junior champion at sixteen, world champion in the two-handed dinghy class for three years after that. As Roy's tactician, he was on the winning boat in the first Citizen Cup, in 1979. Chris Dickson's greatest moment had come in Fremantle, where he skippered *KZ-7* for Michael Fay; though the Kiwis lost the challenger series to Dennis Conner, Chris Dickson returned to Auckland a national hero.

Among his earliest memories were those acquired sailing on *Tuahine*, Roy's forty-three-footer. He had sailed ever since, and at twenty-eight he had a record of victories as long as some sailors decades older. He ranked first on the world match-racing circuit, a position he would defend for years afterward. Chris Dickson was compact but well proportioned, like his father, and his eyes were the same piercing blue. He had surrendered more of his hair to the sun and wind than Roy had, and his self-consciousness about it gave away a streak of uncertainty that could otherwise be missed. Sailing wasn't a sport to Chris Dickson. It was a profession. "I'm not obsessed with winning," he once told an Auckland reporter. "I'm obsessed with survival—survival in a very competitive career."

He had sailed for Sir Michael, but he never would again. In Fremantle he was known as "the U-Boat Captain," partly for his determination and partly for his style as a helmsman. There were unquieted rumors of fist fights and shrieking fits during the event. Later it was said he had cracked up in the last two races of the challenger series against Conner. "The quicker boat won at the end of the day," Chris would shrug. That wasn't how others saw it. *KZ-*

7's reputation for speed was widespread; Jim Blair judged the crew the fittest sportsmen New Zealand had ever produced.

The world began to turn on Chris Dickson after the effusive post-Fremantle welcome subsided—first the insular world of New Zealand yachting, then the larger one. It came to be that he was no longer especially welcome in the seas off Auckland, but from his point of view that was too small a pond anyway. He had overplayed the brilliant-brat card. He was a draw at any regatta, but the crowd bobbing about on the spectator craft seemed happy enough to watch him lose. "There are really tough helmsmen, and there are the smooth, competent types," Gary Jobson said once. "But when you go against the best, and you beat them, it's a kick, it's like beating the Forty-Niners. Not with Dickson. He doesn't just win, he bludgeons. Win or lose, I don't even like sailing against him."

The powerful drive Dickson had acquired in childhood perfectly matched the medium through which he chose to express it. He was superb at the helm, and he handled tactics almost as well. He left crewmates in awe of his ability to jump on an unfamiliar boat and find what sailors call "the groove." But he couldn't control the drive that propelled him. He choked a lot, and his record, for all the victories, showed it. It was spotty, inconsistent. Something happened to his features when the pressure came on, as if he had donned a mask. His face tightened visibly, his eyes suggested that concentration had given way to a kind of mania. Then he would lose control, and time and time again it had cost him.

A Japanese sailor in Gamagori once called Dickson a Komatsu with finesse. As sailors there was no comparison between the two, but the logic was apparent. Dickson was no democrat on a yacht. You didn't get off a boat with Chris Dickson smiling, even after a hard-fought triumph in a major event; you avoided the yachting press, found a beer, and crawled into a corner to recover. Ramming a sailor's face into an instrument was Dickson's style. Or grabbing the sheet from the mainsail trimmer in the middle of a race. "You didn't *see*? You didn't *see*!" he'd shout at a crew member who'd flubbed a maneuver in practice. "Maybe you'll see better without

these!" and he'd tear off the sailor's sunglasses and throw them overboard.

Chris Dickson brought three Kiwis with him to staff his afterguard. There was an Olympic medalist, an experienced big-boat ocean racer, and a sailor who understood sails the way a sculptor understands marble. They had all known victory and defeat, of course. What was singular about the afterguard, in contrast to the man who chose them, was the grace and integrity with which they lived with both.

Unlike their hosts, the Kiwis didn't arrive in Gamagori a unified group. The others didn't hate Chris Dickson—that was too simple an emotion. They were all somewhere along the trail that started with animosity and led through to pity and then to a certain liking for the desolately lonely kid who, at odd, unguarded moments, would briefly appear from behind the persona worn by the man.

·   ·   ·

A real estate company in Chiba, a prefecture of bedroom communities bordering Tokyo, was buying up S & B stock.

Kaori Yamasaki, twenty-six, was getting married.

Tatsu Yamasaki was stepping aside as president of S & B and his brother Masaru was taking over.

The close of the eighties was not an easy time for Tatsu Yamasaki. When he became company chairman after a six-year term as S & B's president, the plan was to move to Gamagori and manage the sailing camp with Roy Dickson. Ken Nomoto, who remained among the *kaicho*'s closest advisers, thought it would make a great combination—the knowing Japanese manager and the *gaijin* expert.

But the *sensei* had little appreciation of Yamasaki's circumstances. The Chiba developers had accumulated almost ten percent of S & B's listed shares, and Yamasaki would spend twenty billion yen, about a hundred and sixty-five million dollars at the time, buying it back. As to Masaru, he managed the manufacturing side all right, but he didn't manage people as well as Tatsu did. Nor did Nomoto understand, perhaps, the elaborate nature of a daughter's wedding in the circles Yamasaki moved in.

Nomoto had his own motives for urging Yamasaki down to Gamagori. Late in June he met the *kaicho* at the Imperial Hotel and asked to take his leave. The boat design was fundamentally in place, he argued, and Gamagori was running smoothly with Dickson in charge. Bruce Farr or other *gaijin* designers might follow their campaigns to the end, but the *sensei* considered his work complete. Nippon Challenge had its boat. It was time for the doctor to resume the work of exploring and documenting the world's forgotten boatyards.

Nomoto would eventually go. Yamasaki would try to spend more time on Nippon Challenge. But there was no leaving Tokyo. Quite apart from S & B and his private life, the syndicate needed him where he was. At Roy Dickson's urging, the board had decided to build two A.C. boats, not one, and Dickson was already pushing for a third. In July he and Eguchi determined to up the ante among the thirty sponsors, from a hundred million yen each to a hundred and fifty million. Before announcing the increase, Yamasaki started an elaborate *nemawashi* campaign. Three or four nights a week through the autumn he would cruise up and down the Sumida River with a few of the executives from the long list of those he had to cultivate. It left him spent, exhausted.

Managing a sailing campaign like Nippon Challenge was something very new to Tatsu Yamasaki. His company, like all others in Japan, consisted of a homogeneous group of workers, each of whom knew down to the finest nuances where he or she fitted. The sailing syndicate was no such thing. Everyone had different ideas, and it was a constant battle to balance them. Yamasaki had to make decisions that departed from the norm in corporate Japan, and he was wholly unaccustomed to it. His friends, like Yoichi Tsuchiya, the fellow partygoer and Sanyo Securities president, started to see the strain. But Yamasaki had his own solution. He wouldn't manage in the Japanese fashion. There would be no strongman at the top. He would delegate to middle management; it was the *gaijin* way, and it would be better for the campaign.

It might have been, under different circumstances. But ideas cannot be imposed until those charged with executing them are

ready. Tatsu Yamasaki saw decentralization, a foreign notion to the Japanese, as a virtue—even if he was making one of necessity. Down in Gamagori, Roy Dickson saw things differently. Yamasaki seemed to be coming his way on most questions, but his absence for so much of the time was one more abdication of responsibility among all the others. Roy was puzzled. As he put it much later, Yamasaki didn't seem to have any guts.

Trouble between the two men first surfaced during the summer of 1989. By the end of August a decision had to be made about the type of winches to be mounted on *Nippon*'s deck. The boat wasn't due until the following spring, but specifications had to be conveyed and orders placed. It wasn't a complex decision; two companies, a United States firm called Barent and a British one called Lewmar, had a lock on the market for racing winches. Dickson favored Lewmar gear. The Kiwis had raced with it on *KZ-7*, and many yachtsmen and hardware specialists considered it ahead of its competitor in terms of quality and design.

There was only one problem. The syndicate had developed extensive dealings with Robert Fry's import concern, the Industrial Suppliers Company, and Isco was the agent in Japan for Barent. Fry was supplying not only hardware, but cloth and other items to the sail loft as well. There were rumors Isco was making profits of as much as forty-five percent on its Nippon Challenge contracts. Fry always denied them, but business was business in Japan, and Isco fought for the winch deal by back-channeling to Yamasaki.

In the end, *Nippon* would sail with Barent winches.

Roy Dickson saw red.

Tatsu Yamasaki saw something else. He had placed his trust in Dickson and had started running the campaign Dickson's way. But the Kiwi moved not at all in his direction. Dickson didn't understand how Japan worked. He didn't understand the importance of relationships in Japan, or if he did, he chose to ignore them.

"It was the point," the *kaicho* said later, "when I started to lose faith and confidence in Roy-*san*."

TATEMAE

"It's like driving a very small car with a very big engine," Chris Dickson said. "It's frighteningly powerful."

He had seen *J-3*, the first *Nippon*, up on blocks in the shed at Gamagori, and he had sailed it a couple of times before taking it into the fresh breezes that prevailed on the official launching day. Dickson had no design sense, by his own admission. Looking at the new craft sitting on its keel, the words that came to mind were simply "fast" and "impressive." Out on the water, "it was a breed of its own." It was "easily driven." The hull shape, Dickson thought, seemed unusually clean: unlike most other racing yachts, there was little distortion in its lines so far as he could see.

Much of that was written into the designers' formula. In many classes governed by the International Offshore Rule, the quest for speed tended to produce strange-looking craft. A yacht would be too broad for its length, for instance, because the designer was working from a set of I.O.R. parameters rather than an idea that originated on his drawing table. The new formula produced no such peculiarities. Here was the unusual combination the rule writers gave sailors in the I.A.C.C. boats: lightness, stability, and huge sail area. Compared with a Twelve-Meter, the resistance curve was gradual. A Twelve needed twenty to twenty-two knots of wind to reach a boat speed of nine and a half knots; Chris Dickson figured the new A.C. class could achieve that in fourteen knots of wind.

The launching ceremony held at Gamagori on Saturday, April 22, 1990, was even more elaborate than the one that had marked the base-camp opening two years earlier almost to the day. Among the dignitaries was Princess Mikasa, a member of the imperial family, who lent the proceedings the desired air of national endeavor. Toshiki Kaifu, the prime minister at the time, wasn't present, but everyone knew that the calligraphy for "Nippon" across the transom was his handiwork:

The craft itself was draped in white down to the waterline, and as the cloth slipped off into the water, cries of "*Banzai!*" filled the air and *komodaru*, straw-bound kegs of *sake* the size of kettledrums, were cracked open along the pier. A huge fleet of sailing craft and motor yachts had assembled. *Nippon*'s mast towered over everything around it like a steeple in a small town.

Chris Dickson, only a few weeks a skipper in Japan, was much in demand, and he took the opportunity to flatter his employers as well as the yacht. "In the America's Cup game, technology is a big part of it," the skipper told one television commentator with all the weight he could muster. "The difference between winning and losing comes down to fractions of knots of boat speed. On that level, the Japanese are world leaders." Another camera, another microphone: "To win the America's Cup, if that means we have to beat New Zealand, well, okay, we'll beat New Zealand. For me, sure, it would be a little disappointing for New Zealand, but I'm part of Nippon Challenge, and winning for Nippon Challenge is the priority."

There were a fair number of foreigners present, among them Gary Jobson. Along with many others, Jobson found *J-3* somewhat more unusual-looking than Dickson did. Its maximum beam was eighteen feet, the limit the rule allowed; from the deck to the water, its freeboard sloped sharply inward, giving the craft a flat, broad look. "It's a very unique design," Jobson said in neutral tones into an ESPN microphone. "The flared-out topside is something we haven't seen before. So there's a potential there that it's quite fast. We really don't know. The smartest thing to do is experiment against the computer and then go against some other America's Cup yachts to see how fast you are."

Although Dickson had been out on *Nippon* before, launch day was more than the Kiwi had braced for. The wind hadn't blown to ten knots on previous days. That morning it was at twelve and picked up to fourteen, fifteen, then sixteen knots. Dickson found the appendages tricky, not easily controlled. The craft looked brilliant: a huge red and white spinnaker barreled out in front when Dickson ran it downwind. But heeling over into the breeze with a carbon fiber mast, with which no one on the boat had any experience, was scary. It all seemed so light and fragile.

"We planned everything well, we did all the preparations we could. The Twelves were out of the water, and the new boat looked excellent," Dickson said on land afterward. "But trying to figure out how not to blow the equipment off it, coming to grips with its power, was a little disturbing. It was like being a theater director and being told you didn't have this much rehearsal time"—he gestured with his hands—"you had three days. At the end of the show you say, 'Yeesh, we got away with it.' "

•   •   •

As his father did at the beginning, Chris Dickson thought Kiwi skill and experience combined with Japanese money and hardware was going to stun them in San Diego. The campaign's management was in place and understood what needed to be done. The technical

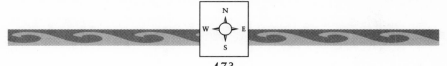

expertise made available was impressive. The design was far ahead of what one would expect of a first-time syndicate. These, at least, were the assertions Dickson made when recruiting his afterguard in Auckland. He had called around town midway in the New Zealand summer, presented his pitch, and asked for replies within twenty-four hours. A week later, Dickson and his three lieutenants were on a plane together bound for Tokyo.

What they found was something different, of course. As time went on their encounters with Roy Dickson would come to seem a little like Marlowe's with Kurtz in *Heart of Darkness*—the discovery of a rational man gone slightly mad, lost in the depths of a foreign jungle. Roy-*san*, since tension with Yamasaki had begun to rise, was beginning to feel his back was pressed against the wall.

Roy Dickson had stopped sailing by early 1990 and was spending all his time, as he put it, "directing, planning, and managing." The crew hadn't seen the stubborn grandfather out on the water for almost a year. When they saw him on land, they thought his face was *panku*, a word drawn from "puncture": his expression had shriveled and twisted up over the months, like a flat tire. Whatever had gone wrong, they knew no details. They knew only that Roy-*san* was trying to change things. In the beginning the object of the game was *asobi*, play, participation, the doing of one's best as a Japanese. Then everything was refocused on winning. "What happened to the Japanese part of it?" Yoshia, the thickly built grinder, wondered aloud one day.

One evening Jin said, "As an outsider who came to teach, Roy-*san* was the best we've ever had. Once he was inside the organization, in management, it just didn't work right."

The I.A.C.C. World Championships, to be raced off Point Loma in May 1991, were little more than a year away. And it was less than a year until they were to move the entire Gamagori operation to San Diego to continue training, testing, and innovating in the waters where the America's Cup would be decided. In Roy's office those events loomed on the calendar as encounters with reality. The Worlds would be the first contest in the new class of yacht. Yet they were sailing with Kiwi-made spars and there was no sign of their

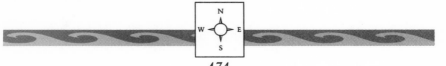

own. *J-3*'s launch, festivities aside, was drastically behind schedule; it had been all show, *tatemae*. The craft had no decently calibrated instruments, and testing it effectively was impossible given the current state of telemetry.

Where did they stand, after all?

The deep divide maintained between the sailing team and the technical people was driving Dickson to distraction. Give and take between scientists and sailors is standard practice in yachting syndicates, something that never even needs to be discussed. Nothing goes on a boat that isn't the product of that process. Not in Nippon Challenge. Nomoto had treated the design process as if it were a state secret. Yamaha and its subcontractors were handling the technical aspects of the campaign at a physical remove from Gamagori. The boat was drawn in Tokyo and built in Arai, some fifty miles distant; other dimensions of the technical program were managed at plants scattered around the Honshu industrial belt. The Gamagori people were rarely invited to any of those places.

Compartmentalization is the norm in Japanese corporations. "A" seldom knows what "B" is doing and wouldn't think to try finding out. The Japanese may switch from department to department within any given enterprise, but each department is a walled castle so long as one is in it. It couldn't work in a sailing campaign. Coordination was of the essence, so far as Roy Dickson saw it. He was still issuing long, orderly memos to the management and staff, and many of them addressed this issue. They would be headed "Development Tasks," and had categories like these:

Spar Program
Boat No. 1 Refinement
Boat No. 2 Building Program
Development Program Boat No. 3
Performance Analysis and Optimization
Summary
Action Required

Sometimes there would be ten subheadings under each category. The subtext, and later the explicit command, was: "Talk to one

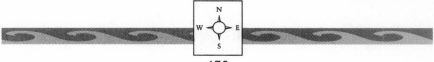

another." Dickson was still trying to break the Japanese mold. But the more intricate these memos were, the more communication they required, the less anyone seemed to pay attention.

Although *J-3* was in the water, Dickson could find out virtually nothing about the design of the hull. Not only did the afterguard and crew need to understand what it was they were sailing; planning future boats was impossible without knowing where they were. On that issue Dickson met an especially thick stone wall. All he needed to know, the technical people told him again and again, was that the hull Nomoto-*sensei* had produced was state-of-the-art. It was so good, in fact, that there might be no need for the third boat Dickson wanted.

Roy Dickson told the story of his own slow descent into frustration in the reports he delivered at intervals to the board of directors. His writing always courteous but blunt, in the Dickson style. "I saw my role as being frank and honest. I couldn't be of maximum assistance otherwise," he said. "And I couldn't see dropping my standards to meet those of the Japanese."

He didn't. "Wind it Up," the electrically charged set of goals declared in the report of June 6, 1989, gradually gave way to undisguised cynicism. The following year's slogan, ominous if un-original, was "Shape Up or Ship Out." Dickson's reports became long litanies of complaints. A deep sense of betrayal bled through all of them.

The campaign, as Dickson saw it, was a mess, and the mess began with Tatsu Yamasaki. He simply didn't understand how to put serious competition before all else, and was therefore incapable of transmitting the proper attitude downward. They were drifting along on illusions. As to Ken Nomoto, who could even tell what he was up to? Nomoto kept hidden as much as he could. But the notion that his work was finished after a single design was absurd on the face of it.

"I'm bitterly disappointed with the building program," Dickson wrote to the board on March 29. "The lack of performance monitor-ing in all areas has led to design, supply, construction, and ulti-mately commissioning and sailing delays. Without change in the

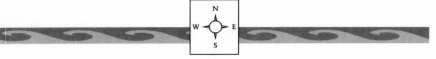

management organization, the probability is that Nippon Challenge will fail."

It was the first of many loaded statements. Months earlier, Roy-*san*'s thinking had taken a turn. When Chris Dickson and the other *gaijin* arrived, Roy had told them immediately that they would be doing more than what their contracts called for. The assumption was simple: there was no more time to instruct the Japanese. In effect, they would be running the campaign by themselves. The hell with Tatsu Yamasaki, Dickson may as well have said, and the hell with the bloated, complicated organization Yamasaki had created to dream his way into the America's Cup. It was a kind of silent coup.

Roy went completely public in June 1990. On a few hours' notice, he summoned the entire technical staff to Gamagori for a four-and-a-half-hour session on a Sunday afternoon. It was a time-tested Dickson tactic: the emergency meeting, inconveniently called.

Dickson announced a radical restructuring of the technical side of the campaign, placing himself at the top of the new organization, reporting directly to the board in Tokyo. Then he made formal the other assignments. The organizational charts issued that Sunday had a Japanese in charge of all departments with a Kiwi's name listed in parentheses under each of them.

John Cutler, who had sailed to a bronze medal at the Seoul Olympics, would be in charge of performance analysis and optimization: the instruments.

Erle Williams, who had sailed on more big ocean racers than anyone else in Gamagori, was to manage the building program and the spars.

Mike Spanhake, who had spent ten years running sail lofts around the Pacific, got the sail program.

Chris Dickson, in addition to sitting on a kind of internal board with Roy and a few others, would manage a catch-all category called research and design.

It was a bald attempt to gain control of the campaign and redirect it, but Roy-*san* had presented Yamasaki with an ultimatum before the session: accept this, he said, or I'm through. Their friendship may have cooled, but the tactic won the *kaicho*'s support. Hideto

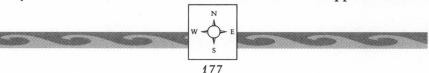

Eguchi, who had driven over from Hamamatsu to attend the meeting, announced at the end, "Anyone who doesn't like this new arrangement should leave now. If you stay, you've agreed to comply."

It looked as if Dickson had triumphed. He would save the Japanese from certain disaster. He would lead them where they wanted to go.

Mike Spanhake, a tall, thin carefully spoken man of forty-one, remembered the meeting afterward as "a huge victory." He said, "It wasn't just another harangue from Roy. It was an excellent presentation. He made it very simple to understand. The message was, 'I'm not just one little cantankerous New Zealander. All I'm doing is telling you what the standards are that you'll be facing.'"

There was only one problem with the pact struck that afternoon. Nothing would change afterward. There are many ways of coping with adversaries, and Tatsu Yamasaki, a veteran of Japanese corporate wars, knew most of them. He had disarmed an enemy by allying with him. The episode probably shortened Roy Dickson's time in Gamagori somewhat, but otherwise it wouldn't make any difference.

•   •   •

Knowledgeable sailors often speak of boats as if they are living entities. Bringing a yacht up to its optimum performance means learning its personality. A boat might be "in the groove" or "humming." It might feel "dead" or "soggy," or it might feel "hot." The language, indeed, is sometimes straight from the bedroom. A sailor will talk about how to "excite" a boat, what "turns it on," or why it "sulks."

That was Mike Spanhake's language.

Spanhake, head sail trimmer in Chris Dickson's afterguard, had seen *J-3* the first day he was in Japan. It was February 27, 1990, a rainy winter afternoon, and he had walked into the shed as soon as he arrived at Gamagori. Compared to the deck of a Twelve, *Nippon*'s was a vast expanse. Standing behind it and looking toward the bow, it exuded power. To Spanhake, it seemed at first glance just as exciting as it had to Dickson.

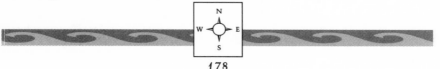

As soon as it was in the water, Spanhake began to think otherwise. "Never in my days have I sailed a boat so devoid of sensitivity," he said of that first excursion on *J-3*. "It's like sailing a corpse. You do things on a yacht—say, trim the sails a certain way—and it says back to you, 'I like this' or 'I don't like that.' This one"—Spanhake started to mix his similies—"gives no sensory return. It's like getting a dead-fish handshake. It's autistic—it communicates with no one. And it's hard to develop any affection for such a child if it's not your own."

On the tow out his first time aboard, *J-3* pitched more than almost any boat Spanhake had ever sailed on. Pitching moment, a yacht's tendency to rock fore and aft when it sails into the wind, is a costly fault once translated into boat speed, and *J-3* continued to pitch that day after the tender released it and the sails went up. Something else also bothered Spanhake during the early excursions on Mikawa Bay. It had to do with *J-3*'s bow and stern.

The ends of a racing yacht are important design features. Because length is a speed-producing factor, design formulas penalize boats judged too long at the waterline. The standard way around that is to design a bow and stern that overhang the waterline at measurement but are in the water when the craft is sailing. Speed is enhanced and a penalty avoided.

J-3 was peculiar. It had extensive overhangs both fore and aft. "But they never got wet," Spanhake explained. "Day in, day out, the boat sailed almost exactly as it measured at the waterline. It wouldn't sink down." What use, Spanhake wondered, were overhangs if they weren't engaged under sail? In time, others started wondering the same thing. Around Gamagori, it became one of the many unknowns about the technical side of the campaign.

Mike Spanhake had sailed almost as many years as he had walked. He had taken an arts degree in Auckland and taught for three years before assuming the first of several sail loft jobs. He was quiet and thorough, the kind of man it was hard to imagine losing his temper, although there were times he did. He brought a painter's sensibility to boats and sails. And he thought *J-3*'s lines were "aesthetically appalling."

When he first asked to see the boat's plans, not long after he arrived, one of the Japanese designers handed him a few ring binders full of press releases—nothing more. Much later, when he finally saw the plans, he commented, "They're like something you'd expect to see in *Popular Mechanics*, at best the creation of a highly insensitive computer." The sheer, the line that describes the deck from stern to bow, has a classical shape on a well-designed yacht. It starts low in the stern, dips about a third of the way up the boat, then begins a long, gradual rise toward the bow along a curve that is always changing in radius; all that is constant are the bow and stern angles. *J-3*'s sheer started high at the stern, dipped well forward, flattened out, and then flicked up at the bow. Nothing was constant in *J-3*'s sheer except the flat section amidships. It looked, to the trained eye, a little like a banana.

Spanhake had trained his eye over many years of sailing in Auckland. He would talk about the look of one yacht designer or another the way someone might talk about a sculptor's *oeuvre*. Bruce Farr built "intelligent, highly strung, finicky boats." Farr stressed technology and function, and his yachts were angular; they reminded Spanhake of Bauhaus architecture. Laurie Davidson, another noted New Zealand designer, did "pretty boats." They were not as brittle as Farr's. They had "gorgeous sheers" and a characteristic curve in the knuckle of the bow. They sailed beautifully, though they tended to have "areas of sulkiness." It was a prejudice, Spanhake admitted, this business of lines. He had seen other craft that were unpleasing to the eye, and he had often understood the principles behind them once he sailed on them. But he found no redeeming features in *J-3* after he sailed it. There was no evidence of a designer's "empathy with water." There were only mysteries.

One day during the early autumn of 1990, Spanhake climbed down the sea wall at Gamagori and looked across to the pier where the Twelve-Meters were berthed. The second *Nippon*, designated *J-6*, had arrived in August, and the two A.C. boats were tied up alongside the Twelves. From the bottom of the wall, Spanhake could crouch to sea level and see straight across the four bows; then he walked down the wall and looked across the sterns.

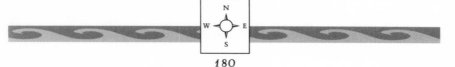

At quiet moments, he repeated the exercise many times over the next several weeks.

"It can't be," he'd say to himself whenever he climbed back up the wall.

Spanhake finally went into the sail loft, borrowed a set square and a set of French curves, and climbed down the sea wall again. Using the square, he determined the angle of entry at the bow, the degree at which the hull lifted from the water, on the Twelves and the new boats. With the French curve, he then found the radius of the bow's arc on each of the boats. Then he repeated the exercise on the sterns; as a last step, he measured the distance across the transoms to calculate the width of the stern as a proportion of each boat's maximum beam. It was a simple but effective way to draw a boat's extemities. With the French curves, his measurements were accurate down to half a degree.

"It can't be," Spanhake said again afterward. "It's too obvious, too stupid an answer."

Spanhake had made a discovery. Nomoto-*sensei*'s hull incorporated exact copies of the Twelve-Meter bow and stern. "Why not?" Spanhake laughed when he later tried to piece together the design team's logic. "They worked in Fremantle." The problem was, the Twelves were almost twice as heavy as the two identical *Nippon*s.

Spanhake mulled it for a while longer, still disbelieving the naïveté such a possibility implied. He finally mentioned it to Roy Dickson. The older man, prepared to believe anything at that point, hauled out his drafting equipment and headed down to the sea wall to see for himself. He took his own measurements and drafted his own set of lines.

Not long afterward, Spanhake was sitting in the office shed poring over the bow and stern lines Dickson had drawn when Ken Nomoto walked in. The *sensei* was no longer managing the sailing camp, but he visited from time to time. "What're you looking at?" he asked, peering over Spanhake's shoulder.

"I'm really intrigued," the Kiwi replied with as much innocence as he could muster. "Why is this bow profile the way it is?"

Nomoto mumbled inconclusively with the patience reserved for a child. It wasn't an answer at all.

"Yes," Spanhake politely persisted, "but this particular profile seems uncannily like the Twelves."

The comparison left Nomoto stunned. "Considering everything else in the design up to that point on the hull, it's not critical what form the bow takes," he responded after a pause. "This bow was obviously successful once before."

Shortly before the end of the year, *J-3* and *J-6* were heading in one evening at dusk after a rigorous day's testing. Off to one side of the dock, a man stood on the deck of a small yacht waving exuberantly at them. The realization came to Spanhake slowly: it was the doctor on another visit, and he had brought his own boat, *Haru-Ichiban II*, over from Osaka.

Spanhake looked inquisitively. Without really thinking about it, he allowed his eye to run over the flat freeboard, the peculiar rigging, the sculling oar, the odd angle of entry at the bow that made the craft look something like a Chinese junk. It was Spanhake's first sight of *Haru-Ichiban*, and he froze. "There are eight thousand keel boats registered in Auckland," he said to himself. "Never have I seen something so . . . crude, so . . . unfunctional." He called it, without being able to explain, "agricultural."

Then he turned to John Cutler, *J-6*'s navigator, who was standing aft next to him. It was a moment both remembered long afterward, like a moment of revelation. "Have a look, John," Spanhake said. "That's the man who designed our boats. That's where these things came from."

•   •   •

You can make as many judgments as you want according to your eye. But an America's Cup campaign imposes a greater discipline. Nobody can complete one without understanding the need for scientific objectivity. You have to know where you stand, even if—especially if—you're behind. Roy Dickson had been trying to reach that point as long as he had been in Gamagori. How does your crew rate against all the other crews? You've built a boat. How good is your boat?

With the arrival of *J-6*, Nippon Challenge became the first syndicate competing for the twenty-eighth America's Cup to put two identical craft in the water. The New Zealanders would do so eventually, as would the Italians. But their pairs came much later. In the fall of 1990, the *Nippon*s gave the Japanese the same advantage the Kiwis had enjoyed going into the Fremantle races.

They would accumulate five hundred hours of tests before leaving Gamagori, a six- or seven-day grind every week, during which one day flowed without distinction into the next. Mikawa Bay presented difficult conditions. It was roughly four miles by ten miles, but they couldn't sail more than three in any one direction before they had to turn around. "Up and down, up and down," Mike Spanhake recalled. "It was among the most boring episodes of my sailing career." Typhoons, which buffet the Japanese islands every autumn, would keep them off the water. Given how fragile the new boats seemed, they would start thinking about coming in if the winds reached eighteen knots; at twenty they would drop the sails and radio the tender for a tow.

On a poor day they would run eleven tests; an average day yielded fifteen and an exceptional one twenty. Some days they would come in with nothing. The winds were so shifty at times that they couldn't keep both boats sailing in the same conditions long enough to make a valid test. For all the effort, they got maybe five good days of tests a month.

What did they test? What did they learn?

In the months before *J-6* arrived, the task was to test *J-3* against the polar diagram produced by Ken Nomoto's VPP to see if the polar was accurate. They did this in a peculiar way. Normally a crew would sail at a certain angle for intervals measured in minutes, say five or ten, each period constituting a separate test. Then the technicians would average the data; over time, the variations would be leveled off and the boat's performance established.

In Gamagori, Yoshihiro Nagami, the wiry Yamaha man in charge of computers, used test intervals of only thirty seconds. If the

average boat speed hadn't changed by a parameter Nagami set, it was considered a good test point. That meant that if the boat was accelerating or slowing, or if the helmsman simply wasn't concentrating, it was a bad point and eliminated from the data. The method yielded a huge spread of results. Nagami then took a leap of faith any saint would envy: he took the top end of the results curve and said, "That's the way the boat performs."

"You use a ten-minute testing method and you'll find a reasonable average over time, a dot on the graph," John Cutler said. "Instead, we ended up with a performance curve for *J-3* that couldn't possibly be achieved."

After *J-6* arrived, the sailors began a test regime carefully mapped by Roy Dickson's technical committee. Mostly it covered the effects of stability and displacement, which were measured by shifting the center of gravity on one boat or the other, or by adding ballast below deck to alter one boat's weight. But they also tested appendages, sail concepts, and other dimensions of the overall design. They tried different rudders, and for a brief time they tried sailing one boat without the *sensei*'s forward canard.

"*J-3* ready for testing." It would be Chris Dickson through the radio when he thought he had the right heading.

"*J-6* ready," Spanhake would reply. Then from the tender: "Five, four, three, two, one. Testing."

Spanhake would stand behind Namba and coach him at the helm all the way through the tests. He sounded like this:

"Okay. Runner down 8.5." That referred to the tension maintained on the mast.

"Namba, try not to let the bow come down.

"More pressure coming in one boat length.

"Up three. Bow up three. Up some more. Up.

"(Ridiculous day for testing. Wind is ten degrees to the right already.)

"Pressure's coming. More pressure ahead about one hundred and fifty meters.

"Kawahara, don't overtrim.

"Going well now. Boat feels good. (Good as this dog can.)

"Another puff coming.

"*J-3*'s hooked into something, a left-hander, but it'll come back down.

"Okay. We're almost back down to the original heading.

"Bow down three. Bow down three. I know it's hard. Keep the bow down and the power on."

Then the tender: "Five, four, three, two, one, zero."

Tests lasted ten minutes during the two-boat period. But, over time, they were no more conclusive than they had been when *J-3* was alone in the water. The telemetry was up and running in a clumsy sort of way, but never for very long without giving out, and the instruments, in any case, were never properly calibrated. Instead of getting results immediately, or even at the end of a session, the crew got them only after the following day's sail. "You could completely forget what went on in a day's testing," Cutler complained, "because you had already been through another full day of it."

Nagami provided no radio feedback from the tender. He would simply hand out the previous day's results in sheets every afternoon. After a while the Kiwis started to find them odd. Every sailor or technician brings a set of expectations to a series of tests. Say a new keel is being tried. If it isn't consistently better than the previous shape, the data can be analyzed to find out why: the wind direction was slightly different; a halyard was looser, a sail trimmed too tightly. Adjustments are made, and the results then look the way they were expected to. It's a tricky procedure. Some syndicates guard against overjuggling the data by allowing only two or three people to know what's being tested on any given day.

Even through the blur of the daily regime, Nagami's sheets seemed off the mark. They always showed that *Nippon* was precisely the boat it was said to be. But they often listed sailing conditions that the afterguard didn't remember as having prevailed.

Late in the autumn, Spanhake arranged with John Cutler to run their own tests. They used a simple laser, a distance gun, that allowed them to sail the two boats exactly parallel, a hundred and thirty-three meters apart. Every thirty seconds, each man noted

wind speed, wind direction, boat speed, and heading. It was exhausting, but at the end of the day they had a mess of handwritten records that Spanhake could put against Nagami's sheets. The exercise brought him to a simple conclusion. "I wouldn't want to take it into a courtroom," he said, "but this was creative accounting. All the testing was doing was producing a result that seemed to have been determined beforehand."

They learned nothing during the months of testing in Gamagori. They proved nothing and they ended knowing little about the craft in which they would compete. The sailing camp was scheduled to close after November's Nippon Cup off Hayama, and the new base camp was to open in San Diego in January. The I.A.C.C. World Championships would then be five months away.

J-6 would sail in them without a single alteration to its hull or its appendages. It never measured up to its polar diagram, which was finally downgraded three times before the Worlds. But little else changed, least of all the mythology, the *tatemae* that held the Japanese boat was "hot," possibly the hottest thing in its class.

"How could *J-3* or *J-6* be the boats to win the America's Cup?" Chris Dickson asked. "No matter how good they are, they can't be. It doesn't work like that. You go on from your starting point."

That question was asked long after *J-6* had sailed against others in its class, however. Roy Dickson and the other Kiwis came to accept that the true story of *Nippon*'s design would never be discovered. They were troubled by the boats' performance. "But we were sailing alone, isolated from everyone else in the competition," Spanhake said. "That means something—that's how you hear things. Down in Gamagori, we weren't hearing anything except what Nomoto told us. We figured it was a new class, a new design. Maybe the rule produced boats like this.

"Besides," Spanhake concluded, "if you hear something long and often enough, you begin to believe it. And we did. Nomoto was a wonderfully charismatic man. He sold us the idea that the boat was perfect. That became the gospel. He had the ability to tell an honest lie and let it become a policy."

·   ·   ·

Once, in the autumn of 1990, Roy Dickson stood up in the briefing room at Gamagori and drew one of his pyramids on the blackboard for an assembled audience of managers, shore crew, and sailors. At one bottom angle he wrote GAIJIN, and at the other, JAPANESE. To one side he listed "sailing team," "shore crew," "physical training," and all the technical programs—sails, spars, appendages, and so on.

One by one Dickson listed the names of the exemplary performers in each category. Stepping back, his blue eyes wide with feigned surprise, Dickson said, "Look at this! They're all *gaijin!*"

Then he said, "Let's go through the activities where there's a Japanese on top." After a pause he drew a large zero on the board. It was almost as large as the triangle next to it.

"Maybe," Dickson concluded, "the answer is this." And he wiped the word JAPANESE off the board.

It was not among Roy Dickson's most brilliant hours.

You had to respect him; it was impossible not to, given all he had accomplished. But Roy-*san* was losing his grip. His management style had evolved into one that was an embarrassment to the other Kiwis. In the design meetings, he rode the technicians so hard they went into themselves. Mike Spanhake called it "the blank features mode." Dickson would hand out assignments—"Bang, bang, bang, bang," said Spanhake, who sat in on all the technical sessions—that were unreasonable given the time available. No one in the shore crew would ever say, "I'm behind." There was simply no performance. It was tempting to call Dickson's manner racist, but it was hardly something that began in Gamagori. Dickson had driven more than a few sailors off Kiwi campaigns, and one heard of the same thing happening in his engineering firm.

The mass address became another technique, whether the audience was comprised of board members or junior sailors.

"Do you really want to win?" Dickson would exhort.

"*Hai!*"

"I can't see it in you. I can't see the commitment."

"Yes. We want to win."

It was a conditioned response. After a while Dickson's meetings had no discernible impact. Except that they created a vicious circle. Roy would shout, more of the faces before him would freeze, and less got done. Sailors would ask the afterguard, "Are all New Zealanders like that?" The polarization of the sailing camp was nearly complete. To some sailors, Kiwi and Japanese, it began to look less like Nippon Challenge than a "Dickson Challenge." The phrase became familiar. Ken Nomoto, although he had been off sailing *Haru-ichiban II*, was in touch sufficiently to conclude, "The two Dicksons together were simply more than we could handle."

Not long after the blackboard display, when the sun was sinking earlier and the winds off Mikawa Bay were growing chill, *J-3* and *J-6* docked in after a day's testing and the crew trudged through the dusk to another daily debriefing. But what took place as soon as they sat down was well beyond the routine. Without much ceremony, and certainly with a lesson in mind, Roy Dickson stood up and fired five members of the campaign.

It was Roy Dickson's ultimate confrontation. To him, such a step was familiar if not routine. Cup campaigns have little room for dead weight; comings and goings are frequent, and when someone is shown the door he is told to walk through it immediately so that secrecy and morale are both protected. In Japan, the sense of community attaching to membership is any organization allows for no such wielding of the ax. There are any number of ways to get rid of people. They can be sent to subsidiaries given up for dead, or they can become *madogiwaseki*, window-sitters, who make an eight-hour art of perusing the daily newspapers. As Nippon Challenge had learned, the unwanted can also be sent to divisions outside the main lines of a profitmaking enterprise. Very rarely, however, is anyone dismissed in Japan, regardless of how egregious the transgression.

Dickson's move precipitated a furor. He had targeted a crane driver, two shore hands, a physical trainer, and a sailor—all with attitudes Dickson judged to be beyond retrieval. They all had to go instantly, straight from the meeting. The sailors were particularly

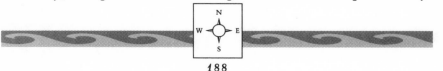

shaken. One of their number, out on the water only an hour earlier, was sacked without warning. His name was Shigeru Fujii, a late-comer to the campaign. To worsen matters, Fujii returned the following day to demand, at the morning session, an explanation of his fate.

Yamasaki and Hideto Eguchi had rushed to Gamagori by then and found that the sailing camp was threatening to fall apart completely.

"This is the way things happen in international sailing, but why did it happen here?" Yoshia, the husky grinder, asked. "No one's been told. We're all saying, 'Maybe we're next.'"

Kazutoshi Isobe, the shore boss, stormed out of the briefing room shouting, "I quit!" as he went. Takashi Kawahara, the pig farmer turned trimmer, stood up and railed. His was a familiar story by then.

"Everyone says this is a turning point in Nippon Challenge," Kawahara remarked afterward. "It isn't. That happened before. When I first joined, people were talking about challenging the Cup. Then the whole direction changed. People talked about winning. *That* was the turning point. This is the result."

After Roy Dickson departed at the meeting's end, others took place in Japanese. Robert Fry, fluent in the language and possessing, like Kaoru Ogimi, two pairs of eyes, criticized what Dickson had done but defended his presence as a necessity in the campaign. "We may not like the way he does things," Fry said, "but he's taught us a lot and he can teach us more." Namba stated more or less the same case. Only Nagami, the shy computer man from Yamaha, stood against the Kiwi and his regime.

Roy Dickson would stay. But not for long.

A few weeks later, at the urging of Ken Nomoto, Yamasaki dispatched Dickson to San Diego to prepare a new base camp near Point Loma for the crew's arrival. He was hardly sitting by the window, but he could stay on, the *kaicho* let it be known, only as a consultant once Nippon Challenge shifted to the United States. Nomoto had delivered that news. The *sensei* then went back to Gamagori to run the camp in its final days.

Years earlier Nomoto had quietly counseled against the hiring of *gaijin*, any *gaijin*, full time. Now he would begin to clean up the mess.

. . .

Settling in San Diego was no easy task. The Japanese had selected a tract of shorefront in a district called Mission Bay. The French and British were to arrive in the neighborhood eventually, but Nippon Challenge was the first syndicate to get there. Mission Bay was owned by the city, which tended to complicate matters. The simplest job— say, putting the sponsors' signboard out front—required enough permits to make you think you were setting up in overregulated Japan; they came to thirty before it was all over. There were construction contracts to negotiate, cargo containers to fit out as offices, supplies to buy in, and apartments to find—several dozen of them—for managers, sailors, and shore crew. By January, with Gamagori closed and the sailing team due soon in San Diego, Nomoto joined Roy Dickson to help out.

Later that month Tatsu Yamasaki arrived for the official opening. He threw two lavish parties in one of the penthouses at the Hyatt Islandia, a hotel located along the bay a few minutes' drive from the camp. Those occasions were milestones for the Japanese campaign and a personal triumph for the *kaicho*. Eight hundred people were invited to one—city officials, yachting heavyweights, reporters—and Yamasaki addressed them in English. He swelled with pride. The campaign was four years old, and so were his language lessons.

By March, however, the festive atmosphere was giving way to worries. Roy Dickson, having declined to stay on as a consultant, would depart completely. Chris would still skipper—he had gone dead quiet in Gamagori after Roy left—and the Kiwi afterguard was still in place. But in some important respect, Yamasaki felt, he was sailing single-handed.

He had never been able to make up his mind about the direction Nippon Challenge should take. He had never really learned to shape events. How the Japanese would arrive at the Worlds, just what their goal would be, had become a game of roulette: whatever situation

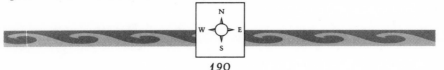

obtained at the time would be it. Now the little ball had stopped
rolling. Yamasaki had tried things Dickson's way, but Roy-*san* had
led them down a road that seemed too hard to travel. Now he was
gone, and the *sensei*, the firmest believer in the Japanese way, was
running the whole campaign.

Familiar problems appeared in a different light. The budget was
getting out of control. Okay, manageable somehow. But the *kaicho*
also had to decide whether to build a third boat. Over and over,
Roy had insisted on it—he had even talked of a fourth—and
Yamasaki didn't know what to do. The doctor, the man in charge
under him, still insisted there was no need for another hull, not even
a third.

Early in April, Yamasaki took his wife, Ayako, and a few friends
to dinner at a restaurant called Tong Fu in the Roppongi district of
Tokyo. It was an elegant establishment, serving Chinese food in a
style best described as "East meets West." Yamasaki owned Tong
Fu, and he was under pressure to redevelop it. The *kaicho* and his
guests dined privately upstairs, in a room Yamasaki had fashioned
"the Cup Room." There were brass lamps, polished paneling, and
wooden models of yachts from *America* onward. "If I sold the land
under this place I could pay for all ten challenger campaigns,"
Yamasaki joked early on.

Money was on Yamasaki's mind. He began to complain about the
syndicate's deficit. The previous evening, out drinking with a few S
& B executives, he had faced the reality that Nippon Challenge
would overrun even its expanded budget. "The spending is endless.
Chris Dickson wants a new boom—it'll save one second on the
course. We need a new keel, they say. Now we're considering a new
boat—one million six hundred thousand dollars just for the hull.
Our goal has been to win the America's Cup, so I can't say no. But
it's a depressing thought."

Midway through dinner, as several bottles of champagne arrived,
Yamasaki changed his tone. "Today I see things in a different light,"
he said. "I realize I was making a mistake. Our goal isn't the
America's Cup but something much bigger—for instance, bringing
Japanese people closer to the ocean. If you think that way, the Cup

is only a stage to a greater goal. It's as if we were climbing Mount Fuji. In the middle of the mountain forest, you realize you only have two thousand yen left in your pocket. But so what? You want to reach the top."

Ayako cut in. "Do you mean getting the Cup isn't the top of the mountain?" she asked. "If you keep thinking it is, you'll be irritated and frustrated. You want to go beyond that."

"Right." Tatsu smiled. "And as we share this experience, people in other companies might be able to generate some new business. I've already discussed it with Tsuchiya-*san* at Sanyo and Tokumasu-*san* at Sumitomo. We shouldn't stay preoccupied with the America's Cup. The Cup is a piece of property, a possession, but that's all."

Roy Dickson had always asked, "Do you want to win?" Less often he posed the other half of the question: "Or do you simply want to be there?"

Tatsu Yamasaki seemed to have made his choice at last.

•   •   •

JAL Flight 062 from Tokyo to Los Angeles was less than half full on the afternoon of April 29, 1991. Kaoru Ogimi, wearing a white windbreaker over a shirt and tie and carrying a small two-suiter, settled into a business-class seat half an hour before the four o'clock takeoff and began to read. He was just back from Osaka, where he'd juried another race from Melbourne, and he was en route to San Diego to watch the I.A.C.C. Worlds.

Once aloft, Ogimi ordered a drink and then spotted a *gaijin* friend a few seats ahead of him on the other side of the cabin. After a while he made his way over and began to talk. Both men had followed Nippon Challenge closely.

"Ready for a race?" Ogimi's friend asked.

"I'm lukewarm," Ogimi said. "With a little luck we might just pull it out, but we'll need it."

"You see problems in San Diego?" the friend inquired.

"I saw problems a long time before San Diego," Ogimi snorted. Then he paused.

"You know, the first time I met Ken Nomoto he told me the story

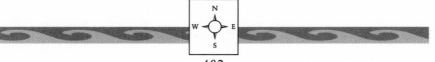

of the admiral during the war," Ogimi continued. 'I think of myself as Admiral Yuzurazu,' Nomoto told me, 'because I'll never give in.' I saw it all coming then."

"Saw what coming?" the *gaijin* asked innocently.

"He's running the bloody place like a Japanese corporation. Everyone's worried about budgets, every department padded out with managers and flimsy timetables in typical Japanese style. Maybe you can run a company that way, or a navy, but you can't win a yacht race."

PART III

REACHING

HONNE

Tatsu Yamasaki, hands tucked into the pockets of his red and white sailing jacket, sat silently facing the stern as *Tariam II* made its way through the swells off Point Loma. There were seven people on board, and everyone else was looking forward. Kaoru Ogimi, legs wide apart, stood aft surveying the horizon through a large pair of field glasses. Shoji Kabaya, from the Yamaha technical staff, was in the port-side seat opposite the pilot, a soft-spoken local named Bill Goodwin. In the stern, long hair blown back from his forehead, was Ichiro Yokoyama, also from the design side. In the companionway, braced against the seats, stood Bruce Peachey, a representative of the San Diego race committee.

Peachey knew the waters around San Diego, had sailed them for years before giving up the sport, and loved to gab about the sea. Peachey, silver-haired and bespectacled, was naturally friendly. When the syndicate executives boarded at Mission Bay Marina that morning he greeted them saying, "This is Bill, and I'm Bruce. He's the quiet one, I'm the bullshitter."

It was a little after eleven on May 1, a cloudless morning with a light breeze in from the southwest. Nine of the fifteen America's Cup boats so far commissioned were about to compete for the first time since the class was created. There was a series of fleet races, followed by semi-final and final match races. That day's contests, and the next day's, were called Pre-Worlds. They were tuning exercises, essentially, in advance of the I.A.C.C. World Championships.

The Italian syndicate was sailing the first I.A.C.C. boat ever conceived, ITA 1, as well as the most recently developed. ITA 15, in fact, was virtually brand new. Bill Koch's syndicate, America³, also had two sloops out, with sails bearing the insignia USA 2 and USA 9. Other entries were from New Zealand (NZL 12), and Japan (JPN 6), France (FRA 8), Spain (ESP 10), and Team Dennis Conner (USA 11). Conner would eventually fight it out with "America Cubed," as Koch's group was called, for the right to defend the Cup.

Among the syndicates and around the San Diego clubs and marinas, the Italians were considered important to watch. They had been on the water longer than anyone else, and they were the first to set up a compound in San Diego to start learning the local waters. Everyone knew the old jokes about the Italians. (How can you tell when the Italians are about to tack? When they throw their cigarettes over the side.) But you didn't hear them this time. Raul Gardini's campaign looked exemplary. The syndicate was already on its third hull. Gardini, the financier bankrolling the syndicate, was said to be spending as much as a hundred million dollars—far more than the Japanese, whose campaign had already gained a reputation for extravagant outlays.

Every syndicate had been living in its own Gamagori. It had all been lab work until then—shots in the dark, theoretical views. May 1 to May 11 offered each its first chance to measure in open competition the path it had chosen—the success of its technology and designs, basic hull concepts, telemetry and sail programs, performance analysis, and a hundred other dimensions of the effort each had made. All the monitors and computer-linked sensors with

which the I.A.C.C. boats were loaded would be switched on all week.
There were other boats on the water this time, and that would make
all the difference.

The Worlds would be tough races to read. The title would be a
decided boost in terms of morale and standing for whoever won it;
nobody could honestly say it was meaningless. But for most syndicates the Worlds were less an event in their own right than a prelude.
There were syndicates like the Spanish, first-timers with much to
learn, that would probably put everything they had into the Worlds.
Others probably wouldn't. The question was: to what extent should
a syndicate reveal its progress? There would be no way to know how
much of what any campaign had to sail with would be out on the
water and how much had been kept in reserve. How much, indeed,
would be sheer fakery?

Dennis Conner's boat—he only had one—was three weeks in the
water. Conner was pleading poverty—limited financial resources,
an underdeveloped boat campaign, a poor sail inventory—and an
aging crew. Who knew if it was true or not? At the launching
ceremony in early April the skirts intended to conceal the hull ran
all the way up to the bow. "This is either the best piece of disinfor-
mation yet in this campaign, or that sucker has wings and a geek,"
a local yachting hack wrote afterward, referring to the keel and the
possibility that Conner had fixed a forward rudder under his bow.
Conner and his navy-blue hull would be followed intently over the
ten days of the Worlds.

Every boat there would also be measuring itself against San Diego
conditions, which were by all accounts a nightmare for designers
and skippers. Peachey was already telling the Japanese aboard
Tariam about the kelp. It grew a yard a day, often breaking loose
and surfacing in clumps the length of small cypress trees. Get weed
on your appendages and you were probably out of that day's race.
The swells were generally heavy and the winds light, meaning a lot
of hull resistance but not a lot of power to overcome it. Nor was the
wind especially reliable. It usually didn't settle in before one-thirty
or so in the afternoon. With twelve-thirty start times, that awarded
luck—a factor in any race—an undue say in the outcome.

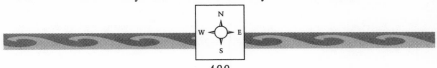

Everyone aboard *Tariam* became more animated as the cruiser neared the racing yachts and the knot of spectator craft. Spread across the horizon, the new A.C. boats looked larger, more delicate, and more imposing than ever. The masts towered. In the sunlight one could recognize the familiar beige of Kevlar sails cambered against the sky. Below them, the hulls seemed like wafers skimming through the chop. No matter how many times one had seen *J-3* and *J-6* on Mikawa Bay, it was no match for that first sight of a Cup-class fleet. They were like kinetic sculptures—monuments to technology, skill, power, money, water, and wind.

"There's Italy 15 far out to starboard. Those are the Kiwis closer in, with the Spanish next to them—no, that's the other Italian boat. Dennis is off to port. . . ."

It was Ogimi calling out syndicates and skippers without taking his binoculars from his eyes. He was not especially looking for JPN 6, the red letters stitched across *Nippon*'s main. But the Japanese yacht would have been just as recognizable as the others because of the unusual cut of its sails. Unlike the triangular shapes flown by most boats, the mainsails on the new A.C. craft were designed to shift area to the top of the mast, where designers expected more wind. That meant altering certain lines. The E of the main, the distance at its base from the mast to the end of the boom, was shortened, and the aft edge of the sail was given lots of roach, or curve. The mains, therefore, looked more like rectangles with rounded corners. The other line that could be altered was the J of the genoa, from the bow of the boat to the mast. *Nippon* went into the Worlds with a lot of sail area pushed upward on the main and a relatively short J.

At twelve twenty-five the committee boat fired the five-minute gun. Ogimi and Kabaya, the Yamaha technician, checked their watches and started their own countdowns. The winds were light—six knots or so—and, at two hundred and forty degrees, from an unusual direction. All nine boats were early up to the starting line, and there was little of the aggressive circling that precedes hard-fought match races. Already it seemed that the new A.C. boats didn't handle at close quarters with the agility of Twelves. From *Tariam II*, behind the committee boat to the right of the line, it looked as if each skipper was engrossed in managing his own craft before the first ever I.A.C.C. race.

It was a split start, and a clean one. *Ville de Paris*, the French entry, was across first, followed by *Nippon*. *Stars & Stripes* was third. But it wasn't an especially fine beginning for Chris Dickson. In a fleet race, a confident skipper will generally steer a conservative course; only if he wants to push his luck will he advance toward the side in search of superior wind. "You'll know if we're fast or not," John Cutler had said the previous evening. "If we are, we'll head right up the middle. If not, we'll be out to the corners as soon as we can." Dickson and Marc Pajot, the French skipper, went immediately on port tack toward the edge of the course; Conner was alone in the center all the way up the first beat.

Dennis Conner's local knowledge, his greatest advantage against everyone else on the water, would prove useful on other days. But Pajot and Dickson lucked out. A wind shift to the right on an upwind leg enables boats on that side of the course to sail closer to the top mark. The French and Japanese tacked over just in time to find both stronger breezes and a fifteen-degree shift. Dickson lifted *Nippon* well. At the first mark, *Ville de Paris* led *Nippon* by ten seconds, and *Stars & Stripes* was two and a half minutes behind; the rest of the field had gone left and was spread across almost eight minutes of sailing.

The course, ten nautical miles, was a sausage—two upwind legs and two downwind. The first race, a yachting hack's worst dream, was virtually decided in those first few moments after the start. Dickson paced Pajot over the entire course, finishing thirty-three seconds behind, while Conner lagged the leader by just under two minutes. All the others simply never found the wind.

Fragility and overdesign were constant worries in San Diego prior to the races, but the casualties were few in the first contest—a blown spinnaker on *Stars & Stripes*, a cracked spinnaker pole on the Spanish boat. The second race of the day was another matter. The breeze was thirteen to fourteen knots, and it quickly picked up to fifteen. The Spaniards snapped their boom even before the 2:40

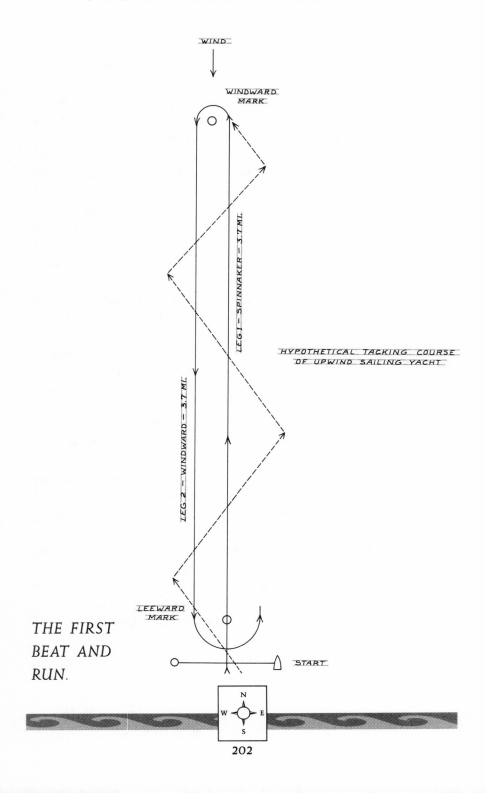

WIND

WINDWARD
MARK

LEG 1 — SPINNAKER — 3.7 MI.

HYPOTHETICAL TACKING COURSE
OF UPWIND SAILING YACHT

LEG 2 — WINDWARD — 3.7 MI.

LEEWARD
MARK

START

*THE FIRST
BEAT AND
RUN.*

N
W E
S

P.M. start. Moments later the newer of Bill Koch's boats, *Jayhawk*, found a crack in its boom and followed the Spanish in. The French lasted less than one leg—a block holding the mainsheet to the boom broke, pulling up a strip of the deck.

The rest of the field was again hugely divided, but there was some good sailing in front. *Stars & Stripes* and the newer *Il Moro de Venezia*, ITA 15, got into a tacking duel while *Nippon* followed closely behind. By the first downwind leg, it was a three-way fight. The Italians held their lead, but Dickson sailed inside Conner just before the downwind mark. Upwind again, Dickson scrapped with ITA 15 in close, swift sailing. As the final downwind run began, it looked from a distance as though *Nippon* had taken first—its spinnaker was first up around the mark—but *Il Moro* kept its lead. At the finish, the Italians were across eight seconds before Dickson. *Nippon* came in almost a minute before *Stars & Stripes*, to take two respectable seconds for the day.

Aboard *Tariam*, Tatsu Yamasaki had been passive most of the afternoon. For a long time he sat below, reviewing papers and eating a *bento* box lunch from the refrigerator. At other moments, he looked as though he had gone to sleep in the stern.

The craft headed in immediately after the second finish. Everyone agreed it had been the perfect outing to test performance under varied conditions. Ogimi, who had been chatting with the *kaicho* as Bill Goodwin turned *Tariam*'s engines up, moved to the companionway and began trading observations with Bruce Peachey. "Dennis looked awfully good," remarked Peachey, who was something of a hometown fan.

In the stern one of the others squeezed one of Yamasaki's deck shoes to get his attention and asked, "What did you think?"

Yamasaki answered slowly. "*Nippon* did well. Light wind in the first race and a harder wind in the second. It looks like we've got a versatile boat." It was his first real judgment on a four-year campaign.

"You must be pleased," someone suggested.

"It's good news for us," Yamasaki said after a pause. "I'm happy."

He didn't look it.

• • •

That evening Kaoru Ogimi attended an open house at the Spanish base camp. Desafio España Copa America, the Spanish Challenge for the America's Cup, sat side by side with the Kiwi campaign on the edge of a pleasant peninsula called Coronado that juts into San Diego Harbor. It was a festive spring evening. There were pitchers of sangria and huge *paelleras* filled with rice, chicken, and seafood. Inside a large tent were tables, flamenco guitarists, and a wooden dance floor, on which crew members took turns with wives, girlfriends, syndicate secretaries, and strangers.

You would never have known it, but the Spaniards had a rough beginning in San Diego. A few months earlier the bulb on *España*'s keel broke off and fell to the bottom during a practice session. The syndicate went into the Worlds with Spanish rigging and sails on a hull borrowed from New Zealand. After only one race, the Spaniards were out a spinnaker pole, which they replaced by borrowing one from the Italians, and a boom, which they wanted to replace by borrowing a spare from Nippon Challenge.

Ogimi was brokering the arrangement with Gerardo Seeliger, the Spanish campaign's director. It was the kind of gesture familiar to anyone who had spent time on the international yachting scene, but Ken Nomoto had stepped in at the last minute with a dozen questions about the transaction. Ogimi, while he waited for Seeliger to finish a long telephone conversation with the *sensei*, moved intently through the crowd, greeting what seemed like half the people there as acquaintances from past regattas.

"For us, there was good news and bad out there today," Ogimi told a friend. "The boat seemed to handle well. But there's further to go. We lost speed in light winds—I noticed that—and we'll have to look further into why."

Ogimi paused until he was sure he had his friend's attention. "But there's more to it than that. It's one thing to go into these races. They're very preliminary. We're all learning from here on out. The question is what you do with the information you get."

Ogimi was confident in *Nippon* after the first day. Before the races, it hadn't been clear whether Dickson would sail to win in San Diego, and Ogimi didn't particularly want him to. For one thing, he still thought Nippon Challenge had enough boat that it shouldn't show competitors all of it. For another, a victory could be enough for the syndicate's board to vote down a third hull. That, at least, had been Ogimi's thinking. Now he felt differently.

"Today's results were bad news for Tatsu from that point of view. If we had been dead last he could've said, 'Okay, we'll compete with what we've got. We have no real chance.' But Dickson sailed beautifully, and the crew work looked good. That means we're going to have to keep competing. Tatsu's going to have to ask for a third boat."

At that moment Seeliger came through the crowd from his office, smiling broadly and holding his hand outstretched. Nomoto had finally agreed to lend the Spaniards a boom, and *España* would be out on the water again the next day.

"Kaoru, I cannot thank you enough," Seeliger said, taking Ogimi's hand.

"*De nada. Con mucho gusto,*" Ogimi replied in the fluent Spanish he kept from his childhood.

Seeliger had organized half a dozen crew members to pick up the spar at Mission Bay, and they stood around him at the outer gate as he chatted briefly with Ogimi under the glare of a security lamp. It was a crisp San Diego evening, typical of the season. Ogimi ended the conversation by wishing Seeliger luck, and both men made for their cars. Then Ogimi turned suddenly and called back, "And don't take any shit from the doctor."

• • •

In a few more days, when *Nippon*'s mast and mainsail were hanging from a buoy halfway to the ocean floor, they would begin to reexamine everything. But there was time left yet for the Japanese to continue believing in what they had all invested so much in.

The course on the second day was a slightly shortened version of what would be sailed for the America's Cup. It was 21.2 miles over

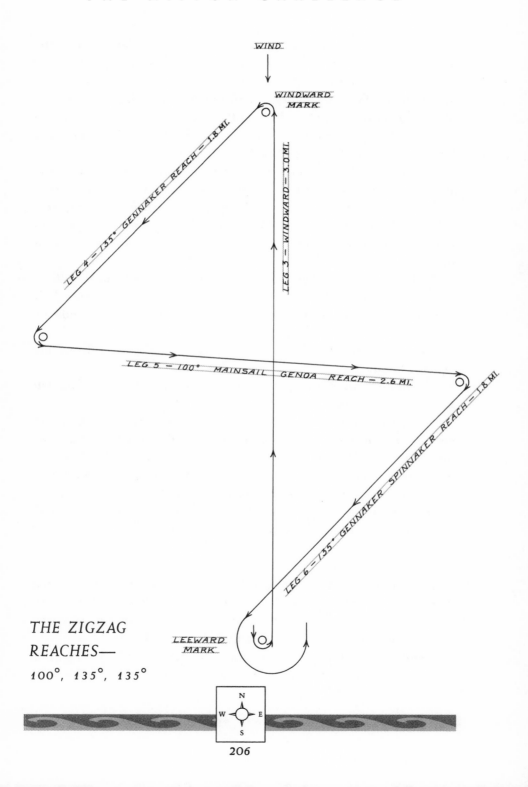

WIND

WINDWARD
MARK

LEG 4 — 135° GENNAKER REACH — 1.8 MI.

LEG 3 — WINDWARD — 3.0 MI.

LEG 5 — 100° MAINSAIL GENOA REACH — 2.6 MI.

LEG 6 — 135° GENNAKER SPINNAKER REACH — 1.8 MI.

LEEWARD
MARK

THE ZIGZAG
REACHES—
100°, 135°, 135°

N
W E
S

eight legs—an upwind beat, three zigzag reaches across the wind, then a series of beats and downwind runs. The breeze was moderate, eight knots, and the circling before the gun was more aggressive than it had been the previous day; the skippers seemed to be getting used to fleet racing in the new class. But it wasn't much of a contest. *New Zealand* and ITA 15 broke out in front almost immediately, and by the first mark the leading positions were set and wouldn't change. New Zealand's apple-red boat was forty-five seconds ahead of *Il Moro* at the finish.

Nippon made more news than either of them: during an upwind beat it rolled over a swell to reveal its forward appendage. The Japanese, along with one of the America³ boats, had gone over the line early and never fully recovered from the penalty. Dickson, after starting again, sailed well but ended third—almost eight minutes behind the leader. It was enough, though, to secure the Japanese first place in the Pre-Worlds.

It hardly mattered, even at Mission Bay. They had sailed well— on some legs better than they had ever sailed *J-6*. But the Kiwis were mumbling that the crew's performance had only masked design deficiencies that could no longer be denied. *Nippon* was pitching too much; it accelerated slowly out of a tack or jibe; it went soft in anything less than ten to twelve knots.

Ken Nomoto saw none of that. He hadn't even bothered to watch the initial races, concerning himself, instead, with a few minor onshore problems. "The first two days were excellent," he smiled after *J-6* came in the second day. "Our basic design principle has been verified."

At the camp on Saturday, May 4, the *sensei* was amused by the various theories in the morning's sports pages about the canard at *Nippon*'s bow. Was it a kelp cutter, the papers wondered, or a forward rudder? Or something only those ingenious Japanese could think of?

"Now the world knows you've got a forward appendage," someone chided the doctor.

Nomoto laughed confidently. "Yes," he replied. "A kelp cutter. That's a very interesting theory."

•   •   •

At Yamasaki's insistence, Nomoto boarded *Tariam* to watch the first
race of the Worlds. He wore his habitual corduroys, sweater, and
woolen cap, and it turned out that he needed them. The winds that
morning were unusually strong. Most designers had worked with
breezes of eight to fourteen knots in mind. Sailors considered it an
unwritten rule that races in the new class would be called at the
start in anything above fifteen knots. Wind speed was twelve as the
yachts approached the line, and the race went forward.

The start was close but clean. Conner reached the upwind mark
in twenty-three and a half minutes, forty seconds in front of *Il Moro*.
Then came a procession from the leeward side of the course: *España*
was third, *Nippon* fourth by seven seconds, then ITA 1, *Jayhawk*,
Ville de Paris, the Kiwis, and USA 2. Dickson was in the middle, but
in the first reach he sailed so hard that John Cutler thought they
were losing control of the boat. They advanced to third over the
reaches, and the tension on board seemed to mount along with the
wind speed.

"Sail call!" Dickson cried as they prepared to enter the third and
final reach. The wind was approaching twenty knots. "What's the
sail call?"

No one on board stood with him after the dispute that ensued.
They were sailing with a brand-new mast, the first carbon fiber spar
the Japanese had ever built, and there had been barely enough time
to mount it before the Worlds began. It was well crafted, but it was
underweight by eighty pounds. Erle Williams, who had been in
charge of the boat since Roy Dickson gave him the assignment in
Gamagori, had seen too much bend in it even in lighter winds. Like
everyone else expected to advise during a race, he wanted a small
sail in front in those winds. As Dickson called for the biggest
gennaker on board, Williams got personal.

"You're mad!" he shouted back at Dickson from amidships.
"You're fucking mad."

It was Kiyotaka Okabe, a tall mastman, at thirty-seven one of the
oldest members of the crew, who went overboard when the number

three gennaker snapped its halyard. There was sailcloth streaming down the leeward side of the boat, Okabe clinging to a line on the other, and havoc on board. Had Okabe held on another minute, they could have hauled him aboard and kept sailing. But he hit a wave and lost his grip, and Dickson had to circle twice to pick him up.

After that the nearest boat was *Ville de Paris*, which was a full minute in front. The other skippers nursed their boats through the next leg, but Dickson tacked and tacked again, chasing every wind shift he saw. He made up some distance, but it was over for *Nippon* after the turn, violent and sudden, around the fifth mark.

Five legs, eighty-three minutes of sailing. Jin, up in the bow for the sail change, heard the mast's sharp crack, and Mike Spanhake the sound of a winch under intense strain. Cutler heard nothing at all. He was working the backstay and was turned toward the stern watching the gauge that measured forestay tension. When you ease a stay, the line gives in sudden jolts around the winch, creating a loud, hollow pop that resonates all over the boat. "Bong . . . bong . . . bong," Cutler heard. And then nothing. Suddenly there was no sound. There was no load left on the stay, and the line went limp in his hand.

Tariam lingered an hour and a half near the buoy Robert Fry had attached to the mast before letting it slip under. The race marks were taken up, *Nippon* was towed, and the cruiser bobbed alone in the swells near the submerged spar. Finally, a rubber dinghy with two powerful outboards arrived from Mission Bay.

"*Kaicho*," Nomoto asked humbly, "shall I stay out here?"

It seemed a peculiar question at the time. Yamasaki, a little impatient with the doctor's insistence on ceremony at such a moment, nodded silently, and Nomoto boarded the dinghy. *Tariam* turned and headed in at full throttle. It was late, nearing dusk, and cold. Apart from Kaoru Ogimi, who had offered a running commentary all day, scarcely anyone else on board spoke. Ogimi had a keen enough eye to know that Dickson had been oversailing, but he saw a lesson in the disaster apart from that.

"It just shows you how unbalanced our program is," Ogimi said.

"We put everything we had into hull design and tank testing, and we neglect the rest of our program."

Cayard eventually took the race and at the press briefing afterward he was beaming. "Obviously this was a great day," he said. "It's a just reward for the time we spent learning to sail these boats."

Everyone else in the room was dazed. There had been roughly three-quarters of a million dollars' worth of damage in a single afternoon. "I think the guys who made the rule and designed these boats are idiots," Bill Koch barked. "These are incredibly dangerous boats and rather foolish. They're a dream for designers and builders and a nightmare for owners and crews."

Koch, who had taken *Jayhawk* out of the race when a jib track ripped away from the deck, had more. "These designs are for what we took to be San Diego's prevailing wind strength, and when you get five knots above that you're in trouble. Some boats aren't insured above fifteen knots. One of my designers said he wouldn't sail one in winds above eighteen."

There was electricity in the room when Chris Dickson cut in with a comment aimed straight back at Koch, the wealthy fifty-year-old with baby-pink cheeks and only a decade's experience on the water. "These boats are at the edge, and the carbon fiber masts are up front on the learning curve," the Kiwi said pointedly. "I feel comfortable driving a car, but I wouldn't feel comfortable driving a Formula 1 racer. These boats are a challenge to the world's top sailors. They're exactly what the America's Cup is all about. But they're not boats the average sailor would feel happy in, not a boat he could step into and do a good job."

Later on, away from the lights and cameras, Dickson explained the day's events in terms he figured would be more familiar to his employers. May 4 is Butsu Metsu Day in Japan, he observed, the only day of the year that Buddha is not on duty.

•   •   •

The shore team stayed up most of the night getting another mast stepped and rerigging *Nippon* to carry it. Nomoto had an hour and a half's sleep. A little after dawn he took the rubber dinghy back

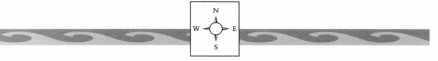

out to the buoy holding the broken mast and the main, but he was unable to bring the whole mess back to shore until later the following evening.

Balance is everything on racing yachts, and *Nippon*'s was destroyed. The replacement spar was of Kiwi manufacture and, like the rest of the gear bought from New Zealand, it weighed too much. It wasn't one generation back in the development program but two. It was roughly five hundred pounds heavier than the piece for which the boat had been tuned.

The implications were several. To compensate for the added weight, the same amount in ballast had to be removed from the bottom of the boat. The weight shift, a total of a thousand pounds, moved *Nippon*'s center of gravity dramatically upward. "You might imagine having two fully grown gorillas clinging to the top of the mast," Kaoru Ogimi said as he watched the afterguard retune the boat from a bluff overlooking the dock. "That's about what we've got."

The gorillas would reduce *Nippon*'s stability, and light winds and large swells would only exaggerate the disadvantage. Its heeling and pitching moments, both of which should be cut to the minimum in San Diego's peculiar waters, would increase substantially. Now *J-6* would hobbyhorse all over the course. The ultimate price would be paid in speed and acceleration.

Nippon sailed badly from then onward. It was dead last for the first four legs of the May 5 race, then struggled to overtake USA 2, the slowest boat on the course. It finished second from the rear, eight minutes and four seconds behind *New Zealand*, which held the lead from the second mark until the end. From any spectator craft astride the upwind leg you could see *J-6* pitch to roughly twice the extent of any boat sailing close to it. Once during the races that followed, Roy Dickson made a study for his son, the kind of analysis no one else in the campaign was providing. He took the downwind legs of one race and analyzed them to determine *Nippon*'s relative boat speed. When all four runs were considered together, the Japanese were exactly in the middle—there were four boats ahead

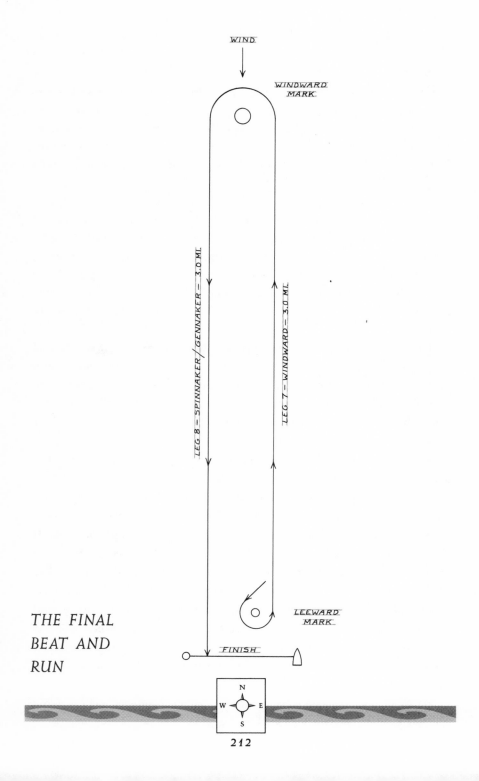

WIND

WINDWARD MARK

LEG 8 – SPINNAKER/GENNAKER – 3.0 MI.

LEG 7 – WINDWARD – 3.0 MI.

LEEWARD MARK

FINISH

THE FINAL BEAT AND RUN

N
W · E
S

and four behind. Isolating the last two runs, when the winds were lighter, there was only one boat slower.

Roy Dickson was more or less *persona non grata* by the time the Worlds began. Dressed as always in shorts, a T-shirt and a worn pair of Top-Siders, he spent his mornings around the camp. But he had to make his own arrangements if he wanted to see the races. Every day he and Marilyn would pack lunches aboard *Plum Swinger*, an elegant cabin cruiser borrowed from a friend, and find a spot in the spectator fleet. Dickson's eye was extraordinary. He could identify a boat by the cut of its sail when the hull and half the mast were lost beneath the horizon. In a calm voice, he kept up a running conversation with his son.

"Almost time to tack, Chris," Dickson would say. Or, "You're going to run a gennaker up and the wind's too strong for it."

Miles away, *Nippon*'s skipper performed as if *Plum Swinger* carried a remote control device. But, no matter how well or badly Chris Dickson did, San Diego was lousy sailing, the older man thought. It wasn't real racing. "After the first beat, the party's over," he remarked. "It's a procession around the course. What kind of racing is that?"

The Worlds made bitter days for Roy Dickson. Almost everything he saw proved that he had been right all along about the Japanese syndicate. To him the boat was a washout, and it had come to threaten the entire campaign.

"Just look at the motion of the thing," the older Dickson exclaimed one afternoon out on the water. "The conclusion is obvious, unless I'm missing something. We need more than a new boat. We need a new design. We've got a lot of wasted time behind us and a critical few months ahead. Unless we see some very big changes, I think we've got a loser."

•   •   •

Mike Spanhake had been worried about racing off Point Loma ever since he arrived and saw the sea. Then all the misgivings had proven to be well founded. One evening in his apartment on a hill behind Mission Bay, Spanhake started talking about a time in August 1990, when he went back to New Zealand to tidy up some family matters. *J-3* had been in the water five months, and its replica was about to be launched. They were sailing daily in the calm, surgeless sea that had first attracted Arthur Wullschleger to Mikawa Bay. No apparent problem with that. The syndicate had dispatched a meteorologist to San Diego, and he was sending back data gathered from the buoys he had dropped along the coast: winds eleven to fourteen knots; smooth water; no appreciable tidal effect.

In Auckland, Spanhake reconnected with some old sailing friends, among whom were a few who had sailed in San Diego for Sir Michael Fay against the Dennis Conner catamaran in 1988. The information popped out rather naturally, Spanhake recalled: "Of course, you're going to be sailing that Japanese boat in some fairly rough water," one of his Kiwi mates told him.

Spanhake was stunned. "Our boat seemed designed with no consideration given to anything but mirror-surface conditions," he said.

Then came the letters. Spanhake was among the more technically adept of the Kiwis in Gamagori, and he had been corresponding regularly with sailmakers, instrument makers, and hardware man- ufacturers about gear *Nippon* would need. Each one had roughly the same pitch: "This piece will be especially useful in the turbulent waters off San Diego," the salesmen would write. Spanhake had reacted swiftly. He recommended putting the entire design team on a plane to San Diego, where they could hire a cruiser and see the conditions for themselves. Nothing ever came of the idea. Now they were sailing in heavier seas and lighter winds than the boat was built for.

Three weeks before the Worlds, and for no reason ever explained, the technical team decided to add two tons of ballast to *J-6*'s bottom. Displacement went from twenty-two tons to twenty-four, and the craft sailed two inches lower in the water. A last-minute response to San Diego conditions? An effort to get the overhangs wet? No one at the base camp knew. The sail loft was thrown into a frenzy: the extra weight allowed *J-6* greater sail area, and the loft had to produce sixteen sails in twenty-one days before the first race on May 1.

They had stumbled into the Worlds like amateurs. The shock of the dismasting, and *Nippon*'s failure to establish its superiority, were forcing Tatsu Yamasaki and the rest of the board to recognize that. If you came here with no real desire or drive, Yamasaki surmised, your campaign looked like a shambles. Only Nomoto, Vice-Admiral Never Give In, could still insist on the *tatemae* that had carried them until then. "We've been depressed since the mast broke," Nomoto said, "but I can't catch any appreciable difference between the pitching of our boat and others."

Everyone else would soon come around to Kaoru Ogimi's view. "We're not out here to prove whether a previous hypothesis is right or wrong," Ogimi exclaimed. "This isn't an academic research institution."

• • •

Thursday, May 8, was a layday, a day of rest before the semifinals. As of the previous day Nippon Challenge was out of the event, having placed fifth in the fleet races behind ITA 1, *New Zealand*, ITA 15, and *Stars & Stripes*. But the syndicate's board, along with dozens of sponsors and suppliers, was in attendance by then, and Tatsu Yamasaki had scheduled a board meeting at the Hyatt Islandia for layday morning. They would do something they had never really done until then. They would start listening to the *gaijin* sailing the boat.

One by one the Kiwi afterguard, along with Namba and another of the senior Japanese crew members, stood and gave the board assessments of *Nippon*. Chris Dickson spoke slowly, with the careful diction he always used with the Japanese, and he ticked off every boat on the course. *Stars & Stripes* and ITA 15 performed better than anyone; ITA 1 and USA 9 were about even. The French were good only in light winds, and USA 2 was slow. As for *New Zealand*, it was faster than *J-6* in fourteen knots of wind, even at fifteen, and slower at sixteen. On San Diego conditions, Dickson figured, they couldn't consistently beat any boat other than USA 2. "Even if we modify *J-6* significantly, *Stars & Stripes*, *Il Moro* 15, and *New Zealand* would be faster," the Kiwi concluded. "Other boats will also be changed. We cannot catch up with them."

Everyone else got in line behind him. The weather readings were obviously all wrong, they said. It wasn't only the heavier mast; the hull concept, the appendages, and the boat's center of gravity were also wrong for San Diego. The board was silent as the sailors commented. But as soon as they finished, Ken Nomoto began to assert his opposition to everything they had said.

Yamasaki cut in abruptly. "Thank you for sailing as a member of Nippon Challenge," he said to the Kiwis. Then he dismissed them before a full-scale argument broke out. It was the first of many to come. Afterward, Yamasaki and Hideto Eguchi walked in the garden outside the hotel until the board meeting was formally convened. The *kaicho* was confused again.

"We may have a problem in the future," he said.

"With what?" asked Eguchi.

"With Nomoto-*sensei*. He is proving very stubborn."

There was no resistance from the Yamaha man. "I agree," Eguchi commented quietly. It was all he said.

That evening, Tatsu Yamasaki attended a reception for the sailing syndicates at a monument high above the Pacific on the tip of Point Loma. Old and new faces were everywhere.

Arthur Wullschleger, who was jurying for the Worlds, greeted the *kaicho* warmly, as did Gary Jobson, who by then was sailing for America[3].

The view all around Yamasaki was spectacular—water on three sides far below the terraces, the city and the harbor off in the distance. Alongside the skyscrapers, you could see the marinas and yacht clubs that crowded the shoreline. It was among them that most of the America's Cup syndicates were based. San Diego seemed, for a couple of hours, the perfect place to be.

Out on the veranda, Yamasaki stood with his back to the sea while three Japanese photographers draped in cameras snapped away at him. Anxious to strike the appropriately informal pose, he gestured

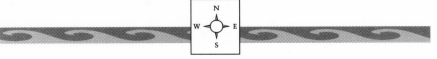

to a *gaijin* friend and began to talk as soon as they were together in front of the lenses.

"I haven't told the crew yet," Yamasaki said suddenly, "but we're going ahead with a third boat. We decided today at the board meeting."

The *kaicho* paused. "Yes," he continued without waiting for a response, "and I'm moving Dr. Nomoto back to Tokyo to take charge of it."

Yamasaki had stunned his friend. "That's a big step, Tatsu-*san*," he said.

"Nomoto-*sensei*, he . . ." Yamasaki trailed off briefly. "He doesn't think much of the way *gaijin* do things."

The two men both laughed. The cameras were still clicking.

•   •   •

"With a little wind and a little luck," Kaoru Ogimi said later that evening, "we could still do well in this."

Earlier in the day, Team Dennis Conner had withdrawn from the semifinals, and Nippon Challenge advanced to fourth place—and into the match-racing segment of the Worlds. It was a cheap way in, but few at Mission Bay complained. The first race, on Friday, May 10, was set between the two Italian boats to insure they wouldn't face one another in the finals; *Nippon* would race *New Zealand*. Once again, the course changed. Expanded to 22.6 miles, it was precisely the layout the challenger and defender would race for the Cup twelve months later.

Conditions that day were the worst *Nippon* could have anticipated: huge swells, winds at six knots. Much was made before the race of Chris Dickson's rivalry with his former syndicate, and in pre-gun maneuvering he was as aggressive as he had been all week. But the Kiwis were all over *J-6*, even behind the line. They were turning faster and more sharply. Five minutes before the gun Dickson hung out his protest flag, claiming he had been luffed—illegally blocked—by NZL 12. But umpires on the water responded with a green flag: protest rejected. Then Dickson went over the line early for the second time, and the mistake cost him almost ten boat lengths at the start.

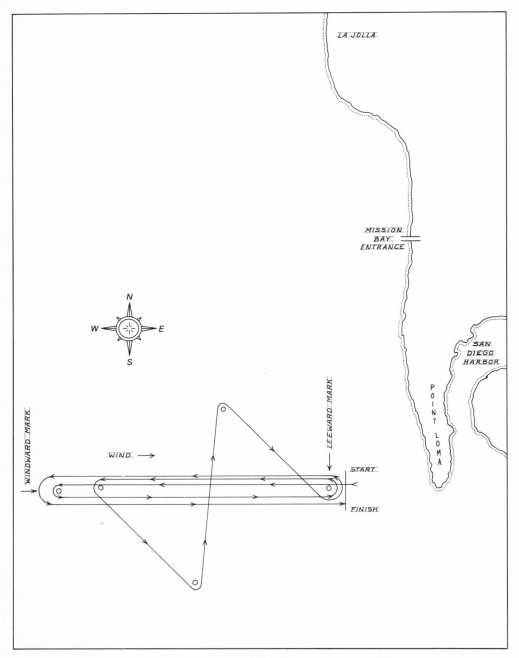

THE AMERICA'S CUP COURSE— 22.6 MILES

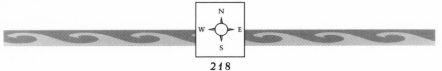

For the rest of the race the craft's weakness in light winds was in full view. By the fourth mark Dickson lagged by more than seven minutes and made no progress in the reach that followed. But in the sixth leg, another reach, *New Zealand* cracked its chain plate, which secures the mast to the bottom of the hull. Rod Davis, NZL 12's skipper, babied the yacht after that, visibly reluctant to jibe or tack; in the upwind beat that followed, *Nippon* narrowed the gap to just over a minute.

It looked briefly as if Dickson had been blessed. He made the most of the break that blew his way, but it wasn't enough. NZL 12, superior all week in light breezes, advanced cautiously but swiftly on the final downwind run, to cross the line two minutes and nine seconds ahead of the Japanese. In the finals, Dickson would fight for third place against ITA 1, the slower of the two Il Moros.

Dickson was deeply discouraged. "I tacked, he tacked faster. I jibed, he jibed faster," he complained to his mother after losing to the Kiwis. "That boat's just no damn good."

But Dickson wanted the third place. And the weather on Saturday, May 11 was perfect for getting it. Conditions had turned upside down from the previous day: shallow swells, winds at twelve knots. Onshore, syndicate executives and the technical team saw the combination as a final opportunity to cast the *J-6* hull concept in a favorable light. That was the last thing Dickson wanted. But he earnestly wanted to demonstrate that he deserved to have made the semifinals, that he wasn't traveling among the America's Cup elite with another crowd of Japanese also-rans.

Fighting for first place, ITA 15 and NZL 12 gave San Diego spectators the best racing they had seen all week. The Italians crossed with better speed and *New Zealand*, skippered by Rod Davis, tacked twenty-two times during the first beat, trying to draw Cayard into a duel. The two boats were close all the way, but they never crossed. Cayard, with Raul Gardini on board, finished a minute and eight seconds in front. It was excellent racing.

Chris Dickson's race against John Kolius, ITA 1's skipper, looked at first like more of the same. They were split at the start, with *Nippon* off on starboard tack. The Japanese sailed closer to the wind than the Italians through the entire beat, but they lagged by a boat length. Like Davis a few moments earlier, Dickson tacked over repeatedly, but every time he tacked, he fell a little farther behind. After coming over ten times, he quit tacking. It was tough, contentious sailing for the first four legs; *J-6* was slower on the beats, but it was faster than the Italians off the wind. Dickson needed a single break, and not a big one, to roll ITA 1 and take his third.

Maybe what happened next put *Nippon*'s final race into that category familiar to all sailors, the decent showing that turns sour and can't be put right again. But there were other interpretations of these last legs, and at Mission Bay they would discuss them quietly, although never publicly, for months afterward.

Completing the first reach and preparing to begin the second, ITA 1 executed a sail change tactic called an early port. It was a conservative move, but Kolius was maybe twenty seconds ahead at the time, and it was what any skipper would have called for. An early port requires the bowman to ease the spinnaker pole well before the approaching mark and pull in the spinnaker underneath the genoa sail on the port side of the boat. The spinnaker is down by the time the boat jibes into the next leg. You lose a little speed by dropping the sail so soon, but the tactic is safe and easily executed.

The call on board *Nippon* was the same. Erle Williams had gone to the foredeck to help pull the sail down and was waiting for the right moment to arrive when the order from the stern was suddenly changed.

"Kiwi drop!" Dickson shouted forward.

This was a maneuver of a different order. Williams, just as he had disputed Dickson's sail call before the dismasting, turned and stared aft over the grinders' heads at the skipper.

"You're fucking crazy!" he screamed. "They can't do it. They're not prepared. It'll turn into a disaster."

The call stood.

Chris Dickson and the *KZ-7* crew had invented the Kiwi drop during the '87 challenger series in Fremantle. Instead of pulling the spinnaker in before reaching the mark, you left it up well into the jibe, then released the pole, floated the sail to the leeward side of the bow, and let it fall back into the boat. It looked untidy to any spectator, and the boat was indeed a shambles as it made the mark. A Kiwi drop added boat speed when it worked, but that was not always. You needed to plan one well in advance, because it effectively reversed a lot of standard moves. Even a crew with a lot of experience with it could run into trouble, and the crew aboard *Nippon* had practiced it maybe a dozen times.

Williams was right. They weren't ready. Jin eased the spinnaker halyard too soon into the maneuver, and the sail dropped too early on either side of the bow. They sailed straight into it. Before anyone knew it, the thing had caught on the keel and *J-6* was sailing with forty feet of cloth trawling off its stern.

They sailed the next leg hoping it would come off. But at the following mark Dickson had to stop, point *J-6* straight into the wind, and float back from the shredded sail. They finished the third reach five minutes and twenty seconds behind, lost twenty seconds more on the final beat, then managed to pick up half a minute on the run to the finish line.

On deck afterward, there was a furor. John Cutler, the Olympic medalist, could recall no time out on the water when he had been so angry as he was in the moments after the last race ended. "We didn't deserve to be there in the first place," Cutler drawled. "But then we make it a public humiliation. I can stomach losing. But why did we have to look so stupid?"

What would they have saved had the drop worked? Half a boat length? They weren't far enough behind to justify a risk with that little reward. There had been a lot of racing left. They knew *J-6* was slower upwind, but they were close enough then, and fast enough downwind, to roll Kolius on the final run. They could have won that race.

Amid all the cursing, nobody on *J-6* mentioned that they thought the error might have been intentional. But several in the crew were nursing the idea. They had seen Dickson do it before: the calculated disaster that looked like lousy crew work and exonerated the skipper in front of the television cameras. They thought, in fact, of the final race of the challenger series in Fremantle, when Dickson faced

Dennis Conner for the last time. Conner was a couple of boat lengths ahead, and there was one more windward leg to go. *KZ-7* approached the final mark as it had hundreds of times in practice: in a Twelve, you can point the bow straight at the mark, since the hull is heavy enough to create a wave that will push the buoy aside. Instead, *KZ-7* hit the buoy and fell out of the race. There had been a furor then, too, not unlike the one that broke out on *Nippon*.

Chris Dickson heard none of what was said on *Nippon*. After crossing the finish line, he sailed briefly past *Plum Swinger* and watched Roy and Marilyn wave without waving back. Then the sails came down, and *Nippon* caught its tow in. Everyone stayed on deck, looking as cheerful as they could under the circumstances. The regatta was over.

Chris Dickson looked as if he was trying as hard as he could to stand among his crew. But he couldn't do it. After a few minutes, someone on board noticed that Dickson's face was falling apart. Then his lip began to quiver, and he hurried below just as some sailors thought they saw the first tears fall. They didn't see him again on deck until *J-6* docked in, its brief racing career over.

• • •

Tatsu Yamasaki had watched the finals from *Tariam II* with Shoji Kabaya from Yamaha, and Shingaku Takagi, Nippon Challenge's attorney. The result left him in "a state of shock," as he called it. Five minutes and ten seconds! "Look at the weather—wind eleven knots, the swells were down. These were our conditions. But at the first tack they were already ahead of us."

Late, just before the sun started going down, there was a small gathering in the long wooden trailer that contained the syndicate's office at one end and a reception area at the other. Kabaya was there, along with Isao Komiya, the stone-faced executive from Yamaha marine, and Akimitsu Kuroki, the senior managing director at S & B Shokuhin. Yamasaki sat on a low sofa in the center, drawing heavily on a cigarette and saying almost nothing. It was Komiya who began the discussion. "Maybe we have to consider the design of the boat itself, the original concept," he said diffidently. "Maybe we have to go back to the very beginning."

Perhaps it took someone like Komiya to acknowledge the *gaijin* recommendation and put it, finally and openly, on the table. Komiya had been close to the syndicate since the beginning. It was he who had first brought Yamasaki together with Hideto Eguchi. Komiya was an insider. There could be no question of disloyalty to the group. At the same time, he was outside the syndicate's chain of command.

They were just starting to turn Komiya's suggestion this way and that when Ken Nomoto walked into the shed. Yamasaki remained quiet but finally intruded by addressing the doctor directly. It entered him into the kind of confrontation he generally tried to avoid.

"Nomoto-*sensei*," he began, "is our concept right? Please explain to us. Where was the boat speed we should have had in these conditions?"

The doctor didn't answer directly. "*Kaicho*, I'm still waiting to analyze the data collected on the tender."

"We've scheduled a board meeting in Tokyo on May 21," Yamasaki shot back in a firmer tone. "Nomoto-*sensei*, you should be there, and you should be prepared to explain the difference between our ideas and what we now have as facts."

Nomoto stiffened. "It's my design, based on my idea, and we executed it my way," he said. "We've used lots of tank testing and we've done lots of computer work. If the board isn't pleased, *kaicho*, I'll resign."

Yamasaki interrupted again. "We have to know why we lost this race!" he began, but he was stopped by an office assistant who emerged from the other end of the trailer. Taro Kimura was on the telephone asking for Yamasaki.

Kimura, a prisoner of his profession, had remained behind in Tokyo to narrate closed-circuit race coverage for the syndicate's supporting corporations. Now he was furious. "This is a disaster," he shouted into the telephone. "Maybe we've made a big mistake in putting Nomoto in charge of the design side. We've built a Japanese *Mariner*."

"In the end it's our responsibility," Yamasaki replied in a calmer voice. "Remember, Taro, Nomoto gave the board a long lecture years ago, telling us all about how he would proceed. We accepted it. We said okay. After that, we seldom asked him to explain what was going on in the technical team. It's our mistake."

"I want you to tell Nomoto something very clearly," Taro said. "Tell him I'm in an impossible position because of this. We need more money. Now that's going to be tough to get, given our place in these races."

They hung up, and Tatsu returned to the lounge. The discussion had been desultory in his absence.

"That was Taro," Yamasaki announced. "Let me tell you exactly what he said."

And he did.

• • •

Coast Boulevard in La Jolla, the wealthy enclave in northern San Diego, runs along the Pacific for several miles below the village. Expensive apartment houses line the landward side of the street, while opposite them the ocean crashes against the dark, scarred rocks that form the shore. Yamasaki's condominium, number 101, was white, modern, and heavily secured with electronic devices. It was the *kaicho*'s refuge.

Tatsu Yamasaki golfed on Sunday, May 12, and when he finished he was in a somber mood. The day before, Roy Dickson had taken his final leave, and Yamasaki was still turning over their final conversation in his mind.

"Tatsu, I've got only two things to say," Dickson had told him. "One is, if you build another boat under Dr. Nomoto's direction, you're wasting five million dollars. The other is, I have no respect left for you, none."

"I feel the same," Yamasaki had weakly replied.

It was a bitter ending to a three-year partnership, "a shame," as Yamasaki put it. But Dickson had hardly walked through the wire

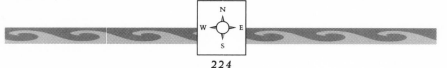

mesh gate at Mission Bay for the last time before the *kaicho* began to sound remarkably like him.

Tatsu and Ayako were to return to Tokyo the following morning, and they had made plans to dine out with several friends on the eve of their departure. When the first guests arrived, Yamasaki appeared in his pajamas straight from a late afternoon nap. Not fully awake, he sat on a sofa and began an impromptu review of the Worlds that was a conversation with himself as much as anyone present.

"Especially after the two finals, a very basic question has come up," he was saying. "Are we going the right way or the wrong way?"

Yamasaki paused. His hands dangled between his knees.

"If I can't reach agreement with Dr. Nomoto in Tokyo, if I have any doubt, if even a single question remains unanswered for me . . ." Yamasaki, still waking up, trailed off.

"I've been sailing more than thirty years," he added, apropos of nothing.

"If there are any doubts you'll change designers?" one of his guests inquired.

Then Yamasaki found his wind. "Change designers, change the organization here, the technical team, the management method—change everything. It's going to be a long, hot summer."

Others arrived—Takagi-*san*, the syndicate attorney, and Kuroki-*san*, the S & B managing director—and the group soon left for a nearby sushi restaurant. Over dinner, the conversation turned to the linguistic struggles they all had had over the previous week. Takagi, a pleasant, plump man who seemed content to have understood little of what he had seen and heard in San Diego, pulled out a calculator-like device that translated words from Japanese into English and back again. It was made by Canon, and it was called Intelligent Dictionary.

"Okay, everybody," Yamasaki said, reaching for the tiny keyboard. "This is our English word of the day."

His earlier mood had evaporated, as it often did in company. He picked a word, punched in its Japanese characters, then pressed the translation key.

Everyone laughed as the machine was passed around. The word he had chosen was *ganko*. Its meaning was roughly the same as *yuzurazu*, "never gives in." The electronic dictionary translated it as "stubborn."

Aloft

One day, a month or so after the Worlds, Makoto Kikuchi sat down at a pair of large desktop computers in one of the cargo containers that lined one side of the base camp at Mission Bay. Next to him was a young software specialist named Jun Nagai. Both of their desks, apart from holding screens, processing units, and keyboards, were littered with papers, loose-leaf manuals, Styrofoam coffee cups, and empty soft-drink cans enlisted as ashtrays.

In his hand, Kikuchi held a single sheet of paper. With it he was going to design a sail, and Nagai was going to draw it for him.

It had a name before Kikuchi gave Nagai the first specs for the first line. If it were a mainsail, it would be called "M," a genoa "G," or a spinnaker "S." Then it would get a numerical code. A sail designed for very light winds would be numbered "1"; one intended for the strongest winds *Nippon* was prepared to face would be "code 5." Last came its lineage: an "A" sail was the first of its type to be built, a "C" the third, an "F" the sixth. If you were allowed to look inside the base camp's two plywood-and-cloth sail sheds, one alongside the sprawling sail loft, the other down on the dock, you might find, for example, a long sailbag labeled "M1C," or another marked "G3A."

The sail Kikuchi started to design in June 1991 was a gennaker, a type designated by the letter "K." It was his first design since the Worlds, and it marked the start of the final and most important phase in Nippon Challenge's sail program. This was to be among the lightest sails in the inventory. It was called K1E: the fifth gennaker the syndicate had made for winds of six knots or below.

"Most people use spinnakers downwind and gennakers for reaching. K1E is a downwind gennaker," Kikuchi explained at his desk one afternoon. "Only once, in Gamagori, have we tried a downwind gennaker, and it didn't perform well. Earlier this year, we didn't have enough time for more testing, so we went into the Worlds with spinnakers."

It was a logical choice. In the same way the I.A.C.C. yachts were in a development class, the gennaker could be called a development sail. Cruising yachts had flown them for years. But they weren't used in America's Cup racing until 1987, when Tom Schnackenberg introduced them in the Australian defense. Schnackenberg was regarded as a genius among sail designers; his use of gennakers attracted much attention. But they were still very new in the match-racing scene; apart from the Kiwis and the Italians, no syndicate in San Diego had had much experience with them.

A gennaker is simply an asymmetrical spinnaker: its forward edge is longer than its aft edge. In sailing terminology, the luff line is longer than the leech line. Like the huge, colorful spinnakers skippers call for on downwind runs, gennakers are used instead of genoas or jibs. They are, in effect, hybrids, as their name suggests. They were attractive because they were less likely than a spinnaker to interfere with wind entering the mainsail. Cruisers found them easier to handle because cruisers didn't need a pole to fly them. But gennakers were unwieldy on I.A.C.C. boats. There they needed a

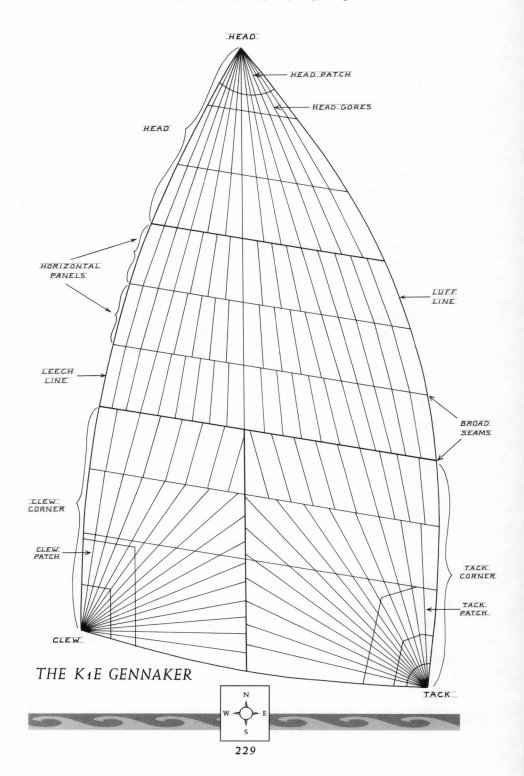

HEAD

HEAD PATCH

HEAD GORES

HEAD

HORIZONTAL
PANELS

LUFF
LINE

LEECH
LINE

BROAD
SEAMS

CLEW
CORNER

CLEW
PATCH

TACK
CORNER

TACK
PATCH

CLEW

TACK

THE K1E GENNAKER

pole more than thirty feet long, and they were no bowman's favorite sails.

K1E was an experiment. Even before the Worlds, up in a hired helicopter or following the other syndicates' practice sessions in the rubber dinghy, Kikuchi noticed that the Kiwis were, as Mike Spanhake put it, "heavily into gennakers." The Kiwis flew narrowshouldered gennakers not only on reaching legs but downwind as well. The Italians seemed to be going roughly the same way; they had mixed gennakers and spinnakers throughout the races.

As resident sail designer, Kikuchi huddled regularly with Spanhake and Chris Dickson. The three of them, along with John Dibley, the sail loft's manager, made up an informal committee that determined the sail program's direction. After the Worlds, they were happy enough with the quality of their sails, but they knew they had made an important error. They had been building sails for flat water and moderate winds—the same conditions Nomoto had assumed in his hull design. In essence, Kikuchi was now exploring a basic change in strategy, and K1E was a small part of the journey.

Like an accomplished architect, a good sail designer uses the parameters of his work to enhance his freedom rather than inhibit it. There are schedules to be met, and certain assumptions that cannot be ignored. The most important of these has to do with displacement. The weight of the boat determines the sail area: a heavy hull means large sails, a light one less sail. A designer has almost infinite choices as to what he puts on a boat and where he puts it, as long as he uses the same amount of cloth each time. "Development isn't 'area,' and it isn't easy," Kikuchi once said. "It's shape and profile, and there are many possibilities that have to be explored."

In the container, Nagai turned on an Apple Macintosh 11FX 4/80 that was loaded with a software program called Loft. For a moment the screen read, "Welcome to Loft, the program that enables you to design as you want to," and then it changed to a series of selections. Using the computer's "mouse," Nagai worked through them until he produced a blank screen on which the image of a sail came up—a two-dimensional drawing without details or specifications.

For K1E, Kikuchi wanted a higher aspect ratio, which essentially meant a narrower sail, and more twist, which should make the sail more aerodynamically efficient. But how would he get there?

He had two basic gennaker concepts, two extremes. One was a sail that was flat across its center, achieving its depth close to the sides, something like a frying pan; the other would be deeper and curved toward the center, nearer to a cylinder in shape. "We're looking for a flat shape in this sail," Kikuchi said. "We'll test it. Then we'll build K1F the other way, and test some more."

His object, at that point, was to describe a single curved line, an arc that began and ended toward the right side of the Mac and bulged gently out to the left. That would be the center line of the sail, seen from the side. It would determine almost everything about K1E. Most important, it would indicate how deep the sail would be—the chord depth—and where it would be deepest—the draft position, or "maximum camber."

But Kikuchi wouldn't draw the center line. Finding it meant feeding Nagai a series of specs that would produce it by giving the sail the profile he wanted when it was flying. There were the luff and leech curves, the length and shape of the fore and aft edges of the sail; the broadseam shape, the curve sewn into the seams running horizontally across the sail from luff to leech, and the leech hollow, the arc built into the sail along the aft edge, which allows the sail to fly clear of the rigging.

Kikuchi's remaining specs had to do with fabric. He first chose the direction in which he wanted the weave to run. To build the weave into K1E, he then supplied the panel layout. The layout showed the size and pattern of the sections from which the sail would be assembled. A sail will often include as many as six different weights of cloth and several varieties. But because it was experimental, K1E would consist of a single type, a white three-quarter-ounce polyester blend with threads of a new fiber called Power Rip woven into it.

Normally, after Loft gave Kikuchi a completed drawing, Nagai would have taken K1E out for a sail. Jun Nagai was less a helmsman than anyone else at Mission Bay. He usually wore a loose Hawaiian-

print shirt, baggy black shorts, white socks, and scuffed black shoes. Around the camp, he was almost invisible. But Nagai was an expert at CAD, computer-aided design. He could have flown K1E without so much as opening the blinds that dimmed the Nippon Line container he shared with Kikuchi.

From the Mac, Nagai would have shifted K1E to the other computer, a Compaq Deskpro 486/25, and onto another software program called Relax. With Kikuchi next to him, he would have decided what kind of day it was out on the water and how they should fly the sail.

Relax was not a design system, like Loft, but a sail simulation program. Into it went seven more variables. The wind speed defined basic sailing conditions. Then came sail trimming, which was adjusted, as on a boat, through the rigging and various lines: footline, headstay tension, halyard tension, sheet tension, and car line, a track on the deck through which the sheet angle is adjusted. "Sometimes we would make five or six runs with different trims," Nagai said as he went through the program.

"That was initially," Kikuchi interrupted. "Each trim can take an hour and a half. That's an average. It could take more. But we've done enough to know which is the most efficient trim for testing."

"Then we calculate," Nagai continued. "That takes two or three hours."

What Relax took in time it gave back in detail. It first yielded a shape report. It indicated the camber, the draft position, and the twist. It also showed the chord—the distance straight across from luff to leech—the entry and exit angles, which are how the sail assumes its shape on either side, and several other calculations. Relax then listed items in a column:

Stress flow map
Warp stress
Warp strain
Fill stress
Fill strain
Bias stress

Bias strain
Upper principal stress
Upper principal strain
Creasing
Principal strain map
Wind pressures
Shape contours
Fabric properties
True views
Panel layout

Entering any category would yield a three-dimensional drawing with degrees of stress or strain or contour shown all over the sail in different colors, the way a topographical map uses color to depict mountains and valleys. In warp stress, the force exerted on the weave was shown in purple—120 pounds per square inch—at the head of the sail and the clew, and in white—ten pounds—at the tack corner. Warp strain, the extent to which the wind elongated the fabric, looked similar, but it was not quite the same. "Think of stress as power going in," Kikuchi said. "Strain is the effect."

"There are sixteen of these. Which are important?"

Kikuchi started to enumerate. "Warp stress, warp strain, true view, which shows us the sail from every angle—bottom, top, behind." He stopped himself. "They're all important," he concluded abruptly. "But not for K1E."

K1E had no maiden voyage on Relax. Nor did it pass through a third system called SMSW, Sailmaker's Software, a three-dimensional design program that would have supported or questioned Kikuchi's 2-D drawing on Loft. The omissions were explained as a software problem. "The average depth of a mainsail is ten percent or so, and for a genoa fifteen percent," Kikuchi said. "But for spinnakers and gennakers, the depth is twenty percent or more. The computer isn't accurate enough at that depth."

Inadequate software for the sail program had been part of Roy Dickson's daily refrain in Gamagori. There was simply no one in Japan who knew how to write it. What they were using at Mission

Bay had been brought in from a British expert preeminent in his field. Sitting on the desks in the design container was roughly a hundred thousand dollars' worth of hardware and programs. And they still hadn't figured out how to apply it in the construction of some sails.

Nippon Challenge's sail program had turned out to be one of the few areas in which Japanese and *gaijin* had learned to work well together. But Kikuchi didn't think it mattered much that imported technology couldn't always be applied. Electronic design simply wasn't part of the way Makoto Kikuchi liked to do things. "I design from experience," he said. That explanation sacrificed nothing to brevity; it was the best summary of his method that he could have provided.

When he finished drawing K1E, he looked at the screens in front of him. "If you don't have time to see a flying shape, and if you don't have the money to actually build sails, this equipment is excellent," Kikuchi said. "We have money and time. We test on the water."

●   ●   ●

Makoto Kikuchi was a swimmer in high school. Then at university he switched abruptly to sailing. Why?

"Not a good reason," Kikuchi would explain. "There were many girls in the sailing club."

That was Kikuchi's way of keeping distance. Single-handed sailors are often like that, and Kikuchi had been one in his younger days. But his demeanor was unusual nonetheless. It was magisterial. The distance he kept was that of a patriarch, benevolent but firm. One morning in the loft at Mission Bay, the unassembled sections of a new sail began to take shape on the floor. It was another gennaker, and it was out of sequence. "What's this doing here?" someone in the loft asked.

John Dibley shrugged. "A mystery that'll never be solved. One of Kikuchi's secrets and, believe me, there are a lot of them."

Kikuchi was forty. At university in Tokyo he sailed for four years while majoring in economics. In the sailing club, he, too, learned all

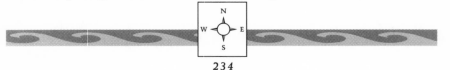

about seniority, hardship, and respect for the dinghies as the immutable property of the school. Then he walked away from it.

When he graduated in 1974 Kikuchi went to work at Taiyo Electric, a heavy-engineering concern. He was in purchasing and specialized in generators for cargo vessels. It was a good start in a *sarariman*'s career that would have made up in length and security what it lacked in brilliance. Kikuchi lasted two years. When he spoke of it at all, it was as nothing more than an inconvenient interlude.

"I couldn't sail much at Taiyo—only on Sundays—and I wanted to be in the Quarter-Ton Worlds," Kikuchi said. "So I decided to join North Sails. That was in 1976, two years before the series. I was lucky. I got involved in the biggest campaign in Japan, the Yamaha campaign."

North Sails Japan, with its headquarters in Yokosuka, was not yet a Yamaha subsidiary when Kikuchi joined it. He knew nothing of sailmaking when he started, but by the Sajima races in 1978 he had produced almost eighty sails, including those flown on *Magician V* and *VI*. Then he trimmed on the winning boat. As they were for other Japanese sailors and designers, the Quarter-Ton Worlds were a watershed in Kikuchi's life. "I had raced at university, but '78 was my first major regatta. I learned to make sails, and I learned to race."

Kikuchi spent the next decade at North. He read all the reports supplied to North Sails Japan by Lowell North, the celebrated American designer who started the company in San Diego in 1958. But those were only documents, sent from abroad.

"I learned on the floor," Kikuchi once explained. "And out on the water. I cut sails, and I did a lot of two-boat testing."

At the time, North Sails was running second in its field. Hood Sailmakers, then headquartered in Marblehead, Massachusetts, was at the peak of its prestige. With franchises in more than a dozen countries, Hood was large by the standards of an industry given to cottage production. The fight for supremacy was bitter. But North Sails did something in the seventies that would eventually advance it

far beyond Hood. In 1974, Tom Schnackenberg developed the first computerized sail program, and North Sails marketed it under the name of Tin Sail.

Sailmakers like to explain what they do by comparing a sail to an aircraft wing stood on its end. Both are foils that produce lift and drive by increasing wind pressure on one side and creating a vacuum on the other. Schnackenberg helped make this more than a comparison. In the seventies and eighties, sailmaking began to look as much like the science of aerodynamics as it did the art sailmakers had long considered it.

It is often impossible to attribute a new idea in sailmaking to a single man. But Schnackenberg, again, was instrumental in showing what the computer revolution meant. In the Australian challenge at Newport in 1983, he used panel layouts that spread odd geometric patterns across the sails of *Australia II*. It seemed eminently simple: he used a computer to keep the weave of the fabric running in the same direction as the load line—the direction in which the wind crosses a sail's surface. Apart from the computer, what made this possible was the appearance of a synthetic fiber, Kevlar, and a synthetic film, Mylar, that were stronger than anything else that had ever gone into sailcloth.

Until Kevlar came into use, racing sails were woven in a plain warp-and-weft pattern, an in-out box weave. Designers knew sails would perform better if they could make cloth with a stronger warp and could align the warp, the lengthwise thread, with the direction of the wind. But they couldn't. Using a stronger thread in the warp produced crimp; building a warp-only fabric was something that had never been done. Kevlar and Mylar changed that. Kevlar was strong and light enough to be used in warp-only construction, and a Mylar coating gave it the stability a cloth with no weft would need. A lightly woven sublayer—Kevlar warp, polyester weft—completed the experiment.

By the mid-eighties, every loft, even small operations that lived on business from the local marina, was using a computer-aided design system of one kind or another. In theory, at least, the avid Sunday sailor could purchase the software, put it in his PC, and design his own sails. North was the undisputed leader in computerized design and production. It took a three-dimensional approach to design, and it cut its cloth with computerized plotters that interfaced with the design program.

This technique had certain implications. On the design side, the method was called mold cutting. You fed the desired sail depth and profile into the computer, and it told you what kind of sail you wanted by producing a mold of it. You drew the center line first. Then the computer produced the broadseam curve and the luff curve, the two most important factors in determining shape. North ended where Kikuchi started. Kikuchi put it in simple terms: he designed "horizontally," on the floor, and North "vertically," as if on a mannequin.

In the sail loft, laser cutting meant that a mass-producer could cut hundreds, or even thousands, of panels at a time. The economic attractions were quickly obvious. The space required to cut and assemble a sail was substantially less. And the loft could hire relatively inexperienced sailmakers because in most instances the computer would compensate for their lack of skill. It was the automation of the art.

Makoto Kikuchi, a valued loft foreman at North Sails Japan, was having none of this. For one thing, the method adopted by North presented certain problems—at the design table and in the loft. You couldn't, for instance, work your way back up the way you had come.

Even the best designer wouldn't know if he had produced a sail of the shape he wanted until it was up on a boat. A computer couldn't duplicate conditions out on the water, no matter how many variables went into it. "In the end," one of the sailmakers at Mission Bay liked to say, "a computer is a dumb animal. It only does what you tell it to do."

Many sailmakers devoted to "horizontal" design argued that with a mold-cut design you couldn't finish a day on the water and go back into the sequence to add, say, four inches to the luff curve. In short, you couldn't do a recut. You had to design another sail. Nor, they said, could you build a precise duplicate of a sail you liked.

The biggest problem in the loft was the kind of thing any sail-

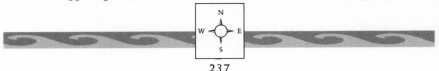

maker who had put in his hours on his knees understood as a given of the art. No roll of cloth is ever straight. Yet laser cutters assumed it was. You could program in a stitch factor, for instance, or any number of other control commands, but not the loose edge on a large piece of cloth. A laser would cut a fair edge on a head panel that was, say, fifty feet by two feet, but when the sailmaker laid it flat again, he'd find a bow a foot deep along one edge of his panel.

It was more than any of this that finally made Kikuchi reject the North system. That had to be explained in more encompassing terms. His method was too deeply rooted in notions such as intuition, experience, inspiration, eye, and an inner sense of what he wanted. There was too much Kikuchi in a sail that went out the door of his loft for him to cede part of the process to a machine. "Design systems compromise everything he stands for," one of his sailmakers said of him. "He'll never concede that they work."

A break with North seemed more or less inevitable as the eighties wore on. Once again, Kikuchi's explanation was brief and elusive.

"Money," he would say.

That was only a small part of it. In practical terms, the final straw was when Yamaha's marine division took over the company in 1986.

"North's way wasn't a bad way," Kikuchi eventually elaborated. "It just wasn't my way. And I wanted to choose my way."

In early 1987 he walked, with thirty million yen, about two hundred thousand dollars, in capital. Quitting was extraordinary enough, in the Japanese context. What came next was yet more notable: ten younger sailmakers followed him out North's door. "The problem was the boss, the way the place was managed—like any other company. Everyone wanted to leave, and they were all excellent. It was difficult. I had to put ten people on the payroll, and I was just starting out."

He found a long, narrow attic, a loft in the true sense, in the commercial section of Kamakura, along the Sagami Bay coastline from Hayama. The room was long and narrow, roughly a hundred and twenty by thirty feet, and the building was crumbling. In the summer, between the uninsulated roof above and a dry cleaner's

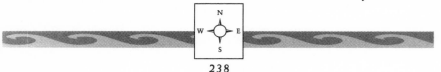

shop below, it was so hot in Kikuchi's loft that they had to stop working.

Kikuchi had secured the Japanese franchise of a Danish loft called Diamond Sailmakers. Diamond would eventually find a place for computers and laser cutters on its mass-production side, but the Diamond system pretty much matched Kikuchi's. Sails took shape horizontally, not vertically. Cutting was done on the floor, by hand. Within a year Kikuchi was running one of the most competitive lofts in Japan. He had no library, no record of what he had done before and how his sails had performed with wind in them. There was only his sense of what the project at hand required. He had computers all over the loft, but they were used mostly for accounting pur- poses—billing, cloth inventory, the budget. It was back-of-an-enve- lope designing, which was by then Kikuchi's established style.

Eighteen sailmakers worked for him. They often stayed well into the evening, stepping over or crawling around one another to produce sails in a space too small for the orders coming in. One of them was a young Australian, the only *gaijin* in the loft, named Andrew Lechte. He arrived from Melbourne in 1988.

"Kikuchi wasn't on the floor that much by the time I joined Diamond," Lechte said. "But he always seemed to roll up when something went wrong. Even a minor thing. He'd walk onto the floor and there'd be twenty sails spread out. Kikuchi would go right to one sail across the room, pick it up, and find some small defect in the broadseam, or a tiny hole in the cloth. I've seen other lofts, but never one like Kikuchi's. As for the quality of what we make, it's the best loft in the world."

Sailors and sailmakers have a term for the heroes and artists among them. They call them rock stars. Tom Schnackenberg was a rock star, as were Lowell North and Tom Whidden, who began with North, split off to launch Sobstad Sails, and then returned to North some time before he started designing for Dennis Conner. Kikuchi was a nobody on the international scene. But, like Kazunori Koma- tsu and Robert Fry, he was something of a rock star at home.

That probably helped when Tatsu Yamasaki first started looking for a sail designer. The bidding was two-way—North and Diamond—

and Yamaha fully expected North to get the contract. But Yamasaki did something very un-Japanese. He gave Kikuchi the job at the end of 1989, specifically stipulating that the Diamond approach to sailmaking would be used. Yamaha was stung. Quite beyond the America's Cup effort, Diamond had by then begun to challenge North's worldwide preeminence, and the shabby loft in Kamakura had made visible inroads into North's business in Japan.

Kikuchi had already burned Yamaha once, when he left North like the Pied Piper with a third of North's sailmakers behind him. He always shrugged it off, but he paid for his triumph. Many months passed in Gamagori and San Diego before the Yamaha people could bring themselves even to acknowledge that Kikuchi was there.

•　•　•

When K1E crossed the camp at Mission Bay from Kikuchi's container to the sail loft, it was a piece of eight-by-eleven paper with four sections drawn on it. The head of the sail consisted of oblong triangles, called head gores, that fanned out from the top. Under the head were "the horizontals," panels that ran across the center; each horizontal was made of a dozen vertical panels aligned at angles. The bottom of the sail was divided in two—a clew corner and a tack corner.

The building in which K1E would turn from paper into cloth was made of PVC supported by steel piping. It was one large room, roughly sixty by a hundred and sixty feet, with a floor of varnished plywood. At the entrance the words NO SHOES were painted neatly on the floor. Six large, gray industrial sewing machines were scattered elsewhere around the room, three mounted on casters and three installed in holes cut in the plywood, like prompter's pits in a theater, so that the machines were at floor level.

There were few windows, but the PVC let in so much San Diego sunlight that the sailmakers sometimes had to wear sunglasses. Next to a couple of metal lockers and a drinking fountain to one side of the vast, empty floor space was a TEAC audio system usually tuned to a "classic rock" FM station. Since the Worlds, the sailmakers had

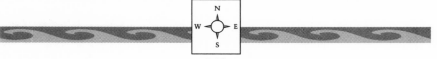

time to stop and talk, and they took a daily coffee break as soon as the boat docked out in the morning.

It was different before the Worlds. They had worked two shifts, ten hours each, to build the new sails *J-6* needed at the last moment—nine spinnakers, three genoas, two gennakers, and two mains. It was a grueling schedule, even for *gaijin* loft hands who had been through previous America's Cup campaigns. They had brought production time for a mainsail down from two hundred man-hours to a hundred and ten; for a genoa, they went from seventy hours to forty. "We were turning out sails, I'd say, twice as fast as any other loft in San Diego," a loft hand named Craig Robinson remembered. "I've never done anything like it before."

K1E would take four days at a leisurely pace, but demands greater than the pre-Worlds schedule were on the way. June was an interlude. The momentum would gather through the summer and autumn until, by November, they would be working at least two shifts again, possibly three. They had made fifty-seven sails for Kikuchi, including the production spurt before the Worlds; through the America's Cup, they were slated to build an additional nineteen mainsails, forty-six genoas, three jibs, fifty-six spinnakers, thirty gennakers, and nine staysails.

Craig Robinson's boast was not idle. There were six of them on the floor every day during the Worlds—a small crew—and they made up what was thought by some visitors to be the best loft in the running. Veterans of the sailing scene had come by and given it good reviews. At that point, the Spaniards were the only other syndicate flat-cutting sails on the floor. Everyone else was computerized; North, in fact, had been well represented off Point Loma. There was no evidence of it, but Kikuchi liked to think the others were "coming our way," as he put it. "Simplest is best," he said one day. "Understanding each shape is easy our way, and improving a shape is easy. We can change quickly and change a lot. It's the best system for the America's Cup."

K1E started in three places at once. At one end of the loft, six lengths of cloth were rolled out, tacked down, and taped together; then six more were layered on top and taped. These would be the

horizontals. In the middle of the loft, Andrew Lechte started on the tack corner. He rolled out cloth, tacked it down, taped it, and went to work on one corner of it. About half the cloth would remain one layer. But from the corner that would attach to the bow, Lechte applied extra cloth in layers. He made a large two-ply section, then a smaller three-ply section. Then it got thicker; at the corner there were twelve layers of cloth when he finished.

Craig Robinson, a stocky man who worked in gym shorts and a T-shirt, got stuck with the head of K1E. "Not really stuck," he said. "We all take turns. This is mine."

The head involved working with panels of difficult shapes. Each of the head gores was about sixty-three feet long and no wider than twenty-six inches at the base. Half of them were straight on both sides: they would add no shape to the sail. The other half would be straight on one edge and curved on the other; each curve would contribute to the depth the sail took when it flew.

"You can spend three years just learning how to handle materials and finding the quickest and neatest way to do things," Robinson said as he prepared to cut his panels.

Andrew Lechte, who happened to be walking by, finished Robinson's sentence. "And they'll still blow the sail the first day it's out of the loft."

Robinson had a long afternoon ahead of him. He would assemble the head panels on a long table to the side of the loft, and he calculated that he would make four trips up and down for each of twenty-six panels.

"The other thing you have to know is where you have to be accurate and where you can cut a corner," Robinson said. He was moving the cut panels closer to the table.

"Are there places?"

"Very few. But there are places you know you don't have to be so accurate in cutting."

"Name one."

"Certain areas of patching." Patching—layering the cloth where it had to be strongest—was what Andrew Lechte was doing at that moment to the tack corner.

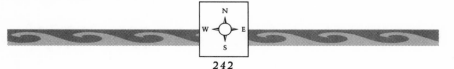

Robinson continued talking as he started to walk the sixty-three feet up and down the table, taking a roll of tape, a box of tacks, a long ruler, and a pair of heavy steel scissors with him.

He was twenty-nine, Auckland-born, Fremantle-based, and he made roughly nineteen thousand dollars a year. He and his wife, Jeanne, were struggling with a new mortgage in Australia. Like everyone else in the loft, and not a few people on the boat, Robinson spent some of his time wondering what he would do after the twenty-eighth America's Cup.

"You don't see too many old sailmakers," he said. "The physical work is tough, and the money's awful. By the time you're thirty, you're either in management or you're out."

"Which way will you go?"

"Don't know yet."

As he taped and tacked his way up and down K1E's head gores, Robinson continued. "I started by taking a four-year apprenticeship at Hood New Zealand. Hood was the best sailmaker in the world, though Kevlar and Mylar changed that. In '86 I joined the New Zealand challenge in Perth. We had fourteen sailmakers at one point."

Robinson laughed at the size of the operation. "At the end we got it down to eight."

He joined an Auckland loft called Lidgard Sails the next year. It was the largest domestic loft in New Zealand, and it was starting up franchises around the country. Using a computer, Lidgard was developing what it called "kit set" sails; it cut panels in volume and shipped them to all the franchises. "It gave the main loft total control over design and cloth."

Robinson was loft manager in Auckland. And when the prospect of a Perth franchise came up, he went for it.

"It was myself at first, and then I got up to three employees. We produced a hundred and fifty sails soon after we started—small stuff, no strain. I met my wife in Perth, too. It all went fine till April '90, when the recession hit."

Robinson found a buyer, sold out, and sat around for a month. One afternoon the telephone rang, and it was Mike Spanhake. "I

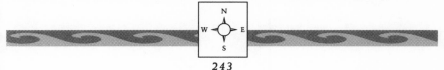

didn't know him personally, but he was a manager at Hood when I first got there. I knew Roy Dickson, though, and I knew Chris. Chris Dickson was best man at my wedding."

Craig and Jeanne Robinson arrived in Gamagori in August 1990.

Working near him in the Mission Bay loft were a Kiwi named Rodger Vinson, Andrew Lechte, and a young Japanese woman named Chisato Asanuma. Another Kiwi, Dave Parr, was temporarily away, and another Japanese, Ryo Komatsu, had gone back to Japan. Why weren't there more Japanese sailmakers on board? Why wasn't this loft more of a tech transfer operation?

"Language is one problem," Robinson said. "It would slow us down a lot if we had to shout across the length of a sail every time we needed to make a point. Kikuchi is another part of it. Kikuchi's on a steep learning curve himself. That's where your tech transfer is. But he didn't want to take people away from his own loft in Kamakura."

By the time Robinson finished taping the head panel, late that afternoon, Lechte had finished the tack corner and was started on the clew. Rodger Vinson had restacked the horizontals so that the ends were aligned, and the following day he would cut a curve into the upper edges to give depth to K1E's middle. Then the sewing would begin—two and a half days of it.

• • •

After the Worlds, the Italian-made dinghy called the rubber duck became more or less Kikuchi's private launch. He took it out to watch his sails on *Nippon*, and he used it to go on spying excursions.

It had a Fiberglas bottom and gunwales made of rubber tubing. Two Yamaha outboards powered it, two hundred horsepower each, and one of the sailmakers once had it up to forty-eight knots. There were back braces for a pilot and a standing passenger on either side. Across the deep swells off Point Loma, Kikuchi drove the rubber duck with kidney-racking abandon.

One morning *J-6* went out to practice against *Ville de Paris*. The French, who had built their camp next door at Mission Bay, usually welcomed a sparring partner as much as the Japanese did. The practice would end as the challenger series neared, but French-Japanese drills and races were a regular event during the summer. Kikuchi liked them too. Every sailmaker in San Diego studied the work of others, although it could be argued that Kikuchi was more dependent than others on what he saw on the water. That morning, he and Jun Nagai docked out an hour after Chris Dickson, got a radio message that *J-6* had broken a batten, and turned back to get a spare. It was sunny, and the winds were fifteen knots. San Diego's usual June clouds were blown into high, thin swirls, like brush-strokes.

After delivering the batten, a support piece inserted in a pocket sewn across the mainsail, Kikuchi dropped behind *Nippon* and trailed it carefully for half an hour. Then he decided to see the French up close and lined up right behind them.

"What do you think?" a passenger asked after a while.

Kikuchi cocked his head. "Nothing special."

Then he sped away. The Kiwis and the Italians were the ones he most wanted to watch, and they were both out that day. New Zealand was testing with two boats a few miles to the south. From where he was, straight off Point Loma, you could just make out the Kevlar at the tops of their masts. On the way to see them, Kikuchi happened to pass an America³ boat, alone on a long reach. He stopped, got behind it, and lingered for a few minutes.

"Same as during the Worlds. Not fast," he said as he continued south.

Kikuchi and Nagai saw immediately that the two New Zealand boats were testing appendages, not sails. They had identical mains and genoas, none of them new, yet one boat was sailing notably faster than the other. Whatever they were looking at had to be below the surface. Keeping their distance this time, Kikuchi swung the rubber duck behind them anyway and waited for Nagai to shoot the sails with a telephoto lens.

ITA 1 and ITA 15 were sailing far out to sea, and the rubber duck pounded over swells of six feet or more toward them. Tracking the two boats, Kikuchi found something interesting. The Italian sails had impressed everyone during the Worlds—huge spinnakers and

genoas, a narrow main with lots of roach at the top. Now they were
going in the opposite direction—wide main, smaller headsail.

"They were quicker during the Worlds—smaller 'E,' bigger 'J.'
Now we're going in their direction and they're coming in ours."

"Why?"

"I don't know. Everyone's trying different things. But our direction is right. Reduce the 'E,' broaden the 'J.' "

They spun quickly around the sterns of the two Italian boats,
lingered while Nagai took pictures, and started on the long cross-
wind journey in.

Amid the many shapes and angles presented by Cup-class boats
under sail, Kikuchi was looking for a very special line. As Mike
Spanhake described it, it was almost an obsession. What mattered
to Kikuchi more than anything else in what he did was the leech line
on the genoa, from the mast down the aft edge of the sail to the clew.
Every designer, loft hand, helmsman, and trimmer has his own idea
of what a sail should look like. Kikuchi looked for a vertical leech.
He would get behind the sail and look up its edge.

"What Kikuchi wants is a line as near as possible to parallel with
the mast," Mike Spanhake explained one evening. "If it's more open
in the middle, it's drawn too close at the head. Then it traps air and
redirects it onto the main. Getting the middle of the leech to hold
and the top to open is extremely difficult to achieve. But if you do,
everything else—draft position, chord depth, distribution, etcet-
era—will be pretty much right."

Years before Spanhake ever thought of working in Japan, he had
learned to value the same criterion. But he never knew anyone else
to judge a sail that way until he met Kikuchi in Gamagori. "At first
I thought he was patronizing me. What's the Churchill phrase?
Absorb your enemies? But I was wrong. We agreed absolutely on
something very few people considered significant. It was the start of
a working relationship."

June 1990, a year before K1E came into being, was the start of
something else. Spanhake had sailed in the Kouros Cup off St.
Tropez and he was back in Gamagori with damaged cartilage in his
knee. He had been out of the sailmaking business for nearly seven

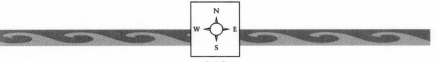

years by then. But Roy Dickson had assigned him the sail loft, and Spanhake started spending time with Kikuchi's operation. "I first thought, There's something I'm not seeing here. But the more I looked, the more alarmed I got. What I saw was all there was, and what I saw was unbelievable—unbelievably bad."

Spanhake admired "Kikuch," as he called him, but he couldn't talk to him about a management structure. There hadn't been one to discuss. Management, for Kikuchi, was one of those troublesome matters that got in the way of the art. He was, in addition, simply overloaded. Forward ordering of cloth and hardware was hit or miss. As he did in Kamakura, Kikuchi was designing on stray pieces of paper that rarely survived the assembly of the sail. It wouldn't have mattered if they had: there were no specs on them most of the time. Kikuchi handled that dimension of things by spreading his hands apart for the sailmakers—"Make it that big across"—or by getting down on his knees and doing it himself.

The simple arithmetic was appalling. The average sail, from design through testing, was taking eight to twelve weeks. In the previous seven months, the Gamagori loft had got ten new sails out the door and done seven recuts. *J-6* was due to be launched in ten weeks, and a set of identical sails was mandatory for two-boat testing. They had scheduled thirteen new sails per boat for the testing program; by the time Spanhake lifted the lid on Kikuchi, that had been cut to five each, a lot of which would be brought in from foreign lofts.

Ten weeks became seven and seven, five. Then four. Yet Kikuchi saw no problem when Spanhake would ask him about the production schedule. Spanhake broke the weeks down into days, then the days into hours. Still no problem. The drill remained as it had been from the start: arrive in the morning, put out what fires were blazing, begin again the next day. "You couldn't call it crisis management because there was no recognition of a crisis," Spanhake recalled.

Kikuchi and his loft were nowhere near an America's Cup standard. Getting them there would involve an enormous leap between the summer of 1990 and the first races. It meant bringing in a management team, and it meant buying a computer system. The

loads involved in the new class, and the pioneering nature of the exercise, made "a more disciplined, scientific approach imperative," Spanhake wrote in a memo to the board. John Dibley, Kiwi-born, veteran of two previous America's Cup campaigns, would come in to run the loft; Peter Heppel, an English specialist, would customize the machinery and software that eventually found its way onto Kikuchi's desk. Kikuch, Spanhake explained, would be left to design. No more inventory, no more scheduling, no more hours on his knees.

Spanhake's effort to put it all in place would evoke sympathy in the most hardened of American trade negotiators. Kikuchi wanted no *gaijin* overseer, he wanted no *gaijin* manager, and he wanted no computers.

Kikuchi and Spanhake would start in the conference room at ten or eleven, take coffee breaks, dash down to the loft every so often, and finish up at nine or so in the evening. Spanhake let the conversation wander: people, attitudes toward life, the abstractions of design—anything. At the end of each day they both felt exhausted but friendly. And they had agreed on the first principle: that there would be changes in the loft.

It lasted six weeks. On Tuesday morning it was as if Monday had never happened. Something would always come up. Kikuchi would be too busy to get to the conference room. When he finally did, Spanhake would have to start with a lengthy recapitulation. "We took three painful steps forward every day, and 2.9 backward every night." It can't be a selling job, Spanhake told himself as the days went by. Kikuchi has to really believe in this if it's going to work.

Fridays were especially tricky. Just before the weekends, Spanhake usually entered what he called "my pink cloud state of mind." He would say, "Kikuch really does want this." Then Kikuchi would go back to Kamakura for two days.

"I always had a sense on Mondays that he had disappeared into the Japanese world. All of the previous week had been lost."

Everything was entirely polite in the formal, distancing way the Japanese cultivate. "He was stonewalling, of course, and after a while I entered into the game. I was sitting on my anger. I started

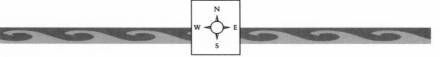

having sleepless nights. I'd think, Nothing in life should be this important. I shouldn't be getting so involved in this. But I was."

The breakthrough came on a Friday. Spanhake was pushing on one of the most sensitive points between them: getting Kikuchi a computer consultant. A system was only as good as the specialist who ran it, Spanhake argued. And he was too tired to wade through the reasoning in the accepted way.

"Look, we've come this far," he finally exclaimed. "You know you're going to have this. It's only a matter of when I get you to accept it."

In an instant, Spanhake achieved what most of the other foreign coaches had pursued and failed to accomplish with Namba and the other sailors. He made Kikuchi angry. In a way, Spanhake felt complimented.

"You *gaijin* are all alike," Kikuchi shot back. "You always push. You always want it your way. How would you like it, what would you do, if I went back to Diamond in Kamakura, if I said, 'I don't need Nippon Challenge,' and if I took the crew with me?"

Spanhake had many reservations about Roy Dickson's management methods. For him, as for the other Kiwis, Roy's eventual loss of control was something he wanted to avoid. But at that moment he took a lesson from Dickson senior's book. He hauled off and hit Kikuchi where it would hurt.

"What we'd do is be very grateful," he shouted. "It would be the first time, after months and months of asking, 'Do you want to win the Cup?' that we would get an honest answer. The answer, of course, would be, 'No.' "

Spanhake kept on, releasing a flow six weeks in the making. "Is that the answer? Are we into a new deal here? Are you saying, 'We don't want the America's Cup. We just want to do things our way'? Maybe you can ask yourself, Kikuch, why the *gaijin* were employed here. I think it was to supply some ideas that you didn't have before. I think you have an obligation to ask yourselves if your way of doing things can win it."

It wasn't the most incendiary of the head-on collisions in the Nippon Challenge's history, but it was among the most constructive.

Progress in the sail program was swift from then on. Spanhake and Kikuchi cat-and-moused over who would name the computer consultant; Kikuchi won the round by hiring Jun Nagai. Kikuchi remained stubborn, suspicious of foreigners, and wary of the computers. But he had learned to strike a balance between art and science. By the summer of 1991, Diamond Japan had adopted the Loft-Relax system in Kamakura, and the Danish head office was talking about using it too.

Spanhake, although he had finally prevailed, although he had redrawn the line, would never be able to move it again. Kikuchi made that clear without saying a word.

"If I was able to do anything," Spanhake said, "it was to make him realize that a genuine wish to win means there have to be sacrifices in terms of how things are done. There have to be compromises. The thing about Kikuch was, the America's Cup wasn't a romantic concept to him. It was a practical matter. He's one of the only Japanese who really wants to win."

•   •   •

K1E got out the loft door at ten o'clock on a Friday, an hour before dock-out the day it was scheduled for testing.

After sewing the panels, the sailmakers strengthened the luff edge with a length of Kevlar cord and stiffened the corners by stitching in pieces of Kevlar cloth the size of dinner plates. Then the rings went on, and the borders—bright green selvage on the luff edge, red on the leech. Two crew members came in to gather it off the floor and into a sailbag. They used short lengths of ordinary knitting yarn to bind it lengthwise—the wind would break the "wools" as the sail was raised—and they let the head and tack corners hang out the top of the bag. K1E weighed roughly eighty pounds and had a designed draft of twenty percent.

It was a two-boat testing day, and there were other things to do before flying the experiment. They put up nearly identical mains—M1D and M1E—and nearly identical genoas—G2C and G2D. Re-thinking *Nippon*'s peculiar appendages was the first step in what

would become a radical revamp of Nomoto's notions about the hull. That day, Dickson was sailing *J-3* with no forward rudder.

To avoid one boat fouling the other's wind, they couldn't sail too close to one another, but they had to be close enough to try staying in the same breeze. Finding the right position could take ten minutes on a tricky day, and this was one of them.

The tests were ten minutes each, as in Gamagori, and there were nine of them. Namba, who skippered *J-6* with Spanhake on board, was silent, but when they were finished testing the rudder he said, "Looks like *J-3*'s faster up to nine knots. Above that it needs more weight underneath, and we're faster."

Spanhake considered this, agreed, then said, "There's an upper layer of air that's quite strong, maybe two hundred feet up, which is different from what we've got down here. What's happening is that air's coming down every so often, hitting the water, and creating vacuums all around us, holes in the road—potholes, basically. What's frustrating is the general telemetry that's feeding back to the tender is coming from equipment maybe a hundred feet up. It bears no relationship to what we're sailing through."

K1E went up on *J-6* in steadier winds of nine knots or so in the middle of the afternoon. The display of panels and seams that had lain twisted on the loft floor that morning became something like a miracle. K1E's middle was flat at the center from the foot all the way up to the head. When the wind skated across it and ran to the sides, blowing the sail full and then letting it ease momentarily, it sounded like the crisp, white tissue in which gifts are wrapped.

Spanhake went up to the bow and stood before the mast to look up the sail's expanse. As the rubber duck came up beside him, Nagai was busy with the camera. Spanhake and Kikuchi signaled one another—they both seemed pleased.

Spanhake was still on the bow, heading in, when he started reviewing the sail aloud. "It's a variation on the basic theme. It's very stable. See the sides? They're parallel like the pillars of a building. The top is very open, and I like the flatness through the middle. Can you see there how clean it is at the foot? Beautifully clean. I'm impressed. Ironically, I think that configuration"—he pointed to the spinnaker on the other boat—"is probably faster, but we'll be testing this, depending on conditions, for several weeks."

J-6 surged slightly forward on a wave, and K1E started to empty.

"Trim," Spanhake called to the sailor working the gennaker sheet behind him.

On the tow in, Spanhake was sitting on *J-6*'s afterdeck.

"You begin to see what's special about sailmaking once a sail is up, once it lives," he said as the yacht neared Mission Bay. He had been talking about who sailmakers were and why they did what they did, subjects that intrigued him.

They were misfits, he figured, possessed of an unusual intelligence that didn't take them far down the roads usually traveled by people as gifted as they were. Pose a question, and a sailmaker in knee pads will usually put down his scissors or tape or thread to range articulately through the science of wind and the art of shapes and lines.

Not much else mattered. However they started out, it became a calling. To make sails was to live in a universe apart. It had its own values, standards, heroes, myths, traditions. It gave sailmakers reasons to respect others, and it let them claim respect in return. Being known in the yacht club bar, being able to talk in familiar terms about "Schnacks" or the other rock stars—those things were important, too.

Spanhake loved to talk about it; the people fascinated him as much as the craft. "My theory is that good sailmakers, those who tend to hang into it, are frustrated artists who found no formally recognized medium to express themselves in."

He was talking about himself to an extent. Although he had started out as an art instructor, Spanhake was sailing and pumping gas when he fell—"quite by accident"—into his first loft job. He was a natural teacher—you could see that on the boat—and that gave him what were probably the most sympathetic relations any *gaijin* at Mission Bay had with the Japanese.

He was forty-three, the father of a baby girl born two weeks before he and his wife, Urszula, arrived in San Diego. Spanhake spoke with extreme care, like a draftsman working without an eraser. To talk about boats and sails, he always reached for broader references. K1E, he would say, was "sculptural." He understood the place science and management had in the trade. But it was an ironic task for him to push a computer into Kikuchi's loft.

"Sailmaking comes down to artistic interpretation," he said. "The route followed by other challengers, and by most large commercial lofts, is to compute by way of a totally physical—as in physics—and numerical approach. I would never refute the value of computers, but I've always been cautious about that approach by itself. There are too many variables on a yacht to be assessed by a computer. No two days on the water are ever the same. Perhaps that's what keeps people like me in this."

Kikuchi's determination to break away had given him star status at home. He was unusual among the Japanese. His attitude was backward in that he favored experience over processes and the technological solution. For the Japanese crew it was something like a privilege to be friendly with Kikuchi. But he was "unattainable," as Spanhake put it after observing the phenomenon over many months. As Kaoru Ogimi would say, Kikuchi was weightless, gravity-free; he was in orbit.

After K1E went up, Spanhake started talking about him again. "He has a way to go with mains, but he has no equal with genoas, and he's damn near there with spinnakers. I've been involved with some of the real stars, Schnackenberg and others. And I put this little-known Japanese man right up there with them.

"But for all his small-time ego, he doesn't realize it. He operates from a position of considerable insecurity. You can see that every time a sail goes out. All the arrogance is gone. Then I see him as a very fragile human being. He's tried his hardest, it's what his life is all about, and he takes in completely what you say. He's deeply suspicious if you patronize him. There's an obligation to be absolutely honest.

"All this is healthy for Nippon Challenge. It tends to make the product extremely good. It's one of our strengths. If Kikuch were publicly acclaimed for his sails, he'd lose that precious naïveté he has, and a part of his considerable talent would be tarnished a bit.

"He's in a perfect situation as someone operating on the international scene. He's trying so honestly to do something that's good."

CHAPTER XI

KAICHO

When Tatsu and Ayako Yamasaki got on a plane for Tokyo on May 13, drained and depressed by all that had happened during the Worlds, the *kaicho* felt he had struck a new vein of determination within himself. After the finals, as he forced a confrontation with the *sensei*, he thought he was ready to change everything. Even as his flight drew closer to Narita, however, "everything" began to seem like a very big word.

As soon as they landed, Yamasaki made for Tong Fu, his Roppongi restaurant, to attend a buffet Taro Kimura had arranged. Freighted with worries, Yamasaki expected a grim occasion. On the telephone and over the fax, Kimura had seemed in an irretrievably black mood. But Kimura, as always, came through, making sure Yamasaki's return was a cheerful event. Still wearing his sailing gear, Yamasaki kept his comments to assembled sponsors and suppliers unusually brief. "We didn't do well," he told them, "but we learned a great lesson. Next year will be different."

What was the lesson? Yamasaki hadn't even bothered to explain. When he finished, Kimura got up and spelled it out. "Sailboats aren't the products of science," Kimura stated. "There's something of mystery in them, something beyond simply the knowledge of scientists and technicians. They're not automobiles. It's frightening to find out that you can't control a product. You don't know what it's going to be like until you sail it. We have to rely on one man's experience—the designer's. One man, and the experience of the sailors. We have to rely on very unscientific methods, even though we don't know how that's done."

That was an important truth for the campaign leaders to grasp, among the most important they would confront. And it was telling that Kimura had led them to it. More and more, as time went on, the syndicate's core leadership would come down to Yamasaki and Kimura. Yamasaki still conferred often with Eguchi. The Yamaha president understood the value of competition and how to grow from exposure overseas. Eguchi was rock solid, and Yamasaki valued his counsel, their walks in the garden. But Eguchi wasn't a yachtsman.

Kaoru Ogimi remained involved too. Within a few days Yamasaki would even ask him to run the campaign as executive director. The logic of such an appointment was apparent enough. The contrast between Nomoto and Ogimi at Mission Bay had been lost on few. The *sensei* had been way out of his depth; he simply wasn't *kokusai*, internationalized. Now Yamasaki was asking for help from those he had pushed to the side long before. It was hard not to see the invitation to Ogimi as an admission of failure, perhaps even an act of desperation. But the *kaicho* had begun to sound different; now he talked about really wanting to win.

The offer, in any case, came too late for Ogimi to handle it as he might have even a few weeks earlier. In the summer of 1991 he began to drift further into the project he had been nurturing for years, through which young Japanese sailors would train aboard an ocean-going square-rigger. Afterward, when Ogimi talked about Yamasaki's proposal, he also gave the impression that he had seen enough in San Diego not to want his name at the top of the syndicate's management. It's Yamasaki's mess, he seemed to say. Let him see it through.

Taro Kimura was the one who really hung in. By mid-1991 he was two years gone from NHK and serving as principal news commentator at Fuji Television, a commercial network. Kimura was famous all over Japan, but his work load at Fuji was heavy. He was appearing on television five nights a week. Between the move to Fuji and the America's Cup, Kimura had had to rent a small apartment in Roppongi and a small office not far away. He began seeing a little less of his house in Zushi. That was a measure of the commitment Kimura had made to Nippon Challenge and to Tatsu Yamasaki.

Before the evening at Tong Fu ended, Yamasaki and Kimura passed a few minutes talking alone. It would be four years the following week since Kimura first walked into the conference room at S & B. "We've spent so much time and so much money," Kimura quietly complained, "and we have nothing to show for it. It's you and I, Yamasaki-*san*, who have to do our best to rebuild this project and recover the spirit of the thing."

Yamasaki smiled. He valued the friendship as much as Kimura did. But he said little. He had jet lag, and he had allowed himself a fair amount to drink. His long, hot summer had begun.

• • •

At S & B the following day, Yamasaki heard detailed reports on *J-6* from Ichiro Yokoyama and his partner, Taro Takahashi, who had taken a train up from their office in Yokohama. The day after that he went through written reports on the same subject by Kikuchi and Robert Fry. Yamasaki understood everything they said, in outline if not in technical detail. *J-6* wasn't it. And no modified *J-6* was going to get them where they wanted to go. Equally important was the honesty of these assessments. None of these men had been encouraged to comment openly on *Nippon* under the *sensei*.

Before he got anywhere near the *Nippon* problem, however, Yamasaki wanted to make a decision about the man who drove it. What stuck in his mind were near identical remarks included in the

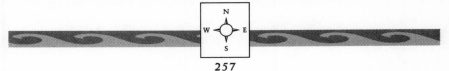

Fry and Kikuchi reports. Both had written wide-ranging assessments that covered the state of play at Mission Bay in general.

Day to day, the place was dismal. Yamasaki knew that: he had seen it for himself. But Kikuchi and Fry went on to say that a lot of the fault was Chris Dickson's. Yamasaki had known that too, if less certainly. Now crew members were talking about it more directly than they had before. Dickson was still precocious, condescending, frequently out of control. Something had to be done, and it came down to Dickson himself. There was too much disunity, and only he could do anything about it. Dickson had sixteen people on *Nippon*, and he had to bring them together, as Yamasaki gently described it, "in one spirit."

Yamasaki hated to admit that another problem even existed at the helm. After Roy Dickson's dismissal, Chris had quieted down, but soon enough he was "at his arrogant best," as Yamasaki put it. One day during the Worlds, Yamasaki had driven over to the America[3] camp to see Gary Jobson. He hadn't forgotten Jobson's help at the beginning, and the American still admired the Japanese effort. "What are you doing here with these people, Gary-*san*?" Yamasaki had asked. "Why don't you come back and join us?" It was no more than a gesture of friendship. "I said it without thinking," Yamasaki recalled later. "But I knew once I said it how unhappy I was with Nippon Challenge."

After putting down the Fry and Kikuchi reports, Yamasaki, alone at his desk, committed himself to keeping the Kiwi on board. It was a lunge for hard ground, a grope for resolve. But for the rest of the campaign, the Dickson question would never be far from the *kaicho*'s mind. He had a master driving *Nippon*. There was no one who could replace Dickson's talents. He was often described as "a near genius"—Yamasaki had heard that frequently enough, though no one ever left off the prefix. But the prodigy was fatally flawed. He didn't have enough character to manage his talent, and the idea of getting rid of him would always linger.

Hard ground wasn't easy to come by, Tatsu Yamasaki was discovering. Changing everything in pursuit of victory was no simple matter.

•   •   •

On May 19, a Sunday, a long message came over Yamasaki's fax machine at home. It was from Taro Kimura, and it arrived sometime after midnight. "Yamasaki-*san*," Kimura began, "thank you for marking the anniversary of our 'inseparable friendship' the other day. Skipper and bowman shouting at one another, the good ship *Kimura* seems to keep going—right up the side of a mountain."

Over the telephone between Tokyo and Mission Bay, Yamasaki and Kimura had agreed to exchange written summaries of the technical side's problems, and Kimura's fax was a neat assessment of where the syndicate stood. It was unusually harsh, but Yamasaki wanted it that way. He had asked Kimura for a tough, inflammatory rewrite of earlier messages Kimura had sent, the more thunder the better. Yamasaki wanted to use it, if he needed to, should he encounter any resistance to his post-Worlds plans during the board meetings.

Kimura had proven more than obliging. Reforming *J-6*, he wrote, was tantamount to "counting the age of a dead child." To continue on the same track meant altering the bow or the stern, "groping for a more effective canard," tinkering with parts to make them lighter. "A third boat made this way won't go beyond first-generation A.C. boats such as USA 2 or ITA 1. It will certainly not catch up with third-generation boats. And USA, ITA, and NZL should by now have already started to draw the lines of the next generation."

Kimura all but rubbed the *kaicho*'s face in questions no one had asked so bluntly or systematically. "Why was the weather data, so central an element of the design, basically wrong?" And, "In two-boat tests in Gamagori and San Diego, almost no tests had been done to change the shape of the appendages. What *were* they testing?" And, "Why did they add ballast just before the Worlds, taking a penalty, pushing the optimum wind speed higher, and narrowing the range?"

And so on, through all of the problems never before discussed. "We can no longer play the trial-and-error development game," Kimura wrote as he started toward his conclusion. "That's okay as

an investment for next time. But there isn't time now. To win the race next year we have no other choice but to seek masterly performance."

Then the punch line: "The existing technical team should be dissolved and the new boat developed by a designer who can judge the dynamic elements of a yacht from experience—who can understand battle conditions without a tank test."

Taro Kimura had given his inseparable friend all the ammunition he would need before the board meetings began. According to Kimura's message, the time for *gambatte* was over.

•   •   •

The first meeting of Nippon Challenge's board turned out to be not nearly the nasty business Yamasaki had anticipated. But that was only because nothing really got done.

Yamasaki's main concern was handling Nomoto; it would be delicate, particularly if the final judgment was that he had to go. The *sensei* had come to the syndicate through Kohtaro Horiuchi, the stout gent who had launched Yamaha's marine division. The corporate connection was strong. And Yamaha wanted to keep its ties with the syndicate close because it wanted to run a corps of technicians through it. To Yamaha, Nippon Challenge was a classroom. How would Eguchi respond if it came to firing Nomoto?

Syndicate directors generally met in the S & B boardroom, which adjoined the small conference room that the inner circle had used so often in the beginning. The boardroom, large and sparsely furnished, was dominated by a long, oval-shaped table, stylishly black, with an empty space in the middle of it. Yamasaki, Ogimi, Kimura, and a few other board members sat patiently through two sessions on the first day: they heard two independent designers in the morning and several people from the Yamaha technical team in the afternoon. Then the *sensei* came in.

Everyone understood that Nomoto would be on the defensive— they had put him there, after all—and he started right in. The race results in San Diego weren't unsatisfactory from an R & D point of view, he began. In fact, the Worlds had gone well from a scientific

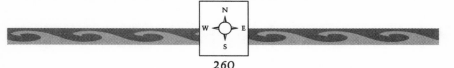

perspective. He had studied the numbers, and they were fine. "If I may make an important point," Nomoto said, "we had a dismasting on the first day of the series, and *J-6* has to be judged with this in mind. We set the boat speed too high."

Nomoto went on to announce his ideas for building the next *Nippon*—it would be a modified *J-6*, as everyone knew—and his schedule for producing it. But all he saw as he stood before the boardroom table were executives shifting in their seats. There was no response until Kimura spoke.

"With that concept, we couldn't even beat ITA 15," he snapped, "and that isn't the Italians' final boat. That's where the Italians were *before* the Worlds."

Ogimi cut in. "Nomoto-*sensei*, it's important we get more feedback from the crew before we go ahead with a third hull. You can't do it without discussing everything you have in mind with the people who are going to sail the boat."

"I understand your position," Nomoto replied. "But I cannot change my concept."

As Nomoto spoke the very words the board was expecting to hear, an old conversation came back to Taro Kimura, and he turned it over in his mind while the *sensei* continued. A month or so before the Worlds, Kimura had proposed ordering carbon fiber panels from SPS in Britain so that they would arrive in time to start construction of the third hull over the summer.

"This is the final boat," Nomoto had said of *J-6* when Kimura approached him on the matter. "We may want to make some small modifications, but there won't be any need for structural change."

"What if we lose the Worlds badly? What if it's a disaster?"

"I don't think that'll happen," Nomoto had responded. Then he had added, "But if it does, I have no alternatives for a third boat. I haven't got any more ideas."

• • •

When the first day of board meetings ended, Yamasaki drove south to Hakone, a region of mountains, lakes, and evergreens a couple of hours south of Tokyo, for a meeting of the National Spice Associa-

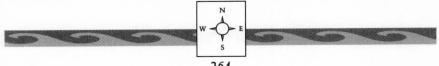

tion. For a few hours at a resort hotel, he mixed with old business friends and, as chairman of the group, delivered his remarks on the state of the industry. It was the kind of obligation Yamasaki needed at the time. It gave him distance, if only for a day. Just as he had in La Jolla before flying home, he stayed up late that night to consider his position.

Yamasaki was nursing a deep sense of anxiety. He had dumped the Americans at Kensaku Nomoto's urging, and he had dumped Roy Dickson, again with the doctor behind the decision. Then he discovered he had taken the wrong path, and now he was going to charge Nomoto with leading him down it. The power of technology had never worked as a substitute for experience. Nomoto's faith had only closed them off from learning, as if he thought the world had nothing more to teach them.

A lot of Japanese were beginning to feel that way. Maybe that was the case in cargo ships, steel, and video gear, but it wasn't true of yacht racing. The world's best designers and sailors had looked upon the May races as a learning experience. They would learn from racing, then they would go home and devise original solutions to take them farther forward. Learning came naturally to the Japanese. But original solutions didn't.

Tatsu Yamasaki was afraid. For the first time, he began to recognize what it was he had gotten himself into. Not all the Kenwood Cups ever raced could have prepared him for what an America's Cup series demanded of those who entered it. It will change your life, Kaoru Sochata, the yachting photographer, had said at the very beginning. This was what he had meant. Why does Nomoto-*sensei* refuse to change his ideas? Why does he refuse to listen to anyone else? Yamasaki had been asking himself those questions frequently. Late that night in Hakone he found the answer, and he couldn't have understood it if he hadn't felt the same emotion Nomoto did. They had entered the deepest water in international sailing, and the sensation, the unfamiliarity of it, was fearful.

Nomoto had no experience in yacht racing, and he was too frightened to allow others who did to change his opinions. Others, like Chris Dickson. Dickson was young enough to be one of Nomoto's

students. Fear, mixed with a certain pride, had forced Nomoto into a corner. Even on the few days Nomoto had watched the races in San Diego, he hadn't understood what he was seeing. He wasn't the slightest bit interested in that kind of competition. Nomoto knew only the old post-Meiji method: erect barriers and prepare yourself behind them. Design mistakes weren't the only consequence; Mission Bay was adrift, without purpose.

The *sensei*'s work is over, Yamasaki concluded before he slept. Nomoto might be able to stay on in some nonexecutive capacity, but Yamasaki decided that night he wanted a new coordinator and a new chief designer. The latter would have to be someone who could learn and then create. That narrowed the field rather drastically, of course. But Yamasaki already had someone in mind, and he would make sure the new man had a completely new design team under him—to the extent, of course, that Yamaha would allow it.

• • •

Early the next morning Yamasaki drove back to Tokyo to reconvene the board. He met briefly with Nomoto before the session began, only to find that there had been no change in the doctor's attitude since they had last seen one another. The two men walked into the boardroom together. Eguchi was late, and when he arrived, he seemed in no mood for niceties. With his arms tightly folded, he launched straight into a discussion of change on the design side. Eguchi wanted Shoji Kabaya, the Yamaha technical man, to be made coordinator of the entire design and construction team for the third boat.

No one objected. Yamasaki then did his duty, relieving Nomoto of his responsibilities. The professor, who was present throughout, walked out without saying a word. It was not, however, his final exit. There were more board meetings to get through—one on the twenty-third open to sponsors and a final gathering of the nine directors two days after that.

Right after firing Nomoto, Yamasaki telephoned San Diego and asked Chris Dickson and Shoji Kabaya to fly to Tokyo for the last meeting. Kabaya, then managing the sailing camp, would have to

address the board and Dickson would explain to them in detail exactly where the campaign stood. Yamasaki also planned to announce a new management structure that day, and both men were to figure prominently in it.

•   •   •

Chris Dickson was midway through a commentary on *J-6* on the morning of Saturday, May 25, when Ken Nomoto, present as an observer, interrupted. Letting the abrasive Kiwi into the boardroom to criticize all he had done seemed too much for the *sensei* to take.

"If Chris Dickson is to take over the leadership of this campaign, I have some advice for him," Nomoto began. He spoke in English, and loudly. "The Japanese way of doing things is important, and I hope you will lead in the Japanese way."

Kimura, struck by the absurdity of such a remark, faced the doctor and said, "Nomoto-*sensei*, you've been removed, I understand. It's for the new design team to determine how to run the technical side."

"I've been living with the crew almost full time for more than two years," the *sensei* shouted across the room. "Who on the board can say that? Is there anyone here who has been as close to the crew as I have? What I've accomplished is being denied."

"Will you please stop all of this," Kimura interjected. "It's a waste of time."

"I'll be finished soon."

Kimura could contain himself no longer. "Your story is all over," he exclaimed.

"It is not over!" Nomoto exclaimed, banging the boardroom table hard enough to overturn coffee cups at the other end of it. "Don't disturb me. I have more to say."

"I certainly will," Kimura countered. Then *his* fist hit the glossy tabletop, and more cups flew.

"Gentlemen," Yamasaki intervened. "This is my boardroom and my table." Then he paused until the room was quiet. "I assume Nomoto-*sensei* has some farewell remarks to make," the *kaicho* said

finally. Turning toward the doctor, he said, "Nomoto-*sensei*, I give you two minutes to conclude."

Nomoto continued in the vein in which he had begun, speaking in a murmur that was barely audible. No one, it seemed, was listening anyway. Then the *sensei* took his leave, with a grace that had rarely deserted him over the previous four years.

When the boardroom door had closed behind the doctor for the last time, Tatsu Yamasaki looked immediately across the table to Shoji Kabaya.

"It's your turn," he said. "Start your meeting."

•   •   •

A certain amount of *nemawashi*, begun in San Diego and finished in Tokyo, had kept Nomoto-*sensei*'s passage back to retirement and the world of antique boats short if not entirely sweet. It also meant that Shoji Kabaya was prepared to table a list of policy alternatives for the board's review as soon as Yamasaki gave him the floor. It was a single sheet of paper with columns labeled A, B, and C:

A:

Participate in the challenger series;
No third boat;
Close the base camp from June through October;
Reduce syndicate members;
Budget:—254 million yen.

"In this case," a footnote read, "the Kiwis will go home."

B:

Participate in the America's Cup;
Improve design and motivation;
Stress *gambatte* in PR;
Build third boat, but keep spars within current budget;

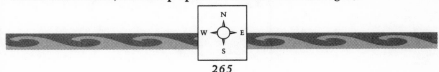

Cut crew to minimum for two-boat testing;
Budget: + 350 million yen.

C:

Win the Cup;
PR stresses that we are very serious;
Build third boat;
Improve spars;
Transfer some people, cut others;
Budget: + 712 million yen.

Beneath these columns, Kabaya wrote: "The expectations are that we can win with a third boat. But other competitors are doing more than just revising their hulls. Nippon Challenge, with no experience, must realize that a third boat alone is not enough."

Then came a single-sentence paragraph: "I therefore propose alternative C."

It didn't take the board long to decide which direction they wanted Nippon Challenge to take—Yamasaki had turned his roots on that point too—but they went even further than Kabaya's C alternative before the meeting adjourned.

Kabaya had budgeted the new-look syndicate this way: third hull, three hundred fifty million yen; three new masts, one hundred fifty million yen; three booms, three spinnaker poles, and assorted hardware, seventy-two million yen; personnel, one hundred fifty million yen. These figures were later refined and revised marginally downward in some cases. But Yamasaki had placed plus signs next to the hull and mast entries—meaning that spending on them would be open-ended. He called the decision taken that day "C plus Alpha."

They had added, in total, just over five million dollars to the budget. As near as anyone could reckon, and excluding the Alpha factor, Yamasaki had his bottom line. Nippon Challenge would end up spending roughly seventy-five million dollars—fifty-two million in cash and twenty-two million or so in hardware and services contributed by suppliers. That placed Japan second in terms of spending, just behind Italy and ahead of Bill Koch's America's syndicate. There would be a post-Cup deficit of six to seven million dollars; Yamaha would pick up half the difference, and Yamasaki the other half.

The new management structure confirmed that afternoon was not unlike one Roy Dickson had proposed before the Worlds. Yamasaki was at the top, and a three-man committee ran the campaign under him. Chris Dickson would manage the sailing camp along with Makoto Kikuchi, the sail designer. Kabaya, in addition to his design role, would also stand between San Diego, Tokyo, and the Yamaha factory in Arai. There was a simpler way to describe the new arrangement. Shoji Kabaya was the new *sensei*, the man in whom newly acquired knowledge was most heavily invested.

It was considered a good choice on both sides of the ocean. Kabaya was much in the Japanese mold as an executive. He was a career technician of absolute loyalty to Yamaha. But he was also respected among both Japanese and *gaijin* at Mission Bay. "Kabaya listens when you talk to him," one of the Kiwis once said. "If he doesn't know something he's not afraid to admit it. Kabaya's one of the few people we've really worked with over the months."

Shoji Kabaya made no outward display of ambition, for either Nippon Challenge or himself. Fragile in build and diffident, Kabaya was, at fifty-two, the antithesis of men like Makoto Kikuchi. Kabaya wanted to win in San Diego because that was what Yamaha wanted; he wasn't afraid to learn from *gaijin* because that was how Yamaha advanced. At Mission Bay it was noted that Kabaya would always volunteer for the dirty jobs. And after the May board meetings, one of the dirtiest was the firing of thirteen syndicate members—five sailors; the meteorologist; two sailmakers; and a slew of managers and technical people. Kabaya handled it, and, so far as the campaign's management could see, there was little fallout.

Kabaya returned to San Diego only once over the summer, chiefly to clean out his apartment on the hill behind Mission Bay. One afternoon during that visit he sat in his office container at the base camp and reflected on the differences between him and the man who

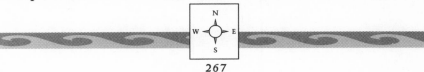

had preceded him. "I liked him on a personal level. He's a man of good character," Kabaya said of the *sensei*. "But he was—what's the term?—a stonehead." Kabaya laughed cautiously. "Not everything is clear in theory, and Dr. Nomoto couldn't understand that. I have to accept the actual situation—in this case, the situation on the water. For instance, we're changing our hull shape because of what happened during the Worlds. Dr. Nomoto couldn't accept that. He said, 'This wasn't analyzed theoretically.' What we're doing isn't proven. Maybe it's not better. But we're trying it."

The man doing the trying, Ichiro Yokoyama, was appointed chief designer the same day Kabaya was elevated within the syndicate. Kabaya, who also replaced Nomoto on the board, had a lot to do with Yokoyama's rise within Nippon Challenge. He had handpicked Yokoyama when the design team was first drawn together in early 1987.

The two men had grown up together professionally. At forty-six, Yokoyama was six years Kabaya's junior, but he was decidedly more worldly than his new superior. That came partly from Yokoyama's father, Akira, the pioneer designer, who had learned naval architecture from American officers during the occupation and then passed the skill on to his son. Later, during Ichiro's decade at Yamaha marine, the company had sent him abroad to study—chiefly in France—and he became part of the design team that built *Magician V*, the winner of the Quarter-Ton Worlds. After that his career and Kabaya's diverged: Yokoyama went out on his own. "There was a limit to what I could do in a big organization," he explained. "You live a stable life, but I felt I should be more adventurous."

Yokoyama's firm was called M D S, which stood for Marine Design System. It was two years old when Yokoyama became chief designer of the next *Nippon*. But both partners, Yokoyama and Taro Takahashi, would bring many more years of experience with them to the third boat. Only a year earlier an M D S design had won the Kenwood Cup. It was a forty-foot sloop named *Matenrow*; it had a carbon fiber hull, and its victory was a high point in Yokoyama's career.

Tatsu Yamasaki drew enormous confidence from Yokoyama's ap-

pointment. It was good politics, given his friendship with Kabaya. More than that, Yokoyama's was another voice that had been silenced under the *sensei*. And the chairman reckoned Yokoyama would bring the syndicate what it needed most. Out on *Tariam II* during the Worlds, Yokoyama had patiently helped the *kaicho* understand *Nippon* in comparison with other boats. He had a superb eye for what others had done. "When we looked at the races together, what he had to say seemed fresh and original," Yamasaki remarked.

After the Worlds Yamasaki pulled Yokoyama aside at a farewell party in a penthouse atop the Hyatt Islandia. It was toward the end of the evening and Yamasaki was, by his own account, well oiled. "Have we seen your best?" he asked the designer. "No," Yokoyama told the *kaicho* as modestly as he could.

"I had the feeling that if I gave him the chance he'd work his hardest and he wouldn't have any of the fear Nomoto had," Yamasaki said when the board meetings concluded. "I didn't want science from Yokoyama. After four years—and what, a billion and a half yen spent on tests?—we had enough science behind us. I expected Yokoyama to use our assets effectively, but I wanted him to add the creative dimension, the art."

•　　•　　•

The kinds of problems Tatsu Yamasaki was trying to solve the summer before the Cup were hardly unique to the Japanese. Virtually every syndicate in San Diego came away from the Worlds with the same sense of having been jarred loose by those first races over the Point Loma swells.

Sometimes the changes that took place all over San Diego made the news and sometimes they didn't. Gary Jobson, in a well-publicized split with Bill Koch, left America[3] to return to ESPN. It was a familiar problem with Koch: he wanted to sail his own boats, and few around him thought he was qualified to do so. Dennis Conner's money problems proved entirely real; even a second hull, to say nothing of a third, a fourth, or a fifth, as others planned, proved unaffordable. There was talk, briefly, of merging the two potential defenders to combine A³'s money with the depth of talent in the *Stars & Stripes* camp. The idea went nowhere; what did emerge was a patriotic arrangement under which American sponsors could contribute to both campaigns. "It means sponsors don't have to pick a winner," Bill Koch said. "We're both going after what's best for the United States, and they can support both defenders."

Things were no better among the challengers. The Spanish syndicate seemed, in effect, to choose something between A and B on a list similar to Kabaya's: they retreated from San Diego for the summer and fired Gerardo Seeliger, Kaoru Ogimi's friend and the syndicate's general manager. The Kiwis apparently had money problems too. Over the summer Bruce Farr, who was designing for them, was boasting of a "breakthrough" boat the Kiwi press termed "different, ugly, and fast." But the syndicate's financial position was rumored to be worsening nonetheless. The Italians were still committed to spending a hundred million dollars or more, by most estimates, but Montedison, the Italian industrial giant, relieved Raul Gardini of his executive responsibilities in the company, and thirty-five members of the syndicate failed to return to San Diego after a long summer holiday. The British syndicate dropped out altogether, and the two Australian syndicates would be late in arriving. The Russians were officially still in, but whether or not they would show remained anyone's guess. They finally dropped out just before the races began. And the Bengal Bay Club gave up the ghost at last. In the end, eight challengers would compete, of the twenty that had originally planned campaigns.

Everyone was tightening up onshore. The sail loft's budget at Mission Bay dropped from a million one hundred thousand dollars to eight hundred thousand, and the production schedule was cut back accordingly. But out sailing it was different. Under the new management structure, Kikuchi's forays in the rubber duck were given a name: he headed what was delicately called "R&D/Other Boats" in one organizational chart, "Spy Program" in another. He had a budget, albeit a small one, of a million yen, about seven thousand five hundred dollars. What he found was encouraging:

like Nippon Challenge, the others were trying everything they could on the water.

The twenty-eighth America's Cup would be a five-hundred-million-dollar race, by Gary Jobson's reckoning, including twenty-three million dollars spent by the America's Cup Organizing Committee and fifty million by syndicates that wouldn't even get there. Those figures reflected gross miscalculations—by the designers who wrote the new A.C. rule and by race organizers who intended to turn yacht racing into the popular spectator sport it never has been. But the miscalculations posed a curious question: will efficiency and experience triumph over money; can smart money win out over a lot of money?

• • •

But the midsummer jibe was different for the Japanese.

Yamasaki rounded a difficult mark when he recognized the need to depart from the accepted ways Japan had of doing things. He had committed himself to a sharp increase in spending, and had introduced a new management structure. He had sacked one of his most elevated executives, and he had rejected Nomoto's inferiority-as-superiority complex and all the "outside" and "inside" that went with it. The *kaicho* had also fired a slew of sailors and staff members—a difficult and radical step that carried the risk of serious demoralization. And no *gaijin* could be held responsible this time. Kabaya had done it, as everyone knew, on Yamasaki's orders. Indeed, the *kaicho* would eventually pay heavily for breaking the promise he had made to the crew after Roy Dickson's summary dismissals in Gamagori.

But had Yamasaki taken the syndicate forward? Had he determined to win, overcoming his years of indecision? Most of what Yamasaki knew about victory he had learned at S & B, not on the water. His was corporate Japan's understanding of the term. Winning the America's Cup at this late date seemed almost like an exercise in product improvement, or something to be added to the boat, like a new set of spreaders imported from overseas.

As Yamasaki's new designer, Ichiro Yokoyama had none of the

sensei's arrogance. As a naval architect, he had about as original a mind as Japan could offer. But the record suggested that he was in essence a copyist. *Matenrow* had won at Kenwood because it was, as sailors familiar with it said, "a very clever clone of a one-ton Bruce Farr design." Now there would be no time for copying. That was one reason the America's Cup was such a curious exercise for the Japanese. All Yokoyama could copy were the boats he had seen during the Worlds, which were outdated before he sat down at his drafting table. "A finished boat," he himself had muttered during the Worlds, "is an old boat."

Tatsu Yamasaki had finally seen the *gaijin* logic that there was only one place to aim in the America's Cup. But did he understand it? Taro Kimura's facsimile message just after the Worlds had urged the pursuit of "a masterly performance," not merely "an investment for next time." But such phrases were bandied about in the interest of boardroom strategy and tactics. It still came down to the same question, two years after Roy Dickson first posed it: did Yamasaki still think that doing well would be enough?

"You can tell Tatsu the score, and I have many times, and you think you've gotten through," Kaoru Ogimi once said of him. "But he always slides back to the comfort level. Is he a great competitor? Yes and no. He likes to compete, but within the Japanese limit."

Once, during a summer visit to San Diego, the *kaicho* stood up during a general meeting at Mission Bay to address the entire base camp. After offering his routine encouragement, Yamasaki switched to an informal report from home. "I had an opportunity to talk with executives from Dentsu the other day," Yamasaki said. "They believe that by the year 2000 the major Japanese media will cover the America's Cup as thoroughly as they now cover the F-1 car races. We're the starting point for the next decade. Think of that, and please do your best to make this prediction come true."

Gambatte. He may as well have spoken the word.

Few present seemed to think the chairman might have acknowledged at that moment that he had abandoned the immediate quest. Not even Yamasaki was immediately aware of the implications of

what he had said. The Kiwis in the afterguard exchanged a few glances. But that was it.

"I came to talk to all of you as much as possible," Yamasaki concluded. "But only about the future. I have no time to listen to anyone looking back."

ON THE WATER

*C*hris Dickson made no secret of his elation when he got back to San Diego from Tokyo. He was beaming. Dickson had a taste for cathartic confrontations, as his father did, because to him there was nothing like one to clear the air. And he had relished every moment of Nomoto's final fall.

"I've never seen them so furious with one another," Dickson exclaimed in laughter when he recounted the board meetings. "Incredible! They were actually angry at one another. I thought, Hey, finally, after all this time, we're really getting somewhere here."

Most people at Mission Bay figured Dickson's mood was also part of a smile campaign he seemed to have begun after the Worlds. Back from Tokyo, the skipper thought it best to raise his own spirits and keep them high, at least publicly. "I've got a lot of people to hold together for the next year. That's my responsibility," he said weightily one night in his apartment.

Yamasaki had had a careful word with Dickson. He had never told the Kiwi straight out that his job had been on the line. Dickson had survived the board meetings, but not by much. When Gary Jobson left America[3], there had been talk that he might move over to Nippon Challenge as a consultant. Nothing came of it, but that, too, contributed to Dickson's anxiety. He was hanging on by thin threads. For the rest of the campaign, Dickson's many masks would be refined down to the basic two: unchecked bluster out on the water, calculated obsequiousness in the presence of shoreside authority.

Dickson did come back with a prize, though. It was his news about the third boat. "We don't have all the answers yet, but they've asked all the right questions," he said with assurance.

To him that meant *his* questions. The morning before he left for Japan, Dickson had walked into the canteen at Mission Bay and unrolled a blueprint across one of the long, narrow dining tables. "Okay, gentlemen, here are the basic lines of our next boat," he said to the few people present. There weren't many details, and it wasn't a boat Dickson ever expected to be built. Rather, it was a rough sketch Dickson had received by facsimile from a designer whose ideas intrigued him.

He was certain he was going to get most of what was in that blueprint. One evening a few days after he got back to San Diego, the entire crew, along with wives and children, attended a barbecue held at the edge of the bay not far from the base camp. The campaign's cooks set up large grills, and there was plenty of steak, seafood, *curririce*, and Kirin beer. Dickson was full of talk, almost to the point of indiscretion, about what the Japanese were going to build. The occasion was actually a farewell for the shore crew and sailors who had been given the gate, but that didn't much concern the skipper; Dickson rarely looked back, unless it was over his shoulder at a boat he had just mauled.

During the evening someone from the sail loft casually asked Dickson what the new hull would be like.

"Radically different," Dickson replied. "You want to know how the bowmen are going to look when they're out there getting the

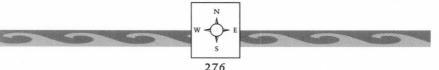

spinnaker up? Like this," and he stretched out his arms like a high-wire acrobat, placing one foot carefully in front of the other as if he would otherwise lose his balance.

As Kikuchi was discovering, every challenger in San Diego was going through the same process of revision. They were all back on the water and in the laboratories testing even their most fundamental assumptions, the things they had considered the strongest points in their programs going into the Worlds.

Nippon Challenge was doing that for the first time. The things they discovered off Point Loma every afternoon could be analyzed, sent back to Tokyo, and incorporated into the development program under Kabaya's direction. What Roy Dickson had worn himself out saying in Gamagori would no longer get you fired. Even Yamasaki was saying it.

"We've been pushing hard for this for years," Chris Dickson said early in the summer. "This is the way programs happen. We've wasted a lot of time and a lot of money, and now we've got to make up for it."

How much wastage there had been was continually shocking. The crude surgery through which *J-3* and *J-6* inherited the bow and stern of the Kiwi Twelves was long ago understood. So was the futility of the five hundred hours of tests they had run in Gamagori. Now came a discovery yet more curious.

Erle Williams, the Kiwi in charge of the boat, made it on a trip to Tokyo to confer with the technical people. Years earlier, when Nomoto completed his testing program, he had discovered that he had underdesigned *Nippon*. Nomoto was going for a long hull, but if Yamaha built according to his models, the boat would measure below the length allowed by the I.A.C.C. rule. They would be giving away advantage and getting nothing for it. His solution was as inelegant as it was secretive: the *sensei* had simply scissored his design sheets in two and added almost two feet of length in the middle of the hull.

"No wonder," Spanhake smiled, "it had that peculiar line when I first saw it come out of the shed."

How it had happened, as Spanhake concluded, was another tale that would never be told. The best anyone could make out was that

the deed had been done just before construction began at Arai. After all the millions spent at Mitsui Akishima, neither *J-3* nor *J-6* had ever been tank-tested as they were actually built. It was still not a favored topic within the syndicate. But you now had to speak of a notional *Nippon* and the real one that sailed in the Worlds.

"The new design's going to take us a long way from *J-6*," someone would say.

"Which one?" would come the reply. "Notional *J-6* or the one at the dock?"

They often spoke of the notional boat. In a way it was more real to them than the boat they had sailed in the Worlds because they knew more about it. It was finally possible, though, to begin figuring out the actual hull. One morning in the canteen, a group of sailors were discussing models being tested for the third boat. Williams interrupted the meeting to fetch a set of drawings from his office across the camp. They would show *J-6* in comparison with rough ideas for the new boat. It was the summer of 1991, and it was the first anyone outside the technical team had seen of *Nippon*'s lines on paper.

Line drawings are simple to look at. They are not cluttered with specifications; in fact, none are given. They show a hull from various perspectives—from above, laterally, and lengthwise—and enable one to slice through it, so to speak, to see its shape at any given section.

Any yacht's lines represent the designer's effort to balance two theoretically opposed objectives. He wants to give water the easiest passage possible around the hull—the least obstructed "entry" and "exit"—but he also wants to build in stability, which slows the passage of water. The aim is to design a hull that combines speed and stability while producing the minimum drag. The result is asymmetrical, because a boat always heels when it sails. In essence, a yacht is a series of constantly changing curves from bow to stern. It is closest to straight in the bow, becomes rounder as it approaches maximum beam, and then begins to straighten out again toward the stern.

When Erle Williams returned from his container and tacked

J-6's lines up on the canteen wall, the Worlds were far enough in the past—and the third boat enough of a reality—to allow those present an entirely spontaneous reaction. These were men who had looked at lines for all of their adult lives and in some cases a good part of their childhoods.

What they saw prompted immediate and unrestrained laughter. Within a minute or so they were holding their sides. Someone said, "They forgot the Plimsoll line"—the depth mark painted on the side of a cargo vessel.

J-6 started with its borrowed bow, had a ruler-flat section on the top side, and went straight back along the sides, with no variation, for fifty-five percent of its length. Then came the borrowed stern.

Well-designed yachts become more powerful when they heel, because the form built into the hull shape gives them greater stability. *J-6*'s lines added almost no stability when it heeled; the consequences in speed were evident.

"What we were sailing," Mike Spanhake said with a grin after the meeting, "was a supertanker."

•   •   •

That was the past. Now they were starting another race, the race against time that everyone in San Diego was running.

By the second week in July they knew at Mission Bay that the next boat would be a narrower, lighter, more maneuverable hull, and that it would be built to sail in San Diego conditions. They could ask Kabaya for whatever they wanted and count on a fair hearing. But they had to ask for it by July 24; that day, the twenty-fifth in Tokyo, Ichiro Yokoyama was to present the hull's basic lines at the Yamaha production facility in Arai.

Testing was intensive by early July. Shore crew and sailors gathered at nine each morning in the base camp canteen. The canteen was both conference hall for the entire camp and midday dining room for the shoreside people. Long lists were read there every day—things done, things delayed, things to do. The easy routine that had set in after the Worlds was gone. There was, more or less, no routine left. Each session announced new experiments, new schedules, new ways to finesse the deadline.

"France and America³ start racing today," Makoto Kikuchi began one morning. "Spanhake will watch from the rubber boat. Grinder tests start tomorrow."

It was Wednesday, July 10. Along with Dickson, Kikuchi was six weeks into managing the camp. The two of them sat opposite one another at the center of the long, Formica-topped tables that ran, end to end, the length of the trailer. Kikuchi spoke in Japanese, keeping his voice slightly louder than Hideko Morita, a front-office assistant who translated simultaneously into English.

"Keel tests have begun, and acceleration is good. Maneuvering is easily managed, speed is consistent, helming is easy. These are the first conclusions. We tested on Monday and Tuesday. *J-3*'s mainsail shape was too flat, so we shortened the checkstay Tuesday, and test performance improved. We can't judge the keel tests if the sails are different. Trimmers, you must check that stays are the right length.

"Regarding the jib, the tack lengths on *J-3* and *J-6* are different. Please consider this. Trimmers, please ask how this should be managed.

"In winds of more than thirteen knots, *J-3* is softer. To check this, at the end of this week we will switch the masts between *3* and *6*. But the hull itself seems softer on *J-3*." Kikuchi paused. "Mike Spanhake has today's weather."

Weather reports were something of a joke. In the summer months they were always identical: cloudy and breezeless in the morning, sunny with winds picking up in the afternoon. Spanhake had that day's San Diego *Union* spread out in front of him. "Patches of light rain possible this morning. Clearing up, with winds of ten to twelve knots, later on." For a moment, everyone laughed.

Dickson was next. As usual, he spoke slowly and in simple language. Dickson had the habit of leaving out his articles when addressing foreigners.

"Winning Winches tests start tomorrow," he began. "Grinders, please have meeting with Jaime Marina so that during tow back today you can start taking winches off. Jaime."

Jaime Marina was a shoreside maintenance man, a straight-to-the-point Australian. "We're looking at Winning Winches, pedestals and drum systems, for two reasons," he explained. "One, for the company's information, and two, to see if they're as good a product as they say. They're very light. Could be good."

Dickson cut in. "To think about which winches we need for the third boat, very important for grinders to meet every day to discuss. What is good? What is bad? What should be changed? Think about gear ratios. Do you want lower gear or higher gear? Everything"—Dickson paused to let the word sink in—"we can change.

"Keel testing," he continued. Very important for third boat. There's big difference between E type and F type. Keel, mast, forestay will change.

"Karasawa, Jun Nagai. You'll be watching A³ and France with Mike Spanhake. We know *J-6* against France. Watching France against America³, we can see what changes A³ has made—whether they've moved forward, stayed same, moved backward. We are watching boat speed, trimming, crew work, how many grinders, different systems. Racing is six months away." Dickson paused again. "Not so long," he said, stretching out the words. "We now must take each opportunity we can to make our own progress.

"Mainsail trimmers," Dickson concluded, "a very short meeting after this one."

•　　•　　•

That day and the next, and many after that, were as frustrating out on the water as any at Gamagori had been. Either there was no wind, or it was too patchy to allow for reliable tests. "We've had two days of the last thirty with wind of more than twelve knots," Dickson complained one afternoon behind *J-3*'s wheel.

The winch tests began at the assigned time on Thursday. "Grinders," Dickson reiterated during the nine o'clock meeting, "make sure you know everything possible about winches so you can make the right decision."

Spanhake gave a long report on what he had seen watching America³ race against the French. Koch was on the defensive from

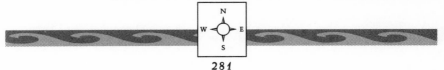

the prestart gun onward, so much so that *Ville de Paris* was visibly "being kind," as Spanhake put it. "America³ did look good. There was no difference between the two downwind. We saw good crew work, and they looked fast. On the zigzags, they had a very interesting gennaker. Downwind, we saw they were using very light spinnaker wools every three hundred millimeters up the sail. They broke very quickly. They were fully set four boat lengths around the mark. The French need almost three times that. Another mark, America³ was fully set in twelve seconds. We have videos. We can go over this.

"But we saw very violent helming on A³," Spanhake concluded. "When Koch tacked, he came full over so fast that the boat stopped completely."

Everyone laughed. Bill Koch, his afterguard a shambles, was becoming an object of some derision all over San Diego as the summer wore on.

Aboard *J-3* and *J-6* there was little time for the problems of others. They still couldn't get the readings they needed.

J-6 continued to carry the same appendages it had through the Worlds: a keel strut of average area, a large bulb at the end of it, and a forward rudder. This was known as an F configuration. Very few changes would be made to *J-6* throughout the testing period. It was the control, where they had come from, while *J-3* took most of the alterations. Most of these were E, or single-rudder configurations, and there were numerous alternatives to be tried. At that moment *J-3* was sailing on what was called "the Yokoyama keel," which required no forward rudder.

Dickson figured, preliminarily, just what Namba suspected after the first day of keel testing and what Kikuchi was indicating in the meetings. "*J-6*, with the forward keel, is faster in fourteen, fifteen, sixteen knots, but it slows right down in lighter winds," he said while helming *J-3* through a dead patch. "The Yokoyama keel is always quicker in seven, eight, nine, ten knots. Eleven and twelve knots, they're closer to the same."

They were looking for "the cross," the crossover, the point at which the two *Nippons* sailed exactly the same with each keel and

rudder configuration. Then they would know what they wanted. A series of good tests would tell them which appendages sailed fastest in light winds but gave up the least speed as the breeze developed, crossing with *J-6*'s appendages at the highest wind speed. How would they find the cross in ten days' time?

Sailing with Dickson was always magic. No matter what the conditions, he had a touch that was effortless yet exact. He was never uncertain of it. He pointed perfectly. Yet he worked *J-3*'s wheel as if he were rocking a cradle and reading a book at the same time. He was like any true master of any craft. "I expect to learn something about helming *Nippon* every time I go out in it," he said once. He meant it; he knew instinctively that there was always more to learn. It wouldn't be something he could point to. It had to do with an understanding that went beyond articulated knowledge and into the realm of sense.

But he was bored with the conditions. In a good test, when conditions were identical for each boat, one would gain roughly twenty meters on the other over the course of the ten-minute testing period. But they were getting differences of several times that, from which they could conclude nothing.

Dickson started watching for whales out ahead. The previous day there had been some that came within twenty yards of *J-3*, and one that seemed to be chasing *J-6*. They sent sonar signals bouncing off the keel—six notes, like a seaman's whistle, in pairs on an ascending scale. The notes echoed below the deck, and you could hear them clearly up on top.

"How many weeks do you need to judge these appendages?" I asked as we waited for enough wind to start another test.

"Weeks? In two really good days we can do fifteen to eighteen tests. That's enough. But we don't get them. On a bad day . . ." He stopped and pointed his thumb toward the deck.

•　　•　　•

The Japanese do not make winches. They never developed the industry because there wasn't a domestic market. Equally, there was nothing to gain by manufacturing winches for export; one was

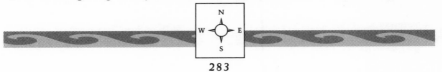

the same as another, and Lewmar and Barent virtually had a lock on the worldwide market for racing winches.

J-3 still sailed with its Barent winches, and the other boat had Lewmars. Both systems were heavy; at roughly four hundred and eighty kilograms each, they were by far the heaviest gear on the deck.

There were high hopes for the equipment brought in by Winning Winches. There was a new Barent system, designed and built since *J-3* and *J-6* were launched, that took two hundred kilograms off the deck, and a new Lewmar system that was two hundred and fifty kilograms lighter. Then came Winning: it offered a winch system that weighed a hundred and fifty kilograms, less than a third of what the J's were carrying, and Erle Williams wanted to cut that down further.

"It's the same all over the deck," Williams explained one day out on the tender. "That steering system, the pedestal and wheel, is made by an American company called Harkens. It weighs almost fifty kilograms. We're putting one on that weighs nine. We're probably going to take five to six hundred kilos off the third hull. The center of gravity on it will be way below the bottom, halfway down the keel. Anything you carry above that means heeling. It comes right out of speed."

He had been trying to throw things off the boats since the first one was wheeled out of the shed. *J-3* had even started out with some kind of electronic bilge pump.

"It's perfectly understandable. The Japanese have never been through this kind of exercise. We have."

The Kiwis were always saying that. Burying their own frustrations had become second nature. Williams, square-jawed and with a football player's build, was thirty-two and noted for his temper. You felt, talking to him, as if he were barely containing himself, and the Japanese crew feared him almost as much as they did Dickson. But he understood big yachts better than anybody at Mission Bay. Williams had confidence in the third boat, chiefly because he was intimately involved in planning the spars and hardware it would carry. "Oh, it'll be a much faster boat, all right," he said as we headed in from one of the winch tests.

The very brief history of Winning Winches was the story of the tremendous injection of energy the America's Cup gave to the technology of yachting. The Cup condensed into a matter of months developments that would require years to evolve in the commercial market. "It's the only context in which you go back and back and back again until what you've made is perfect," Craig Robinson once said about the sail loft. It was the same with the rest of the yacht.

Chris Chambers, the managing director of Winning, was twenty-four. He wore his title like a suit that was too big. What he was selling in San Diego in the summer of 1991 was essentially his senior thesis from his university days.

Chambers, thin, unassuming, English pale in the California sun, grew up on the Isle of Wight. In the summer of 1988, a year away from graduation at Sheffield Polytechnic, he was casting around for the project he needed to fulfill his degree requirements. Almost everything on a sailboat had taken a technological leap in either materials or design and sometimes both, he thought. Sails, hulls, appendages, spars had all undergone revolutions in the previous ten to twenty years. But no one had looked closely at winches.

"Winches rely on very basic, very sound engineering principles. There's no subtle twist," Chambers said one day at Mission Bay Deli, an outdoor sandwich place next door to the base camp. "A winch is first a bollard, a post around which lines are secured, and second, it rotates to tighten or ease the lines. That's about it."

During his years at Sheffield, Chambers once spent a couple of months at Lewmar Marine, on the English Channel near Portsmouth. It was enough to inspire him. "They weren't doing anything innovative. They were simply honing their concept by machining off weight and using titanium wherever they could. I set out not knowing what my idea would look like. It's a fact that winches take high loads, but so do a lot of other things on a boat. They still seemed too heavy for what they had to do. I thought, There must be a more elegant solution, a better way to do it."

Chambers presented his thesis in the spring of 1989, graduated,

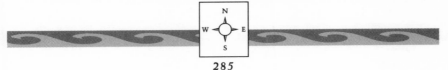

and spent the summer showing his designs to friends and friends of friends along the Isle of Wight waterfront. " 'If it weighed this much,' " I said, " 'would you be interested? Would it sell?' " He got enough affirmatives to begin begging and borrowing cheap time in old British machine shops to build a prototype. It was ready in September 1990, by which time Chambers and two friends had formed Winning Winches Limited.

Winning's innovations achieved the elegance Chambers sought because they were simple. Chambers looked at the drums on standard winches and decided that by making them larger in diameter he could use thinner material without reducing the load they could take: a textbook principle of industrial design. Winning Winches were called "top hats" because of their size, which was three to four times the dimensions of comparable Lewmars or Barents. He also rearranged the gears so that the heavy casing normally required to hold them could be brought down substantially. That, too, was based on a fundamental law of machine engineering. In the process of these changes, Chambers made his winches modular; any part could be changed, repaired, or redesigned without, as was usually necessary, taking the whole system apart.

Earle Williams wanted to do more. Williams proposed building parts of the drums and the drive shafts out of carbon fiber instead of aluminum, which had never been done before. And he wanted to try stacking one winch drum atop another, which would mean the third boat might carry two principal winches instead of four. Chambers said, "Our main winch, which we call the 'Sub^{20} Primary' because of its weight, is seventeen kilos at the moment. We estimate we can get it down to twelve and a half."

Chambers, along with his partners, Mark Turner and John Farmer, were packed into a phoneless thirty-five-dollar-a-night Point Loma motel room for two weeks while they made the rounds along the San Diego waterfront. For a day or two at a time, Winning Winches were going on and off other boats, including *Stars & Stripes* and *Il Moro de Venezia*. But Nippon Challenge looked as if it would be Winning's first sale.

All Chambers seemed to have against him was his track record. He didn't have one. How good was the engineering?

Erle Williams thought it was fine, and he was plainly impressed with Chambers's ideas. He hadn't yet made a decision, Williams said one day in his container, but he had worked out a schedule: yes or no by July 16; a month, until mid-August, for design and development; production to begin August 16 for delivery in Arai October 30. That was Williams's deadline for deck hardware. "There's some flexibility in there, but I did that on purpose. What if some of the other syndicates decide they want them? Then you risk manufacturing delays and late deliveries."

Chambers, who installed the testing winches on *J-6* himself, was doing his best to hide his anxiety around Mission Bay. He knew the America's Cup was perfect for him. At home, Margaret Thatcher had already awarded Winning eighteen thousand pounds' worth of prizes for industrial innovation. And the weight sensitivity of the I.A.C.C. boats played right to his strong point. But he hadn't filled an order yet.

"Five years from now," Williams said once as he watched *J-3* and *J-6* in a test, "people won't believe the kinds of things we had on these boats. It'll all be different."

After the tests, the grinders complained that they hadn't liked the Winning Winches but that the *gaijin* wouldn't listen. The *gaijin* complained that the grinders never made their criticisms specific. "They just griped," John Cutler said, waving the matter off.

In some respects, not much had changed within Nippon Challenge.

On July 18, two days behind his schedule, Williams told Chambers that Winning had Nippon Challenge's business. It was worth a hundred and thirty thousand dollars. Whether the grinders liked it or not, Japan's third boat would sail with the most advanced winches on the market. In a few years' time, Williams figured, the Japanese would be building winches of their own.

• • •

It was a Thursday, and there were only a few days left.

When *J-3* and *J-6* docked in, a little after five, an inner circle gathered in the canteen for the weekly planning meeting. Dickson and the Kiwi afterguard were there, and so was Makoto Namba. From shoreside, the group included Kikuchi and Jun Nagai, Robert Fry, and John Dibley.

The Thursday sessions were tedious much of the time. They simply reviewed the current week and scheduled the next. But apart from certain strategy meetings that followed the nine o'clock sessions, they were the most important gatherings at Mission Bay; they were the point from which San Diego communicated to Tokyo.

"Okay, testing this week," Chris Dickson began energetically. "Today, let me tell you, was very, very shifty, so the results are not so accurate."

John Cutler took over right away. Beside him, a white plastic drawing board was tacked to the canteen's wall; another was propped on a chair behind him. He drew a rough graph with two lines that converged at certain points but never met.

"We're getting a huge spread of results. There's still more time, but what we're coming up with is no more than a varied range."

"So we might be into a ten- to eleven-knot cross rather than a nine to ten," Dickson said while studying Cutler's lines.

"You can see *J-3* almost cross over at eleven to twelve. The problem is we have only one test at that speed."

"We have to identify good and bad tests, don't we?" Dickson asked.

"If we start averaging, bad tests will move the average only a little bit," Cutler replied.

"What if we go four bad ones to one good one?"

"We have to be careful, but we have to hope the trend comes out." Cutler paused and thought. "If we know a test is bad, we could scrub it at the time."

"On the water."

"Right."

While the others continued, Dickson began dictating in a low voice to Hideko Morita, who sat next to him. "If we conclude on the

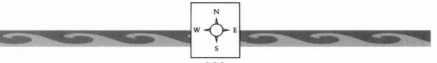

water that a test is no good, do not record the test." Morita screwed up her face.

"Test again," Dickson said somewhat louder. Then he turned back to the others. "The swing at the moment is ninety meters for one boat and a hundred and thirty meters for the other. We're not seeing our twenty-meter differential."

The floor went to Jun Nagai, which meant Morita would translate simultaneously. Nagai had been filling in a large chart on one side of the plastic drawing board. It showed various combinations of appendages that needed to be tested before the third boat's lines could be decided. It looked like the chart below.

"The big question is whether we want a forward canard or not," Nagai said, still half turned to the board. "So the tests with no canard are the most important for Yokoyama."

Nagai paused, then picked up again. "I want to talk about the schedule. The problem here is we have only one forward rudder. For example, if we run this test"—he pointed to the one that required the very small canard—"what should we use for comparison?"

	Canard	Keel	Rudder	Total area (sq. m.)
J-6 (Worlds)	1.13	3.67	2.72	7.52
med strut small rd.	—	4.99	2.05	7.04
med strut Yoko rd.	—	4.99	1.75	6.74
med strut small rd. v sm cnd.	0.40	4.99	2.05	7.49
small rd. Yoko cnd.	0.58	3.67	2.05	6.30
Yoko rd. Yoko cnd.	0.58	3.67	1.75	6.00

The design and shape of appendages were still to come—they were Tokyo's affair. At Mission Bay they were testing sizes. The most effective combination of appendages would be sent back to Tokyo and Arai. Using dimensions sent from Tokyo, the shoreside crew could build mock-up keels of various sizes that were good enough for tests. But they couldn't build rudders and canards.

"Yokoyama's idea is to cut our small canard down to make the very small canard," Nagai said. "His canard can't be ready in time. He says test with the 0.58 canard and then cut it to 0.4."

Cutler seemed to ignore this. "When will we receive Yokoyama's forward rudder?" he asked.

"July twenty-fifth if we're lucky," Dickson said.

"That's the deadline. We can't do any of this unless we push the whole schedule back."

Dickson calculated. They wanted to decide on the basic lines by the twenty-fifth, but mold construction probably wouldn't start until the end of the month.

"We might be okay," he said. "Yamasaki has been pushing this schedule, but he's seeing creative things happening. If that means the boat's going to be late, he'll vote for it. That's my thinking."

Kikuchi eventually left to telephone Yokoyama at M D S, and he returned with good news. They could continue testing appendages through August 15 if they would get as much as possible done before then by reordering the tests so that they could cut down the canard they had.

There were other decisions to make. Cutler had worked out a new weather system with local meteorologists that would be used during the races. Using a weather buoy and one or two boats at the edge of the course, it would deliver hourly reports that covered general weather conditions, along with reports every thirty minutes indicating conditions at each mark. To make it work, he wanted to buy an on-board data system called a B & G 690. B & G (Brooks & Gatehouse) was a British firm that competed with an American company called Ockham much the way Lewmar did with Barent. In Gamagori, they had installed an Ockham system but had never made sense of it.

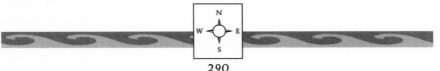

"Let me play devil's advocate," Dickson said. "Any reason we shouldn't buy it?"

"Several," Cutler replied. "One, we have lots of parts from the old Ockham system. Two, the Ockham is very simple. If it needs repair, it's easily done. Three, compatibility. All the testing equipment can accept straightaway what the Ockham puts out. But none of this outweighs the benefits of the B & G. I've never used it, I've seen it once. But looking at the specifications and the way it's calibrated, it looks a long way ahead of what Ockham is up to.

"I look at it this way," Cutler concluded. "The next boat arrives and we're going racing. If we buy it now, we can fit it into the third boat a week or two before the next mast arrives.

"Anything else?"

The meeting was dragging on. Figuring out the right order for the keel tests was like solving a riddle. That alone had taken more than half an hour; it was nearing seven.

"The spar program," Dickson said. "We need an update from Kabaya. They've scheduled three masts, two booms, and six spinnaker poles."

"There's a boom missing," Fry observed. "They're talking about two booms and we were supposed to get three."

"Who's making the booms?" Dickson asked.

"Mitsubishi Rayon," someone said.

Dickson held his face in his hands. "They've never made one before," he sighed through his palms.

•   •   •

"You work backward," Dickson once explained. "During the America's Cup, you can change genoas overnight—you can change sail strategies overnight. In between the round robin and the semifinals, you can change ratings—that means the basic parameters. You can move the mast, change the rudder, make it five tons lighter. Now go another stage back. What you can't change is the hull. Before the first race, that has to be presented in San Diego for measurement. After that, the hull's the hull."

On both sides of the ocean, Nippon Challenge was learning what

it meant to abandon all that had been arduously prepared beforehand. Flexibility in a dynamic situation—Roy Dickson's phrase—
was coming hard. The Japanese had lost a generation since *J-3* left
the shed and Nomoto's technical team concluded that its job was
done. "We should've started the third boat last December and the
fourth just after the Worlds," Chris Dickson complained. "But
people had to be proven wrong before we could move ahead."
Dickson would change directions often. He had told his Japanese
partners after the Worlds, "Don't worry about maneuverability,
just give me a fast boat." But by the summer he was helping to
determine just what the new yacht would look like largely on the
basis of tacking and acceleration.

Dickson was fighting deadlines from two directions. He had to
meet those of the Yamaha factory in Arai, which were tight, but he
also wanted the new boat in San Diego as late as possible—as close
to the official measurement date as Arai was willing to deliver it.
When was that? Defenders had always enjoyed an advantage: they
could present the boat in which they would race the day before they
met the challenger. For much of the summer, there were rulings
back and forth about when the challengers had to be measured.
First it was January, then December, then back to January.

Next-generation I.A.C.C. boats were already arriving. America[3]
took delivery of a new hull in late July; others followed as the
autumn arrived. Dickson wanted to be last. "We won't start sailing
seriously until April, when the semifinals begin," he reckoned. It
wasn't arrogance. Making the semis probably meant beating the
Spaniards, the Swedes, one of the two Australian syndicates, and
the French—the last being the most serious threat. "It'd be nice to
have the new one for a month of sailing, but we have the first round
robin to figure out how to sail it. What's worse is getting a boat in
November with the wrong design and construction. Then we're out
of the game."

In the end, Dickson got the worst combination he could have
anticipated: official measurement was fixed, finally, for January 24,
the day before the challengers started racing. But Yamaha wouldn't
budge from its schedule: the boat would roll out in Arai on Novem-

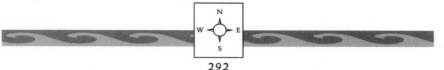

ber 15 and would leave from Nagoya aboard a cargo vessel eight days later. There were schedules to keep, and Yamaha had a budget to meet. Chris Dickson had wrung as much flexibility out of the Japanese as he ever would.

·   ·   ·

Mitsui Akishima's tank tests, which began in late June and extended into early July, involved three models. One was of *J-6*—the notional *J-6*—and the others represented new designs. The second was made from the rudimentary ideas put forward by Ichiro Yokoyama; the third came from an outsider, John Swarbrick, who had designed *Kookaburra* with Iain Murray for Australia's '87 defense in Freman-tle.

Swarbrick was a respected designer whom Chris Dickson had introduced to Nippon Challenge. It was Swarbrick who had sent Dickson sketches at Mission Bay. The designs he was working with for the new I.A.C.C. yachts were impressive, if unorthodox, and Kabaya's team stood to gain substantially from his presence in Tokyo. Swarbrick's response to San Diego conditions called for an extremely deep hull, narrow at the waterline, with a bow that was straight up and down as if it had been chopped off. Swarbrick's model was a kind of reference point, as Bruce Farr's generic design had been for the *sensei*.

Yokoyama could also keep pace by learning from Swarbrick, but that was a tricky business. The America's Cup rule stipulated that designs had to be domestic in origin. The problem was not insurmountable. Huge areas of gray enveloped the issue. As anyone familiar with Cup politics knew, with finesse and sensitivity a Swarbrick design could be sufficiently domesticated to satisfy the rule. Literally or figuratively, Swarbrick would simply have to sit by Yokoyama's side while the latter drafted the new boat's lines at M D S. More to the point was whether the Japanese had enough time to absorb a *gaijin* concept and turn it out as one they were satisfied was their own.

In any event, the tank tests they ran told an interesting story. In the important range of wind speeds, seven to ten knots, *J-6* was last

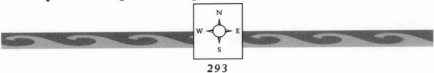

by a long way, Swarbrick's design placed in the middle, and Yokoyama's came first. In higher wind speeds, the Swarbrick design improved, but it lacked stability.

There were problems with the tests, however. Ichiro Yokoyama had scarcely had time to think through a design. And the model for Swarbrick's boat, based on a very preliminary drawing, was modified at M D S from what the designer had in mind. The test results were questionable, but M D S was moving, nonetheless, in a definite direction. The *sensei* was right, Yokoyama concluded, to go for the top end of the graph in terms of concept: a long, heavy hull that pushed sail area near to the maximum allowed. But in terms of shape and volume distribution, there would be important differences in the way the new hull looked and functioned.

It would be narrower from bow to stern and from top to bottom. The new yacht would be slightly shorter than *J-6*, overall and at the waterline, but that would include an extended bow and a shortened stern. The rounded *J-6* bow would give way to something sharper, and the stern would slope at a lower angle to the waterline. Both would get wet under sail. Kabaya wanted to modify the bottom the same way. It, too, would be sharper than *J-6*—moving, very roughly speaking, from a U shape to something closer to a V.

In sailing terminology, *J-6*'s banana-like outline in elevation meant the boat's buttock-line profile carried a lot of rocker. That, too, would change. The shape was known not only to be slow; in no small way, it also contributed to the pitching problem. Correcting that meant moving closer to what the Italians and Team Dennis Conner had: their buttock-line profiles sloped straight down from the bow to the center of the boat, and straight back up to the stern.

Overall weight would actually rise slightly from *J-6*'s weight during the Worlds, to twenty-five tons. The real changes were in where the weight was placed. Including the weight cuts Erle Williams was making, the new hull would be some sixteen hundred pounds lighter. The keel strut would lose an additional five thousand five hundred pounds. The object was a lower center of gravity. All the weight saved, plus a little more, would go into the lead bulb at the bottom of the keel. On *J-6* it weighed just under forty thousand pounds and looked like a pudgy bomb, four and a half meters long and nine hundred millimeters at its widest. The new boat would carry a bulb more than seven thousand pounds heavier. And it would look very different. Longer and thinner, it would produce less resistance.

J-6's center of gravity was located just below the midpoint of the keel, a meter and a half below the waterline. The new boat's would be 2.2 meters under the waterline, just above the point where the bulb and strut are joined. The differences could sound modest to the layman, but they would fundamentally alter the next *Nippon*'s trip around the course off Point Loma.

· · ·

Just before the period of intense testing was over, Yoshihiro Nagami, Yamaha's overconfident computer man and a survivor of the post-Worlds purge, ran a simple test at Mission Bay. It wasn't of his own devising—he had been quietly asked to do it—and it was conducted outside the formal testing program.

Afterward, the test was never discussed. Even Chris Dickson, who combined supreme cynicism about the capacities of Japanese designers with a deep desire to know all that could be known about the craft he would take into the challenger series, seemed to shrink from the result.

Using a computer, Nagami compared *J-6*'s performance with that of ITA 15. It was based on a well-rounded sampling. Nagami used the three Pre-Worlds races and the portion of the first of the series up to the point when *J-6* dismasted. That took in light, medium, and fresh breezes. He entered in each boat's time around each mark, wind conditions, sea conditions, and the tactical positions both boats sailed on each leg.

Nagami arrived at a differential and converted it into a simple percentage: ITA 15 had outperformed *J-6* by roughly nine to ten percent. The next step was to add how much the Italians could be expected to improve on ITA 15, whether they worked on the existing hull or superseded it with another. Conservatively estimated, that came to three and a half to four percent.

The question that popped out at the end of the process was simple: would the third *Nippon* outperform *J-6* by twelve and a half to fourteen percent, the calculated minimum required even to pace the Italians during the challenger series?

It didn't seem even close. It seemed an impossible target to achieve.

There were developments as the summer wore on that allowed for optimism. Kikuchi's sail program was making more difference than anyone had counted on. And the new boat's displacement would allow him slightly more sail area than he thought he had—he could lengthen his J without giving up much of his E.

There was a surprising breakthrough in the appendages tests. The forward rudder that measured 0.58 meters, known as the "Yoko canard," had beaten the boat without one by a wide margin over a number of days. Then there was the third boat. Yokoyama's design, combined with these other advances, could be enough to make up the percentage Mission Bay reckoned it needed to match and overcome the winner at the Worlds.

The second half of 1991 was a long season of more or less constant change. Some other configuration of appendages would displace the Yoko canard as the object of optimism. Or they would begin to think again that no canard was best. Kikuchi would have further discoveries to make in the sail program. Who knew where those things that could be altered would be when the time for experiment drew to an end?

Optimism ebbed and flowed. Others were making discoveries, too. As new boats arrived, it looked as though everyone had learned a lot about sailing off Point Loma.

During one of his visits to Mission Bay over the summer, Tatsu Yamasaki went sailing on *J-3* while Chris Dickson helmed it through the day's experiments. It was the usual San Diego day: big swells and patchy, shifty winds that were never very strong. Stretched across the afterdeck, the *kaicho* rapped the hull with his knuckles and said confidently, "I built a boat. Now I want a racing yacht."

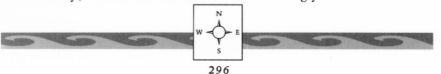

Maybe he would get a yacht. Maybe he hadn't wanted one badly enough to do everything required to get it. Maybe Tatsu Yamasaki had finally found something in his life that he wanted but could not have.

DEMOCRACY

One day toward the end of the summer, as the season's heat and haze were giving way to the clarity of early autumn, Kaoru Ogimi sat in a coffee shop a few blocks from his office and looked back over all that had gone into the Nippon Challenge campaign. Ogimi had never allowed himself to assume defeat, even when his instincts told him it was due. Now Ogimi was detached and a little depressed as he stared across a busy avenue at the Imperial Palace; he had come to look upon the twenty-eighth America's Cup as if it had already been raced.

" 'There is no second,' " Ogimi pondered. "They never understood that."

The phrase was familiar to anyone who knew much about the America's Cup tradition. A hundred and forty years earlier, the Queen of England had watched *America* from the deck of *Victoria and Albert* as it was about to take the Hundred Guineas Cup. No boat was near as *America* approached the finish line.

"Say, signal master, are the yachts in sight?" the queen had inquired.

"Yes, may it please Your Majesty."

"Which is first?"

"The *America*."

"Which is second?"

"Ah, Your Majesty, there is no second."

The exchange had long ago entered the realm of cliché. But the sailor's final response had taken on a deeper meaning to everyone who had ever sought the Cup *America* won. To Kaoru Ogimi, it held a special lesson for the Japanese.

"Whether to win or not—that has been the problem from the beginning," Ogimi said.

It had been almost five years since Sumao Tokumasu, the chairman of Sumitomo Marine & Fire, offered his spirited opinions on the value of friendly competition in the pages of *Nihon Keizai Shimbun*. It had been nearly as long since Kazunori Komatsu, the hazel-eyed skipper, began his search for "the individual Japan needs for the twenty-first century."

Ogimi had listened then and had decided that Japan was ready for the race. He had awakened from a dream, he had said, and he figured others had, too. He had recognized from the beginning that Japan couldn't enter the America's Cup the way Toyota got into the auto market or Hitachi into televisions. People would have to change; the organizations would have to be different. Commitment on command would have to give way to commitment from within. A few others in the campaign knew that because they understood the nature of the event. It was the levelest playing field there was. Others knew it only because that was what they had been told. But they would come to understand, Ogimi thought.

"We can show a new Japan to the world," Sumao Tokumasu had written hopefully.

That had become an article of faith. But they hadn't kept the faith.

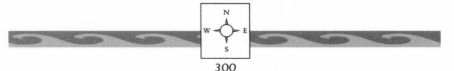

When it was over, most people would see no reason to speculate as to how much of what they had set out to achieve had actually been accomplished. Cleanly and conclusively, the race results would be taken as the final gauge of where the Japanese were, how well or badly they had competed, the way the box score of a ball game was understood to tell you everything that had happened on the diamond over the course of an afternoon.

But the truth of the five years Japan devoted to preparing for the twenty-eighth America's Cup could never be so enumerated. To Kaoru Ogimi it was clear enough as the first race of the challenger series approached that those in the Japanese syndicate had reached only a kind of halfway point in the drive to transform themselves and therefore, in some small way, to begin to transform the rest of the nation. Nippon Challenge was not wholly within the Japanese tradition, but it was very far from opposed to it.

It was a deep disappointment. Ogimi had put his faith in all the ambitious ideas advanced as the syndicate got under way. He believed that the *shinjinrui*, the new species an emerging generation had produced, represented the embodiment of those ideas. But he was wrong, mostly—about the sailors, the executives and managers, and the sponsors who paid for it all.

Sumao Tokumasu thought art and science, as he had defined the terms, had been successfully combined in San Diego. The symmetry was there, but it meant nothing very new. After Nippon Challenge arrived at Mission Bay, Sumitomo opened a branch office in the city, located in a Japanese-owned high rise, and was soon writing a fair amount of marine insurance. As to the sailing campaign, the art of the equation, Tokumasu himself had emerged among Nippon Challenge's most faithful supporters. "The world of competition is full of unexpected events," he had messaged Mission Bay just after *J-6*'s mast went over. "Risk is also opportunity. Never give up." He was the only one to have made the gesture.

Sumao Tokumasu's deepest ambition was a simple one. He wanted Japan to feel at home as it sought the America's Cup. The notion behind the event was an old one in the East, he insisted, and he spoke in Zenlike riddles to explain the idea. "The pursuit of the

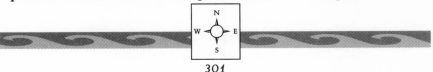

America's Cup is a Western thing, but it's seen as a contradiction in the West because the Cup is an economically worthless prize. To the Eastern way of thinking, there's no contradiction in that. Pursuing something with no value is to pursue something that is priceless. Something without worth has no price, correct?"

Call it arrogance or call it innocence. But there were bigger questions than that. The Japanese had entered among the most intense of all athletic competitions. On every level that mattered, you had to be out front to win it; you could never triumph as a follower, no matter how assiduously you followed. In its gentlemanly way, the America's Cup is as riven with dirty politics, cheating, and underhandedness as any sport in which the prize at issue is great. Japan's global influence, from the conduct of business to the prices of real estate, had become enormous by the early nineties. But the notion that there was anything especially Japanese about international yacht racing's premier event was no more than another dream from which the Japanese had yet to awaken.

At home there was a budding awareness that Japan was turning itself again into a sailing nation. This was part of the larger impulse to explore that came under the heading of *kokusaika*, internationalization, and it had taken hold. Sailing had become by the early nineties the fastest-growing sport in Japan. Nippon Challenge was partly a reflection of that and partly a cause of it. And Tatsu Yamasaki and Taro Kimura were preparing to push the phenomenon in their countrymen's faces. Among other things, the syndicate planned to display live coverage of the Cup on a giant television screen in Tokyo Station.

But all the television cameras in Japan couldn't show that Nippon Challenge had learned the most important lesson. They wouldn't show that sailing—competitive sailing—asked more of a human being than a *sarariman* was required to give his company. Those who controlled the campaign saw no need to disrupt either the group as it functioned in Japan or the hierarchy that existed within it. Indeed, so far as management was concerned, the notion had never truly been grasped. Yamasaki had attempted a kind of decentralization that relied on the inner drive of the shoreside managers.

Then the *kaicho* discovered the hard way that there was no such drive to tap; without direction from the top, there was no direction. At best you had to consider the syndicate's management a messy, unsuccessful modification of the Japanese corporate model.

Many Japanese corporations faced the same problem as they expanded overseas in the years since the campaign began. They wanted to put *wakon yosai*, the long-tested principle by which the nation had modernized and prospered, to an entirely new purpose. Could you apply "Japanese spirit, Western technology," to encourage the development of individual creativity? The notion was absurd.

Hito, *mono*, and *kane*—people, things, and money. They had done what they could with them, or at least what they wanted to do. But at their most impassioned, the Japanese had gone to San Diego to glean and go home, not really to win. And most of them did not understand the difference. Kaoru Ogimi was a resolute man. But he did not represent the Japan of the late eighties and early nineties as accurately as Tatsu Yamasaki, an indecisive figure who had glimpsed a world larger than his own but could never bring himself to enter it.

The distinction was more important on the water, finally, than it was anywhere else. They had hired some of the world's best sailors. Had they produced through them the kind of human being Kazunori Komatsu had sought, the kind Japan would need if it wanted to compete?

•　　•　　•

A few of those who crewed *J-3* and *J-6* seemed to pass, one by one, into the new and unfamiliar world of the America's Cup. Not all of them would make it. Not all of them wanted to. A lot of the men who trimmed, ground winches, and raised *Nippon*'s sails looked at their circumstances as the Cup drew near and still figured on the old percentages. You had to put that group at something over half the crew. "This is like three years in the corporate mailroom for most of these guys," John Cutler once said. "It's just lost time."

A handful, because they had been at loose ends when they joined the campaign or because there was something waiting within them in

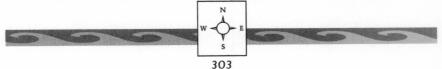

the first place, had let themselves be changed. They had gone to San Diego knowing nothing but ready for anything. They stayed open to what was all around them and they had gone inside themselves when they had to. They would end, as Ogimi might have put it, by defying gravity, by going into orbit.

They earned nine hundred dollars a month plus room, board, and an additional three hundred and fifty dollars in spending money. Most cared about the missed promotions at home and the lousy salaries in San Diego, and the handful didn't.

"It's not about money. Sailing's about winning," Ken Hara said not long before the races. That was roughly the view he had voiced five years earlier, when he stood half terrified before Kazunori Komatsu for the interview that got him the job.

Jin had been lucky. The moment that changed him had happened early on, when he fell off the Stewart 34 in Auckland and came out of the water embarrassed and determined. Jin discovered things about himself after that. For others, the event that made the difference was sometimes so small and inconsequential as to go unnoticed by anyone else who might have been there. Once, in the autumn of 1989, Kiyotaka Okabe, the tall, quiet mastman, traveled south with the racing team for the Australia Cup. Finishing the first downwind leg, they hauled the spinnaker in and, following the custom in match races, left it on the foredeck for the next run. "We had always put the spinnaker back in the bag," Okabe remembered. "But from then on, we left it out. We weren't different from other racers. That's when I felt I had arrived."

Jin, tall, deeply tanned, his hair cut shorter, had opened like a flower in San Diego. He was a leader, and in recognition of that he became boat captain on *J-6*, which meant he was responsible for seeing it was properly maintained. Jin was always moving, always animated. When you were around him, it was as if his body had trouble containing the personality that had burst forth within it. He was quick-witted and irreverent, and nothing was sacred. At every Nippon Challenge party or barbecue, Jin's impersonations were a high point. There was one of Nomoto, one of Roy-*san*, another of an unnamed afterguardsman angry with the crew. It was as if he were

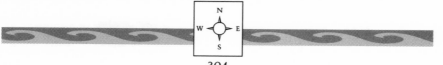

celebrating the individuality of his subjects. He would stand up in front of the whole campaign and wouldn't quit until he had them all roaring.

"Nippon Challenge has given him a vehicle to express himself," Jim Blair, the physical trainer, once said of Jin. "He's a performer. And if you can perform one way, you can perform another."

Jin had made himself, indeed, into a pretty good pitman.

Late in the summer, Jim Blair paid a final visit to the syndicate at Mission Bay. He had seen the crew before in San Diego, but he knew he wouldn't see them again before the challenger series started—and then only from a distance. Racing in the Worlds, and being around the other syndicates, watching *gaijin* crews train a few miles away in the sea off Point Loma, had transformed them, Blair believed.

"Before, when all they had were America's Cup videos and the descriptions of others, you didn't get the fierceness of competition," Blair said. "You just never saw it. Now that they're here, they're seeing other sailors every day. They're starting to realize the relevance of all the drilling. They're starting to realize what it is they have to do."

But Jim Blair never sailed. He never saw the crew he had trained physically perform out on the water. And there it was a different story.

•   •   •

"The America's Cup tradition," Chris Dickson said as the races approached, "is that you win on boat speed first." The young skipper was relaxing in the living room of his apartment behind Mission Bay. As did his father, Dickson tended to state things in the form of immutable rules. "If you're lucky, you have the only fast boat. If you're unlucky, there are two or three others with fast boats. Then other factors come into play."

Other factors included crew work. There was some truth in what Dickson said. Because he was a survivor, he lived by what he had learned on the water. A superior machine might even carry a lesser crew first across a finish line. But you couldn't win consistently, you

couldn't operate the machine well over time, unless you had sailors able to do it. Chris Dickson missed that. To him the helmsman was all that mattered. The rest were so many hired hands. Once, after winning a match race series with some of the same Kiwis in the Nippon Challenge afterguard, there was a dispute over how the purse would be divided. Midway through the argument, Dickson compared his crew with students of an Auckland sailing coach noted for his youth programs. "I can get a bunch of Harold Bennett's kids and the results will be the same in any regatta," he had shouted. "I don't need you." To most of those who had heard the story, that said everything you needed to know about what Chris Dickson thought of those who crewed for him.

Dickson's view fit well with all the images surrounding a skipper on a yacht. But they had flowed long ago from popular ideas of a sea captain on a sailing ship, and the imagery was out of phase. The skipper's role on a racing yacht had changed fundamentally over the previous quarter of a century. Partly that reflected the increased complexity of boats and the technology that went into them; partly it had to do with the diversity of the effort that racing campaigns had come to require.

"A skipper is simply the one whose name ends up listed on the racing sheet," Mike Spanhake observed. "That tends to be the helmsman, but it isn't always. The helmsman must be skilled, but his function is very, very focused. Who is the skipper? He is the one who's responsible within a certain larger organization. He's the buck-stops-here man."

There could no longer be a rigid hierarchy among the crew in a sophisticated, well-run campaign. You could have a gifted helmsman, but he wouldn't survive the mistakes a bad bowman made. Everyone's performance in a race is too reliant on the person next to him. Dennis Conner, the preeminent skipper-as-rock-star, demonstrated his understanding of that every time he raced. Conner's imperious manner onshore was well known. But those who had sailed with him said it was different on the water. "He has a marvelous ability to involve everyone in every aspect of the race," wrote the Australian

John Bertrand, who had sailed with Conner before defeating him in '83. "He will suddenly shout questions to inappropriate people—he will ask the bowman what he thinks of the shape of the mainsail. He will ask the port trimmer whether we are going fast enough. . . . A guy who has a routine task suddenly finds himself involved with the master about overall cockpit strategy. It makes everyone feel great, and Dennis Conner was the first skipper to show me how effective his method is in producing tight team spirit."

From this perspective, the Japanese had made some unfortunate choices. Roy was one. His distinctly military style had become the established method by the twenty-eighth Cup. Like yachting technology, however, you had to consider whether it was outmoded as soon as it was perfected. Something more "level" was required, some experienced sailors believed, something more democratic.

Chris Dickson was another error. He knew nothing about team spirit. If *Nippon* were going to win the twenty-eighth America's Cup it would be he alone who sailed it to victory. That was how Dickson seemed to see it. He felt that way with all-*gaijin* crews, and he was more deeply convinced of that view when the crew was made up of Japanese beginners.

But then Chris Dickson had never skippered to victory in a major yachting event. By the end of 1991 he had been on the sailing circuit for almost fifteen years. He had been through Admiral's Cup campaigns, One-Tonners, Southern Cross Cups, Kenwoods. But he had never gone home with the chalice. All of these regattas were miniatures of the big marathon—a Kenwood involved a campaign of roughly two months, an Admiral's Cup three or four. You structured the management, chose your design, figured how you wanted to approach the formula, developed a sail concept, assembled your crew, drilled, and entered into the nasty business of whittling down your sailors to those who would sail the race. Above all, a keelboat campaign meant working with people and getting the best out of them. But Chris Dickson had never seriously figured in a keelboat campaign.

He was a match racer, and match races are weekend events. Pulling a crew together and showing up is the extent of the organi-

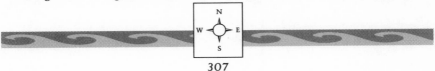

zational challenge. You choose your sails by drawing from a hat. There is nothing remotely like boat development. The race committee tells you everything, sometimes down to whether you could clean your yacht's bottom; the rigs were tuned and couldn't be changed. Dickson excelled at that kind of racing. Jump on the boat, compete savagely, get on to the next series. He delighted in recounting how he had won the '85 Citizen Cup. "I was in L.A. and got a phone call from Auckland saying there had been a dropout entry. I flew back, organized a crew, had one day's practice, and won the series."

After the twenty-eighth Cup, where would Dickson sail?

Nippon Challenge, whether it won or lost, began to look like a peak in Chris Dickson's career. He wouldn't race for the Japanese again. That was clear. And he had already been more or less blackballed at home. When he applied to join New Zealand's Admiral's Cup campaign in '89, he was dismissed after one trial race that most Kiwi sailors saw as a token gesture anyway. What was left?

"He'll always win the weekend regattas," one of the Kiwis at Mission Bay said. "But he'll never take a big one. In the complex machinery of a campaign, he's a loser."

•   •   •

"How did we acquire confidence?" Kiyotaka Okabe wondered aloud late one afternoon. His hair was windblown and his cheeks were reddened. He had just finished an autumn day during which Ken Hara had skippered *J-6*. It had been a novel experience for everyone on board.

"It's different in your world," Okabe continued. "For us, senior people are always superior. It's as simple as that. But to win we have to be equal."

Neither Chris Dickson nor Roy assisted the crew in that crucial psychological transition. Consciously or not, they discouraged it. Chris's authority among the crew was enormous, unassailable. And it derived from the very assumptions that the crew had to struggle to overcome. While sailors were trying to learn how to function within a democracy, he was running the boat on the basis of rank within a hierarchy. It was something to which the Japanese were trained to respond, and naturally they did.

That cut two ways, however. When Dickson was skippering you could sense a certain restraint among the crew. They were afraid to make mistakes, and that kept them from achieving their best, or going beyond it. But Dickson was away frequently during the summer and autumn of 1991, either match racing or conferring with the technical people in Japan. And that made a difference as night to day at Mission Bay. During one of Dickson's trips, Mike Spanhake once announced to the crew at the nine o'clock meeting, "It's your day, organize it yourselves."

They went Japanese immediately. Under Dickson there was an enforced specialization that allowed almost no movement on the boat. The crew hated it. The first thing they did was switch every sailor to a different position, as if they had all suddenly been transferred to other corporate departments. Then they organized a jib-packing contest: the *J-6* crew was divided in two, and each team appointed the other side's foredeck hands. There were cases of beer for the winners. Ken Hara skippered, although he didn't helm because he had cut his knee badly in a previous practice session.

"The point is for everybody to understand one another better," Hara said as he sat, out of the action, on the afterdeck. "Another reason: every man must learn to think individually. On a boat this size, that's important. It's not only the helmsman you have to understand. You should also know what each man is thinking in each position." Hara paused. "More pressure coming just ahead!" he shouted forward.

The crew continued switching positions even after Chris Dickson returned the following week. Possibly Dickson saw virtue in the practice, or possibly he calculated that ending it would make him too unpopular around Mission Bay. Ken Hara was placed permanently in charge of the crew. Jin noticed a change in the way Dickson treated him as boat captain. Dickson wasn't over his shoulder quite so much. "I think he's learning to trust us," Jin said, "a little."

Jim Blair figured they deserved it. "They've climbed a mountain

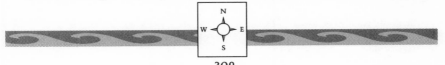

in terms of performance and responsibility to each other," he remarked during his final visit. Blair's understanding of the job at hand had evolved over the years of his visits. As he finally saw it, the crew faced an emotional and psychological exercise more complicated than any undergone by sailors of the other syndicates preparing to race. It involved a kind of betrayal. "The nettle they have to grasp, as traditional Japanese, is that they won't succeed in the America's Cup until they act, albeit for a short time, non-Japanese. They've virtually got to adopt a Jekyll-and-Hyde attitude. 'I'm one person during my work on the boat, and then I revert back.' "

It was the only way, he considered, that the sailors he had worked with would connect with "the emotional thing," as he put it, required to prepare for international sports competition.

"Let's take rugby, for instance. It's a collision sport. On the basis of cold analysis alone, you're not going to take the risks involved in winning. You've got to have that wee part of emotion. There's always an emotional dimension to a successful sports performance."

"And you're saying the Japanese don't have it?"

"Most people don't. It has to be stimulated. Put Carl Lewis in an empty stadium and see how fast he runs. Then put him in a stadium with a hundred thousand people. I think the Japanese are ready for that. But if you wait until the day, it's like not training until the day. You're not prepared. When you first feel the surge of emotion, you leave the analytical part of you behind. You need time with it, so it doesn't diminish your skill or the analytical part, it enhances those things."

•　　•　　•

The exercises initiated in the days Ken Hara skippered *J-6* had gone well enough. But the boat was too slack—in Blair's terms, without emotion. Cigarettes during easy moments were perfectly acceptable; when there were errors, no one was called to task. The first day Hara skippered, someone on the foredeck had lost his grip on a line and it had wrapped around the keel. It was the kind of thing that could happen to any sailor. The difference on *J-6* was that nothing was ever said about it. By all appearances, they were back to the comfort level. Not even Namba had learned, after all the years he had sailed for Nippon Challenge, to raise his voice.

In mid-autumn, Namba skippered *J-6* against the French. The wind was fresh, twelve knots or so, and the swells weren't too high. They were *Nippon*'s conditions. Up the first beat the boat did well, reaching the weather mark several lengths in front of *Ville de Paris*. Then the breeze lightened and *Nippon* fell behind as the two yachts headed downwind.

Over three races, *J-6* beat the French on only one other leg. As a helmsman, Namba displayed a new sense of seriousness and command. "Trim. . . . Bow down. . . . Overtrim! Overtrim! . . . Bow down. . . ," he would call, sounding every inch the skipper. He had learned certain things about his craft. But the crew work got sloppier as the day wore on, and Namba did nothing about it.

At certain points it was as if they were in Hamanako again and it was day one. At the leeward mark in the third race, the foredeck crew had trouble handling the spinnaker pole and fell into a pathetic mayhem. The takedown line wasn't ready to get the gennaker in and the genoa wasn't ready to go up.

"They're fine as long as the routine holds, as long as there's no pressure," Jaime Marina commented with some disgust in the stern. Marina, who rarely left his shoreside duties to sail, was the only *gaijin* on the water that day, and he was working the backstays. "Let something unexpected happen and they just fall apart."

Up the next leg, the bowman lost the spinnaker halyard and it floated gracefully in the wind off the starboard side until Namba helmed around the next mark and it drifted within reach. As a consequence, the gennaker didn't get up for several minutes into the final run. *Nippon* remained under sail a few minutes after crossing the finish line. No one said a word. The day was over. It was a little after four.

"When I sailed on the maxi circuit," Marina said as they waited for the tender to arrive, "we'd sit around the forward hatch after a race and go over every move. 'That was a good spinnaker set, that was a bad one, that was a fine set of jibes.' And *why* each time. You

learn from that, if you want to. Here, it'll be jokes, smokes, and sleepin' all the way in.''

It usually was the case when Dickson or the *gaijin* in the afterguard weren't on board, and that day was no different.

• • •

What winter there is in San Diego approaches almost without announcement. The morning gloom is slower to burn off, the sun is less intense. But the rain remains reluctant, and the leaves don't turn. Apart from a few brisk days, there aren't many signs of seasonal change.

The routine at Mission Bay continued with few alterations as the autumn neared its end. The sail loft began changing shifts: sometimes the sailmakers would sleep days and work nights so that recuts ordered after practice one day would be ready the next morning. But the drilling went on as it had all summer, as did the testing on components that could still be changed: the appendages, the sail shapes, the rigging.

A closer look at the base camp revealed it as the field of battle in a war of attrition neither side could win. Other syndicates were working ten-, twelve-, fourteen-hour days to get all the programs as near to right as they could be brought in the time remaining. Not at Mission Bay. After a period of post-Worlds unity, the campaign was splitting again into camps that were estranged at best, and in some cases perfectly ready to resume fighting.

Yamaha was reasserting itself: Shoji Kabaya and Chris Dickson were at odds over the unresolved aspects of the boat, Kabaya and Kikuchi over the sail program. Maybe it was because the end was finally in sight. There were, once again, *gaijin* and *nihonjin*, foreigners and Japanese. The joint venture had never really held.

Yamaha, in fact, was already preparing for the next Japanese challenge. Late in the autumn it launched an information hunt that lent perverse new meaning to the concept of learning from abroad. Well before the first gun had gone off, the files of all the *gaijin* at Mission Bay had been pilfered and in some cases stripped bare. A Kiwi sailor would walk into his cargo container to find a Japanese

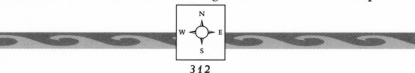

technician entering his computer or searching his desk drawers. It lent the place an almost sordid air, but everyone knew why it was happening. The Japanese were dependent on copying even in an event where the method did not work. Yoshihiro Nagami, the Yamaha computer specialist, once explained the company's plans to John Cutler. The next campaign was to be run very differently: it would concentrate even more heavily on research and technology, and it would prepare at home as long as it could. There would be no base camp abroad until the last minute, when a small crew would show up with a single boat. In essence, it would be another search for invincibility behind closed doors.

•   •   •

"I felt a lack of ambition to win," Tatsu Yamasaki complained after a visit from Tokyo. "It's a team, but it's not competitive enough."

Japan had discovered a vein of confidence in the 1980s. The yen was powerful and the nation was rich, at least on paper. Everything seemed possible, suddenly. But not everything was, as the Japanese were discovering by the early nineties. The era of cheap capital was over, and where the Japanese had invested so heavily—in Hollywood, for instance—they sometimes began to feel like fools. Nippon Challenge was no less a product of the times than was the Sony Corporation's purchase of Columbia Pictures. Tatsu Yamasaki had gotten carried away, not unlike Japanese investors who had paid too much for paintings or property only to discover their investments didn't work. The *kaicho* had learned the hard way what competition was like when easy money didn't make all the difference.

Toward the end, when he began to recognize what the desire to win was all about, the issue immediately transformed itself: should Japan win with a *gaijin* at the helm anyway? Feelings ran high on the issue as the races approached. Many of the *gaijin* at Mission Bay thought they detected a kind of silent sabotage in the crew's uninspired performance. Why look good this time, the sailors seemed to ask, if all it means is that we'll have to match the performance, or better it, to prove ourselves in four years' time.

As gradually as the sun grew pale, it became clear at Mission Bay that these were the *gaijin*'s final days of sailing with the Japanese. The next time around, whether you assumed it would be another challenge or, optimistically, the Nippon Defense, the Japanese would do without foreigners. Almost no one liked to talk about it, but the reality was stark. Kaoru Ogimi saw it, and even he understood the sense of it. "It'll have to be done by Japanese from here on out, particularly with a Japanese skipper," he concluded. "It's the only way it can mean anything to the Japanese side."

Namba-*san* was once again skipper designate. There were even those who believed Nippon Challenge would be better off with Namba at *Nippon*'s wheel in the 1992 challenger series, never mind the next America's Cup. Chris Dickson had always represented a trade-off. He had the skill, but he so intimidated the crew that many reckoned his cost had come to outweigh his benefit. Late into the year you could still get even money around local yacht clubs as to whether Dickson would make it to the start of the series without getting sacked. Namba had a tiny fraction of Dickson's talent; but some of the most qualified sailors at Mission Bay wondered whether he could drive *Nippon* at least as well as Dickson, assuming there was a certain democracy in the afterguard and the crew did closer to its best. Doubtful, they concluded, but maybe.

But you could make no assumptions about the crew. Tatsu Yamasaki had detected the demoralization that had set in at Mission Bay, but he showed no sign of understanding the extent to which he had caused it. After Roy Dickson dumped some of the dead weight at the sailing camp in Gamagori, the *kaicho* had promised the crew it would never happen again. But it had, when the operation was trimmed over the summer of 1991, and the price turned out to be heavy.

"If there's another America's Cup for Japan, I couldn't enter," Jin said one evening in a conversation with a few other sailors. "I couldn't trust Yamasaki-*san*."

"Do you think he knows you feel that way?" someone asked.

"I'm not the only one," Jin replied. "Attitudes around here have changed so much, he must know."

"People don't feel very good about Yamasaki," said Yoshia, the heavy-set grinder. "He lied."

"I feel sadness, and bitterness, too," Ken Hara put in. "To have someone at the top telling lies, you can't identify with him."

Their gaze remained inward their entire stay in San Diego. They never sought to explore the city or its lively social scene, as the sailors of other syndicates did. How much had they learned about competition? These were among the best Japanese sailors the campaign had produced and they had still not grasped what the America's Cup meant. They did not understand that nothing could be allowed to get in the way of a campaign's journey toward victory, and that there could be no place for those who did not show the drive to make that journey. If anything, the knife Tatsu Yamasaki wielded after the Worlds had not gone deep enough—not on the technical side, and not on the crew side. The *kaicho* glimpsed the principles by which a successful campaign had to be run, but he was no match for the ingrained Japanese traditions by which his people lived and worked. In a word, he wasn't a leader; he hadn't shown the way.

"Relaxing is okay for this period," Yamasaki told himself in the summer and autumn. "In mid-November we'll learn to have the atmosphere of winning." In another of his speeches at Mission Bay, close to the start of the challenger series, the *kaicho* had proudly announced that there would be a second Japanese challenge. There would be a next time. That, after all, had been part of Yamasaki's private agenda from the beginning.

"I regret saying that now," he reflected afterward. "I worry. Maybe they'll think I'm not concerned about winning."

• • •

Long after Roy Dickson had left Mission Bay and picked up his life in Auckland again, Jim Blair still thought about all that his old Kiwi friend had done during his years with Nippon Challenge.

"If there's a good measure of success," Blair said, "Roy Dickson will be the unsung hero. He took them from scratch and very early set the objective, knowing it wouldn't be easy."

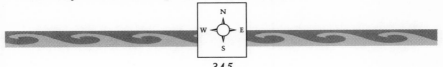

Blair thought for a moment before continuing. "But I wonder if they ever sat down and said, 'Why is he doing this?' As they can expect us to make an effort to understand how they feel, they should reciprocate."

Jim Blair finally accepted that a decent showing in the challenger series would satisfy the Japanese—a place in the semifinals, as Ken Nomoto had long ago said was secretly the goal. "I don't think anyone else is coming here just to do well," Blair said. "It's wrong. If I only want to do well, it means I'll stop when I've decided I have."

Like many other sportsmen, Jim Blair spoke often about past experiences and the lessons he had learned from them. He remembered, for instance, watching Michael Fay's syndicate, in a huge, heavy maxiboat, compete against Dennis Conner's catamaran in 1988. Blair had trained the Kiwi crew. "We knew we stood no chance, but those Kiwi sailors were sailing as hard in the last ten minutes as in the first. That's what I mean when I say latent passion."

"You're saying the Japanese don't have that, either?"

"Can they come back from two or three defeats, pick up, and come back winning?" Blair asked in reply. "You never know until you're sat down at the bottom and you have to get up each time. It'll only be proved in competition."

. . .

The freedom to compete and the autonomy of the individual are the essence of the American ideal. To put it another way, they are basic rules in the game as Americans play it. The promise of these things, the promise that "latent passion" can be discovered and brought to bear, is part of what has made America so powerfully attractive in the postwar era. Perhaps this is now changing. Not everybody believes in these ideals. Arguably, the extreme to which Americans have taken their beliefs has contributed to the decline of our civic life and to what might be called our psychological privatization—an unattractive self-absorption and a pronounced lack of concern for anything outside our front doors. So the ideal becomes less alluring—and maybe was never quite so compelling as we thought it was in the first place. We thought, indeed, that we had taught the Japanese all about democracy and free markets after the war. Then it belatedly became clear that they were interested in learning our lessons and applying our model only in the most superficial fashion.

As Kaoru Ogimi recognized, the Japanese are engaged in a great struggle, not only with the rest of the world over trade surpluses and international responsibilities, but with themselves. They have been magnificently successful in the modernization project upon which they launched themselves in 1868. But in important ways success has left them with no knowledge of who they are or what they are made of. Apart from money and material goods of high quality at low prices, they do not know what it is they can offer the world beyond their shores. *Nihonjinron*, "the theory of the Japanese," is veritably an industry in Japan, the stuff of scholarly treatises, books, films, and television specials. *Nihonjinron* asks and seeks to answer, Who are we? Where did we come from and, by implication, where are we going? Where else on earth could such preoccupations thrive?

The Japanese cannot be understood so long as one thinks of them only as predators in search of prey. They can compete murderously in some things, but only if they have gathered sufficient advantages before the competition begins. They possess no key to the kingdom so far as the conundrums of human management are concerned. They often flounder when placed in unfamiliar territory, which is most of the world outside Japan, including San Diego. Standing out, accepting responsibility, does not come easily to them—not on shore and not on the water; they do not understand what it is to distinguish themselves as individuals. But, as Kaoru Ogimi understood, we can no longer speak, with radical simplicity, of "the Japanese," at least not since the first Japanese sailor said, "I want to win."

PART IV

RUNNING

IN NAGOYA

The train from Tokyo south to Nagoya speeds past all the familiar scenery of contemporary Japanese life: cramped office blocks that seem to tilt too close to the tracks, overpasses, monorails, tunnels, standstill traffic, tiny houses, sprawling factories, parking lots, patchworks of tile rooftops, urban rice paddies, and everywhere the tangles of telephone and electricity lines that dip and rise between preformed concrete poles. It's a backdrop available through any train window in the country. Japan never seems to change, as visitors often complain. Yet there is something wholly temporary about the things of which Japan is made, things that suggest a makeshift world where change is incessant and unstoppable.

Nagoya was jammed on the morning of Saturday, November 23, though most of the traffic was headed for the annual auto show. About a hundred people had inched their way through the gridlock to enter the city's sprawling port. At Dock R1, they saw stacks of metal containers waiting to be loaded aboard one or another of the massive vessels moored nearby. *J-26*, partially covered by a shiny gray tarpaulin, looked small and sleek among them.

Most of Nippon Challenge's top executives had made the journey. Tatsu Yamasaki was there, as were Taro Kimura, Kaoru Ogimi, and a sizable contingent from Yamaha: Hideto Eguchi, Shoji Kabaya, Isao Komiya, and several others. At the sailboat's stern, Yamasaki mounted a wooden stage to deliver a short address, and then Kabaya said a few words. Yamasaki handed flowers to Captain Takashi Itoh, whose ship, *Hira II*, would carry the craft across the Pacific. Between them, the two men briefly held a flag with the "Nippon" logo on it. Then Yamasaki stepped down. *J-26* was on its way.

"Honto sugoi!" the *kaicho* exalted as he gazed at the newest *Nippon*. "Really amazing." Over the next hour the phrase was repeated often.

Off to one side, Ogimi watched as stevedores wrapped green slings under *J-26*'s fore and aft sections. Then a crane hoisted the boat slowly toward the deck of *Hira II*.

"To the trained eye, the difference between this and the first two boats is radical," Ogimi said. "What strikes you immediately is the difference in bow and stern shapes. The angle of the stern is completely different, and this one has a very straight sheer line. In the first ones, there was a very broad flair at midships, but this one has much less flair. The max beam appears further aft than on the first two."

It was Ogimi's first sight of the craft, and his commentary ran nonstop for several minutes. Notably, the boat had an open transom, an innovation that was part of the effort to shift weight downward. The Italians were the first to try it, and Ichiro Yokoyama had been impressed enough at the Worlds to adopt the feature.

"I saw the mold, but in the factory you don't get a perspective," Ogimi continued. "It certainly has a leaner, meaner look to it. It's a quantum leap from the others."

Yamasaki seemed even more pleased. "She's so beautiful," he gushed with a broad smile. His neck craned upward as *Nippon* hung

suspended above the dock. "We learned a lot from the first two boats. I have a good feeling about this one."

Taro Kimura was less ebullient. "It should be a good boat, but I can't tell," he said. "At least now I can tell Chris Dickson, 'You've got what you wanted. Now it's up to you.' "

J-26, narrower in profile than its predecessors and with a strikingly shiny surface, would travel immediately forward of the wheelhouse on *Hira II*'s main deck. For everyone who had come to the dock, and for many in San Diego, the third *Nippon* represented a small piece of the future.

At Mission Bay twelve days later, Mike Spanhake was one of the first to see it. "It might not go down as a piece of yachting history," he said, "but it's got the indelible stamp of its designer instead of a computer. It has its own characteristics. It has the logic of a yacht."

•　•　•

"There's nothing to worry about," Tatsu Yamasaki said at the sendoff. "We just have to wait for the start of the Cup."

He hadn't waited, though. He had already laid "the lines of retreat," as Ogimi put it. Yamasaki had decided in the autumn that the second Japanese challenge would be part of a larger business venture, the company for which would be formed in April 1992, a month before the America's Cup finals. There would be a sports academy, an interest in a marina project in Gamagori, and a broadcasting network. Challenge Channel, the new network's name, was to televise the twenty-eighth Cup as a debut event; broadcasting the Worlds, in fact, had been intended as a kind of dry run. Taro Kimura would be Yamasaki's partner, and in a joint venture with Yamaha they would mount the next America's Cup campaign. "We've decided to keep a permanent challenge," the *kaicho* explained.

Roy Dickson and Ken Nomoto had no such ambitions. They each turned back into their private lives after leaving Nippon Challenge, both with evident relief. "I've done nothing," Dickson said six months after his departure. "I hadn't realized how much it all took out of me." Dickson sounded weary. His only project was the construction of a cabin cruiser with his wife, Marilyn, and a friend.

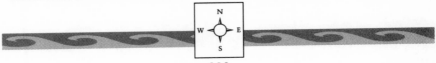

Nomoto-*sensei* took up where he had left off four years earlier. In search of old boat designs, he began sailing *Haru-ichiban II* around the Japanese archipelago within a few weeks of the painful board meetings in May and was rarely to be found in the apartment in Kobe to which he retired.

Even amid the intensifying pre-series schedule, the future began slowly to insinuate itself into the sailing camp at Mission Bay. Craig Robinson, one of the Kiwis in the sail loft, was discussing a permanent position in Makoto Kikuchi's operation in Japan—not on the floor, he hoped, but as a loft manager again. Kikuchi, in turn, was thinking about opening a second loft in Japan or a Diamond franchise in Australia. Robinson had already run a franchise in Perth for Lidgards, and Kikuchi seemed interested in him.

Others among the sailmakers were happy enough to stay on the floor with their scissors and knee pads. "I want another Whitbread and another America's Cup," one said. "Then I'm going to hoist an oar over my shoulder and walk directly inland. When someone asks me, 'What's that?' I'll know I've found home."

Chris Dickson was disappointed with the prospects available on the match racing scene. It had seemed the place to be for several years before he joined the Japanese, but then the whole thing slowed down as evidently as *J-6* did just after a tack. "Match racing hasn't continued to grow the way I hoped it would. New events have had trouble getting off the ground," he remarked. "But we'll see more America's Cup class racing, maybe a grand prix. My own direction is where I decide the opportunities are likely to be. I'm in the game of professional yacht racing, so I move in the direction of the leading edge."

The rest of the afterguard wasn't so certain about the future. Mike Spanhake felt no need to make any decisions before racing for the twenty-eighth Cup, but he thought he would probably keep sailing. Returning to Auckland right away didn't seem to appeal. Erle Williams was looking for another big-boat campaign, and John Cutler, tired of sailing, wanted to complete a graduate degree in business that he had dropped to join the Japanese syndicate. But he

had to make a living, and the New Zealand economy looked unpromising. So he might stay on the water, too, he figured.

Jin, Ken Hara, and Yoshia thought of little other than how to
keep on sailing. "I'd like to try a Whitbread," Jin said one evening,
"if someone would invite me. Or another America's Cup. But next
time, not as pitman. Trimming or afterguard. After that I'll think
again." The three of them had already been planning together.
"The notion of sea sports is still completely lost on the Japanese,"
Hara explained. "It's not an encounter with the sea. For them it still
means spending a lot of money, getting dressed up, and hiring
people to do the sailing."

Hara seemed unsatisfied that he had made his point and stopped
to think a minute before continuing. "When you go to a marina
here, what do you see? People in old clothes working on their boats.
They might be millionaires, but they do the work themselves. It's a
love of the sea. If we hadn't come to a foreign country, we never
would have seen that. A Japanese will buy a boat, but he'll miss the
point. Now we've acquired that feeling, and we have the knowhow.
My dream is to bring that back to Japan, maybe in some kind of
marina business. We've had long talks about that. Now we need the
money to do it."

They worried, though, about going home. "Last time I was back,
it was so different to be in Tokyo," Jin said. "It was hot and humid,
and there were all the *sararimen* in jackets and ties, scurrying and
sweating. I thought, Can't do it anymore. This year had changed me
a lot."

"How?"

"No more *tatemae*. I've forgotten it. I have more confidence in
myself now, and I speak very honestly. From now on, only *honne*."

•   •   •

One Sunday in the early autumn, Kaoru Ogimi took a fifty-footer
and a crew of eight out into Sagami Bay off a village called Misaki.
It was up the coast from his home in Ninomiya, and the occasion
was the Yujiro Cup, a local event named for Yujiro Ishihara, a much-
admired actor who had died tragically of cancer some years earlier.

Ishihara's brother Shintaro, by this time the celebrated author of *The Japan That Can Say No*, was much in evidence that day. Ogimi finished first, a few lengths ahead of Ishihara's yacht, but the fifty-footer's rating was the highest of any on the water, so Ishihara took home the cup.

Afterward, Ogimi repaired to a small boat docked in the marina to change for the award ceremony. It had a tiller instead of a wheel, and it needed paint badly. Plastic bags, bottles, and other bits of debris floated all around it as if clinging to the sides of the hull. It was twenty-four feet, seven inches, the tax-exempt limit when it was built in 1962. The craft's name was *Serena*. "After we built it, Father sailed it for a year and a half before he died," Ogimi said as he stepped aboard. "Since then I've taken it out regularly, though it needs some work at the moment."

Below deck, Ogimi began to expand on his own plans for the future. He was still organizing—races as well as campaigns. Together with three New Zealander friends, Ogimi was planning to launch a Whitbread entry, and Yamaha was interested in backing them. It had even accepted the stringent limits Ogimi proposed on its role: a Yamaha technical team would participate in the construction phase, but the company wouldn't build the boat. And there would be no Japanese crew. This reflected a deep and startling conviction that had developed at Yamaha. The company's top managers seemed to have concluded that sailing—world-class competitive sailing—was not an activity for which the Japanese would ever be suited. It was simply too unpredictable, and big campaigns required too much flexibility.

Nonetheless, Ogimi saw Yamaha's support of a Whitbread campaign as a step to something else. "My primary interest in the Whitbread is to get a Tokyo-to-Tokyo race going that would alternate with it. You would have the Whitbread Cup starting and ending in Southampton every four years and the Tokyo Cup running two years after it."

Kaisei, the square-rigged barquentine Ogimi had worked for years to bring to Japan, was nearly refitted and about to begin its long delivery passage from Weymouth, in the south of England. It

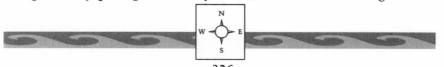

would cruise the British Isles for two months, winter in the Mediter-
ranean, and then take part in a tall-ships regatta that was to trace
Columbus's route across the Atlantic. Late in 1992 it would arrive
in Misaki, the base camp for Ogimi's training program.

"The ship isn't the object, it's the means," Ogimi told a friend he
had invited on board *Serena*. "I want to give Japanese youngsters a
chance to be buffeted by wind and sea and go face to face with
nature. It's teamwork, cooperation. The principle of competition
that pervades society isn't it, either. In that sense, it's 180 degrees
from yachting, and especially the America's Cup. The object isn't to
teach sailing, but to discover their own strength and whatever they
have within."

The conversation lulled briefly, and both men turned their attention to the boat in which they sat. *Serena*'s cabin was minute, but
Ogimi was inordinately proud of the craft. Together with Yosoe, he
had crammed everything into it that a much larger boat would
carry—weather and navigational systems, a forward stateroom, a
galley equipped with dented pots and pans, a head. Through a
porthole not much bigger in diameter than a coffee cup, the sun was
starting to go down.

"Everything works," Ogimi said as his visitor's eyes wandered. As
if to demonstrate the truth of what he said, he reached into a corner
and flipped on an overhead light. "It's at least a ton heavier now
than anything else in its class. She can't really compete, but she still
moves beautifully. I'll sail her forever."

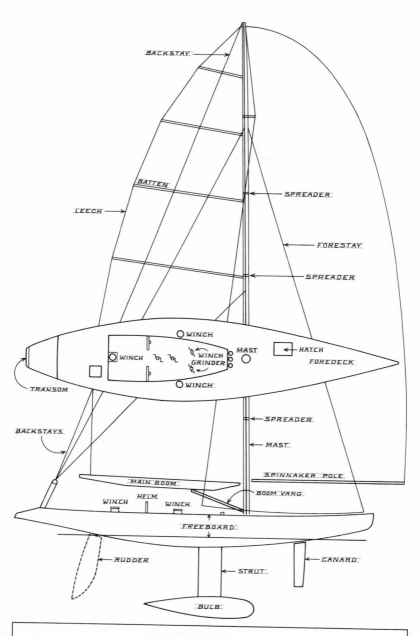

BACKSTAY

BATTEN

LEECH

SPREADER

FORESTAY

SPREADER

WINCH

WINCH

MAST

HATCH

WINCH
GRINDER

FOREDECK

TRANSOM

WINCH

BACKSTAYS

SPREADER

MAST

SPINNAKER POLE

MAIN BOOM

BOOM VANG

WINCH   HELM   WINCH

FREEBOARD

RUDDER

CANARD

STRUT

BULB

SPECIFICATIONS J-26

	SAIL AREA	
LENGTH (OVERALL) : 23.4 M		DISPLACEMENT : 24.5 TONS
LENGTH AT WATERLINE : 21.5 M	MAINSAIL : 215.5 M²	DISPLACEMENT (MNL) : 22.5 TONS
MAXIMUM BEAM : 5.3 M	JIB : 94.4 M²	MAST : 32.5 M
MAXIMUM DRAFT : 4.0 M	SPINNAKER : 480 M²	CREW : 16 M

ACKNOWLEDGMENTS

My debt to the management, crew, staff, and sponsors of the Nippon Challenge sailing syndicate, particularly in those passages that required reconstruction, will be apparent. Less so is all I owe to the many outside the syndicate who helped and to family and friends in many different places. My gratitude to all.

Those who assisted directly in preparing the manuscript are Kay Itoi, colleague, keeper, and guide in Japan from the beginning; Doune Porter, supporter and patient researcher in Tokyo; Lynn Dennison and Tom Smith, respectively finder of facts and close critic (and siblings both); Judith Evans, reader and critic; Paul Bayfield, who helped from Hong Kong; and John Roberson, adviser from Fremantle. Bob McCabe of the Paris *Herald Tribune* offered rigorous editorial judgment in the final stages of production. *Domo arigato gozaimasu.*

Philip Pochoda, literary agent extraordinary, generously gave his attention, advice, and support throughout. Thanks are also due to Bob Gottlieb and Chip McGrath at *The New Yorker*, where a portion of this book appeared in different form shortly before publication.

And special thanks to my Great Explainer, whom I also count a great friend.

ABOUT THE AUTHOR

PATRICK SMITH, a former editor at the New York *Times*, has been a newspaper and magazine correspondent in Asia for eleven years. In 1985 he won an Overseas Press Club Award for his coverage of South Korea. He served as bureau chief for the *International Herald Tribune* in Hong Kong and Tokyo from 1986 to 1991. He now writes on Japan for *The New Yorker*.